Sitting in Oblivion

The Heart of Daoist Meditation

Livia Kohn

Three Pines Press

Three Pines Press
P. O. Box 609
Dunedin, FL 34697
www.threepinespress.com

9 8 7 6 5 4 3 2 1

Printed in the United States of America
This edition is printed on acid-free paper that meets
the American National Standard Institute Z39. 48 Standard.
Distributed in the United States by Three Pines Press.

Cover Art: "Meditating Daoist." Traditionally attributed to Chen Zhitian (14th
c.): *Fourteen portraits of the Daoist Priest Wu Quanjie from when he was 43 to 63 years
old.* Museum of Fine Arts, Boston (#46.252). Used by permission.

Library of Congress Cataloging-in-Publication Data

Kohn, Livia, 1956-
Sitting in oblivion : the heart of Daoist meditation / Livia Kohn.
    p. cm.
Includes selections from the Zuowang lun by Sima Chengzhen translated into
English.
Expanded ed. of: Seven steps to the Tao. 1987.
Includes bibliographical references and index.
ISBN 978-1-931483-16-2 (alk. paper)
1. Meditation--Taoism. 2. Taoism--Doctrines. 3. Sima, Chengzhen, 647?-735. .
I. Kohn, Livia, 1956- Seven steps to the Tao. II. Sima, Chengzhen, 647?-735.
Selections. English. III. Title.
BL1923.K685 2010
299.5'14435--dc22
            2010025486

Contents

Acknowledgments

This book began when my earlier work on the *Zuowang lun, Seven Steps to the Dao* (1987), went out of print and the editors at *Monumenta Serica*, who had published it in their monograph series, generously granted permission to reuse the materials in a new format. The texts, then, are republished from the earlier book in the "Translation" part with a few minor changes in terminology and annotation, but no serious alteration. Three new texts—since then translated and found relevant—were added into the mix, again with some changes in format and terminology.

The "Discussion" part of the book is entirely new. I have tried to retain the basic descriptions and references used in the earlier book, but a lot of it was simply outdated, superseded by research in the past twenty-odd years, or formulated in ways I would not use today. The book still retains the same focus as the earlier one: the *Zuowang lun* by Sima Chengzhen of the eighth century. The text is both first in the "Translation" section and at the center of "Discussion." This part of the work is designed to build up to the central work, beginning first with a general placement of "sitting in oblivion" in the larger context of the phenomenology of meditation and Chinese religious history. From here, two chapters present historical forerunners in pre-Han Daoist materials and the scholastic vision of Twofold Mystery. The next two chapters present the biographies of the main Tang masters and technical information on the texts. After that, the work places the practice outlines in the *Zuowang lun* in its Tang context by looking at the complexities of the integrated meditation system and examining advanced practices. The last two chapters, finally, move again away from the *Zuowang lun* proper, relating it first to contemporaneous Buddhist concepts and practices and second to modern scientific explanations and the use of meditation in healing and stress reduction.

I am deeply grateful to the editors of *Monumenta Serica* for their kindness both in helping with the original work and in giving permission to have it reissued in this manner. I am also deeply indebted to Mario Poceski, Halvor Eifring, and Michael Saso, for reading through the manuscript and providing comments and suggestions for improvement. In addition, I benefited from the support of Liu Ming and Shi Jing, who made materials on modern *zuowang* practice available; from the help of Harold Roth, Richard J. Smith, Brook Ziporyn, and Jeremy Zhu in securing relevant resources; from the expertise of Shih-Shan Susan Huang, who suggested Chen Zhitian's painting for the cover; and—last but certainly not least—from the enthusiasm of numerous scholars and practitioners who never tired of urging me to complete this new exploration of sitting in oblivion.

Discussion

We are focus-points of consciousness, enormously creative. When we enter the self-constructed hologrammatic arena we call spacetime, we begin at once to generate creativity particles, imajons, in violent continuous pyrotechnic deluge.

Imajons have no charge of their own but are strongly polarized through our attitudes and by the force of our choice and desire into clouds of conceptons, a family of high-energy particles which may be positive, negative, or neutral.

Some common positive conceptons are *exhilarons, excytons, rhapsodons, jovions.* Common negative conceptons include *gloomons, tormentons, tribulons, miserons. . .*

Every nanosecond, an uncountable number of concepton clouds build to critical mass, then transform in quantum bursts to high-energy probability waves radiating at tachyon speeds through an eternal reservoir of supersaturated alternate events.

Depending on their charge and nature, these probability waves crystallize certain of these potential events to match the mental polarity of their creating consciousness into holographic appearance. The materialized events become that mind's experience, freighted with all the aspects of physical structure necessary to make them real and learningful to the creating consciousness. This autonomic process is the fountain from which springs every object and event in the theater of spacetime.

As we fasten our thoughts on positive and life-affirming values, we polarize masses of positive conceptons, realize beneficial probability waves, and bring useful alternate events to us that otherwise would not have appeared to exist.

—Richard Bach, *Hypnotizing Maria* (2009)

Introduction

What is Zuowang?

Zuowang 坐忘, "sitting in oblivion," signifies a state of deep meditative absorption and mystical oneness, during which all sensory and conscious faculties are overcome and which is the base point for attaining Dao. I translate *wang* as "oblivion" and "oblivious" rather than "forgetting" or "forgetful" because the connotation of "forget" in English is that one *should* remember but doesn't do so, or—if used intentionally—that one actively and intentionally does something in the mind. None of these holds true for what ancient and medieval Daoists were about. This is borne out both by the language and the writings: the word *wang* in Chinese consists of the character *xin* for "mind-heart," usually associated with conscious and emotional reactions to reality and the word *wang* for "obliterate" or "perish." The implication is—as indeed described in the sources—that one lets go of all kinds of intentional and reactive patterns and comes to rest in oneness with spirit and is ready to merge completely with Dao.

Zuowang first appears in classical texts from before the Common Era, then forms the title of a key treatise on Daoist meditation in the Tang dynasty (618-907), and still serves to indicate Daoist contemplative practice today. In all cases, moreover, the state of mystical oneness is not isolated, but texts and practitioners describe its surrounding features: which methods to use for attaining it and what to expect after one has reached it. This, then, makes *zuowang* the heart of Daoist meditation.

As a meditation practice, sitting in oblivion shares the same fundamental definition as other forms of meditation as a way of resting the mind within to attain healing, purification, and spiritual transcendence. In its medieval heyday when its procedures are formulated in most detail, it also matches their basic characteristics, such as an emphasis on breathing, a basic ethical code, a strong focus on the mind, and a communal setting for training and practice. Unlike other

1

forms of meditation, however, which make use of certain sense organs (vision, hearing) or the conscious mind to access the subtler layers of the person, *zuowang* demands the complete abolition of all sensory perception and conscious evaluation, insisting on "immediacy" in attitude and lifestyle.

Defining Meditation

Meditation can be defined as the inward focus of attention in a state of mind where ego-related concerns and critical evaluations are suspended in favor of perceiving a deeper, subtler, and possibly divine flow of consciousness. A method of communicating with deeper layers of the mind, it allows the subconscious to surface in memories, images, and thoughts while influencing it with quietude, openness, and suggestions.[1] Typically, and commonly among its many different forms, it works with breath awareness, has ethical rules or requirements, creates social communities, and aims at mental transformation.

Breath awareness forms an essential part of all meditation. It may be a count that accompanies inhalation and exhalation, a counting of only the exhalation, the silent repetition of "in-out" as the breath comes in and goes out. Or it may involve a physical awareness of the feeling of the breath—either at the nostrils where it enters and leaves, or at the abdomen which rises and falls with it (the preferred location in Daoism). The practice may also involve a pure awareness of breath, with no specific counts, vocalizations, or kinesthetic locations. Or it may be a special effort at lengthening or holding the breath, making it work in various ways. In all cases, the breath is a bridge between body and mind, as an expression of mental reality, closely linked to emotions, nervous conditions, and peace. The more the breath is deepened and calmed, the quieter the mind becomes and the easier it is to suspend the critical factor and enter into the serenity of the meditative state.

Ethical rules may be highly detailed regulations or a general encouragement to cultivate goodwill and compassion. The idea behind "meditation as an ethical process" (Brazier 1995, 34) is that one cannot connect to the ultimate goals as envisioned by the tradition—however defined—unless one reaches a certain level of purity. This purity carries an ethical dimension and is, at least in the beginning, often expressed as moral rules and precepts. Most common are the four great moral rules against killing, stealing, lying, and sexual misconduct (see

---

[1] This is the definition used in this book as well as in my earlier work, *Meditation Works* (Kohn 2008a). There is no consensus on a definition of meditation applicable to the heterogeneous practices usually called by this name. Scholars and scientists tentatively agree that meditation in general is a self-induced state that utilizes a clearly defined technique with a specific anchor of concentration and invokes muscles relaxation as well as the easing of logic and preconceived assumptions (Cardoso et al. 2004; Ospina et al. 2007, 9). Some also define it as a "family of self-regulating practices that aim to bring mental processes under voluntary control through focusing attention and awareness" (Walsh and Shapiro 2006).

Gert 1970), but most traditions—and thus also Daoism—have extensive and often highly specific precepts and regulations.

The community-building aspect of meditation reflects the fact that is best taught in direct contact with a master and most efficiently practiced in groups. Traditionally organized in monasteries or hermitages, they were located at a distance from the ordinary world but today also appear in various kinds of centers in the cities. Communities tend to be hierarchically organized, with the master or teacher and his assistants at the center of command and various kinds of administrators managing the group.

All forms of meditation, moreover, share the dualistic vision that the mind we carry in our ordinary life is not the pure mind necessary to realize oneself or the divine.[2] The practice thus sets out to transform the mind from its ordinary tendencies, which include various emotions and negative feelings, into a purer, gentler, and more positive agency. A powerful way to achieve this is by demanding a complete focus on the present moment. This appears commonly but is emphasized with particular strength in *zuowang*. By being in the present moment, consciousness becomes clear and lucid, and each and every aspect of perception stands out vividly while any fixed identity and any limiting sense of ego are bound to dissolve. This effect is also enhanced by an awareness of death: death, when accepted fully in the midst of living, can provide a strength, an impetus, a preciousness to life that is otherwise hard to find.

Meditative practice, then, usually begins with concentration exercises that tend to involve the breath to allow the conscious mind to rest and thoughts to come to stillness. Beginners are usually be submerged in a torrent of thoughts that jump aimlessly from one to the next, ranging from distant memories of the past to wild expectations of the future. This is what meditators call the "monkey-mind," the "mind like a galloping horse," and what Daoists call "the ordinary mind." It is uncontrolled and wild and does not give the person even a moment's rest (Brazier 1995, 54-63).

Using concentration and breath awareness, old patterns soften or are eliminated. Then new tendencies can be installed—defined in accordance with specific traditions and thus vastly different among cultures and religions. Still, even here certain general tendencies appear: negative emotions are eliminated, thoughts are changed toward well-meaning patterns, and positive feelings are

---

[2] This concept matches the vision of the perennial philosophy, which holds that there is an underlying Ground that pervades and supports all being and which gives rise to a pure level of consciousness or immediate experience that is not accessible with ordinary sense faculties and the everyday mind. For a description, see Huxley 1946; Happold 1970. By saying that meditators typically separate the ideal or pure from the ordinary mind, I do not mean to intend that there in fact is one real universal Ground, but merely that there are highly similar assumptions of such an underlying entity in all meditation traditions.

installed: inner peace, calmness of mind, trust, gratitude, and the like. Eventually practitioners reach a state that goes beyond ordinary consciousness but pervades all levels of the mind—the deep absorption Daoists call *zuowang*.

From here they connect to a wider, greater power, a superconscious way of being, what Daoists refer to as "attaining Dao." The mental state at this level may be called no-mind, wisdom mind, true self, cosmic consciousness, spirit pervasion, complete cessation, pure experience, true thusness, and so on. It is understood as part of an ultimate power or reality underlies the universe and defined differently in each tradition.[3] The usual claim is that, anchored in the joyous awareness of the infinite and firmly established in wisdom, practitioners are constantly aware of their true cosmic nature and remain undisturbed by the polarities of success and failure, pleasure, and pain. At one with a greater power, they often also attain the ability to communicate with, or travel to, the spirit realm, becoming citizens of the universe at large.

Classifications

The traditional way of classifying types of meditation follows the Buddhist model and divides it into concentration and insight (Shapiro 1984, 6): *zuowang* matches neither, although it embraces aspects of both.[4] Concentration is one-pointedness of mind; it involves complete control of attention and the absorption in a single object to the exclusion of all else. The object can be a sound, a visual diagram, or a concrete object. Beginners in most traditions start with the breath, observing it with the help of counting either the number or the length of respirations. The goal is to quiet the conscious mind so that subtler levels of the mind can come forth.

Insight, on the other hand, is often also called mindfulness. It involves a general openness to all sorts of sensory stimuli and encourages a sense of free-flowing awareness with detached observation. Insight meditation usually begins with the recognition of physical sensations and subtle events in the body. It also means paying attention to reactions to outside stimuli, recognizing but not evaluating them. Often associated with notions of deeper understanding or wisdom, it encourages the appreciation of life as flow and lets practitioners see body and self as unstable, ever-changing energetic entities (see Brown and Engler 1984).

---

[3] On the cosmic mind and the true self, see Austin 2006, 359-60; Bucke 1961; Motoyama 1990;. On the mystical experience, see James 1936; O'Brien 1964; Proudfoot 1985; Scharfstein 1973; Stace 1987; Underhill 1911.

[4] The same fundamental distinction, called "stabilizing" and "analytical" is made in Dalai Lama 2002, 118-19. It is also found, supplemented by an "integrated" form in the analysis of meditation by Daniel Goleman (1988).

Developing this fundamental division, the Evidence Report of the Agency for Healthcare Research and Quality proposes a division into five broad categories: mantra, mindfulness, yoga, taiji quan, and qigong (Ospina et al. 2007, 3). Authors acknowledge that this classification is problematic, since it merges a number of different methods into one group such as, for example, hatha and kundalini forms of yoga or breath awareness and chanting under the heading of mantra. It also does not allow visualization as a separate category—as much as the ancient Buddhist system does, which subsumes it under "concentration."

Approaching the problem from a completely different angle and after examining many meditation methods in a comparative, cultural context, I have proposed to classify the various forms according to the venue they use to access the subconscious mind (Kohn 2008a). Most obvious are three ways that match the major modes of human perception: visual, auditory, and kinesthetic. That is to say, the meditation forms of visualization, sound immersion (mantra practice), and body awareness

Visualization is a key method in tantric Buddhism and medieval Daoism as well as the essential working tool of hypnosis. It involves focusing the mind on a specific scene or sequence of events, such as energy flows, deities, cosmic patterns, saints' lives, or potential future events. Scenes are either imagined with complete detachment or involve the participation of the practitioner—in all cases opening awareness to subtler levels of consciousness (see Epstein 1989; Korn and Johnson 1983; Samuels and Samuels 1975).

Mantra practice, which I call "sound immersion," is the vocalized or silent repetition of a sound, word, or phrase. First documented in ancient Hindu sources, it appears as scripture recitation in Daoism and forms an important part of some Mahayana Buddhist schools, such as Pure Land and Nichiren. It approaches the subconscious through the auditory system, creating vibrations in the brain that have a calming effect and, especially if used in conjunction with deity devotion, lead to a sense of selflessness and connection to the divine (see Gass 1999).

Body awareness, sometimes also called kinesthetic practice, centers on the body as it is moved or placed into different postures. Although commonly undertaken in hatha yoga, daoyin, taiji quan, and qigong, most people think of this practice more as a form of body cultivation. Yet, while it does have distinct physical effects, body awareness also has clear meditative purposes. With its deep focus on the movements both of the physical and the energy body, it can release emotional issues and lead to meditative oneness (see Hackett 1977; Kohn 2008b).

Beyond these three fundamental types, three further modes include observation, body energetics, and immediacy. Each utilizes again a different mode of accessing and modifying the subconscious mind, sometimes but not necessarily in combination with one of the main modes of perception (e.g., awareness of physical sensations in observation).

More specifically, observation, used in Buddhist insight meditation and Daoist inner observation, establishes a detached, objective observer or "witness consciousness" in the mind, the "observing self" (Deikman 1982) which is a mental position of distanced seeing, the faculty of taking a step back from involvement with experiences and emotions. From this viewpoint adepts identify, observe, and cleanse negative emotions while cultivating positive states as defined by the tradition: compassion, calmness, and joy. They also see the world increasingly as a succession of changing phenomena and learn to relax into all kinds of different circumstances (see Goldstein and Kornfield 1987; Rosenberg 1999; Brown and Engler 1984).

Body energetics, next, is a form that appears in Daoist internal alchemy, kundalini yoga, and Western alchemy. The meditative refinement of tangible forms of body energy (most commonly sexual forces) into spiritual forms, body energetics activates subtle energetic powers that connect the person to the ultimate. The method works with an intricate network of subtle energy channels, centers, and passes that need to be opened and activated and ideally leads to the emergence of a new spiritual dimension, through which the adept can communicate and ultimately become one with the divine (see Kohn and Wang 2009).

Zuowang matches the last category, which can be described as immediacy and, beyond its development in the *Zhuangzi* and the Daoist tradition, has been adopted also in Far Eastern Buddhism, notably in Chinese Chan, Japanese Zen, and Tibetan Dzogchen. Through its practice, adepts eliminate all sensory perception and the conscious mind as inherently dualistic and potentially misleading, avoiding the use of the sensory apparatus in attaining higher states. Practitioners thus strive to access what they call pure experience or "sitting in oblivion of everything" by letting go of all ordinary perception while strengthening intuition, the potency of the inborn, natural mind—a pure reflection of original cosmos in human beings. Posture and body control become essential; all analytical, dualistic thinking as well as connection to deities are radically overcome. In addition, it has its own understanding of the universe, appreciation of the human role in creation, concepts of mind and body, vision of the ultimate goal, role and importance of the master, and advanced methodology.

Early Sources

The oldest documentation of *zuowang*, as well as the first mention of the term, appears in the *Zhuangzi* 莊子 (Book of Master Zhuang). The classical passage is part of a dialogue of Confucius 孔子 and his disciple Yan Hui 顏回, the latter reporting that he is "getting better" at attaining Dao. When Confucius asks what he means, Yan Hui says he has "become oblivious of benevolence and righteousness," two essential Confucian virtues that, according to the *Daode jing* 道德經 (Book of the Dao and Its Inherent Potency; ch. 18),[5] form part of the later unfolding of culture and thus represent a step away from Dao. Confucius tells him that this is good, but that he has not gone far enough. At their next meeting Yan Hui says he has left behind "rites and music," taking aim at the fundamental Confucian ways of relating to the world, which are similarly denounced as betraying true humanity in the *Daode jing*. When Confucius tells Yan Hui that he still has a ways to go, he leaves, then reports again:

> "I'm getting there!"
> "How so?"
> "I can sit in oblivion!"
> Confucius was startled: "What do you mean, 'sit in oblivion'?"
> "I let my limbs and physical structure fall away, do away with perception and intellect, separate myself from body-form and let go of all knowledge, thus joining Great Pervasion. This is what I mean by 'sitting in oblivion'." (see Watson 1968, 90; Graham 1981, 92; Mair 1994, 64; Roth 1997, 310; 2010, 198)

Zuowang here is an advanced state of meditative absorption, achieved after more common features of worldly connection, social rules and formal virtues, are eliminated. An introverted state and practice, it yet also has an extroverted effect when activated in daily life. Thus the *Zhuangzi* presents various descriptions of mystical states, visions of ultimate ways of being in the world—free and easy wandering, utmost happiness—as well as outlines of the ways people of superb skill and the "perfected of old" live in complete freedom and ease.

For example, "good swimmers . . . are oblivious of the water and its dangers" (ch. 19); "fish are oblivious of one another in the rivers and lakes" (ch. 6); "the snow-goose does not bathe every day to make itself white, nor the crow

---

[5] I translate *de*, usually rendered "virtue" as "inherent potency." The term expresses the manifest activity of Dao, the spiritual potential and inherent power of things and people, the sense of inner truth which is both formless and mysterious as part of Dao but also unique to the individual as it is activated in the world. Moral goodness (virtue) forms part of the concept, but it goes beyond that to include the fulfillment of one's essential inner nature and heaven-given destiny—which may or may not be moral in the common sense.

blacken itself every day to make itself black" (ch. 14). In other words, *zuowang* in the *Zhuangzi*, in addition to being an introverted, absorbed state of deep meditation is also an extroverted way of being in the world that is free from reflection and intentional action. It is a spontaneous way of living in natural simplicity that is realized by being at one with Dao, joined with Great Pervasion—it is in fact the fundamental human birth right that is lost through sensory involvement and conscious categorizations.

As for concrete methods of how to attain this unified state, the *Zhuangzi* speaks of "mind fasting" (*xinzhai* 心齋), which allows practitioners to reduce mental input and replace ordinary perception with the workings of subtler energies, such as *qi*. It also mentions the possibility of being free from emotions and learning how to avoid conscious classifications by "making all things equal." However, the *Zhuangzi* overall remains rather vague as to the exact procedures of meditation. Its commentaries, notably those by Guo Xiang 郭象 (d. 310) and Cheng Xuanying 成玄英 (7th c.), do not give specific practice instructions either. This is slightly remedied in pre-Han literature by the "Neiye" 內業 (Inward Training) chapter of the *Guanzi* 管子 (Works of Master Guan; trl. Roth 1999), which outlines concrete instructions leading to a state of "emptiness" and supported by the *Daode jing* which emphasizes ways of "embracing oneness" and reaching "clarity and stillness" (*qingjing* 清靜).

Tang Works

The other major documentation on *zuowang* dates from the Tang dynasty, when masters of the Twofold Mystery (Chongxuan 重玄) and Highest Clarity (Shangqing 上清) schools wrote extensively about it. They centered their presentations on the same *Zhuangzi* passage but added more subtle philosophical argumentation, vastly more detailed procedures, major Buddhist concepts, as well as visions of the otherworld where Dao is manifest in celestial palaces and immortals. The main source here is the *Zuowang lun* 坐忘論 (On Sitting in Oblivion, DZ 1036, YQ 94; see Robinet in Schipper and Verellen 2004, 306-07)[6] by the Sima Chengzhen 司馬承禎 (647-735). Addressed to a general audience of aristocratic background, it presents seven steps that lead adepts from ordinary consciousness through a variety of practices—including Buddhist-inspired concentration, observation, and absorption—to "attaining Dao," an ecstatic sense of freedom that is reminiscent of the *Zhuangzi* yet also involves the cessation of karma and ascent to the heavens of the immortals.

---

[6] Texts in the Daoist Canon (DZ) are cited by the numbers in Komjathy 2002; Schipper and Verellen 2004. "YQ" stands for *Yunji qiqian*, the Daoist encyclopedia of 1019.

Two further texts are closely related to the *Zuowang lun*. One is an inscription of the same title, dated to the year 829 and placed in front of a temple dedicated to Sima Chengzhen on Mount Wangwu, his latest residence. It summarizes the key features of the other text and is probably an early forerunner. A modern edition has been provided by Wu Shouju (1981), but it is also contained in Zeng Zao's 曾造 *Daoshu* 道樞 (Pivot of the Dao, DZ 1017, 2.7a-8a).[7] The other is the appendix to the *Zuowang lun* in its edition in the Daoist canon (DZ 1036, 15b-18a). This is identical with the *Dingguan jing* 定觀經 (Scripture on Stability and Observation, DZ 400, YQ 17.6b-13a; see Schipper in Schipper and Verellen 2004, 332), an outline of mental transformation in forty-nine verses signed by the otherwise unknown Lingxuzi 泠虛子. Also summarized under the title *Guanmiao jing* 觀妙經(Scripture on Observation of the Mystery, DZ 326; see Robinet in Schipper and Verellen 2004, 558), it has been cited in longer or shorter parts in quite a number of other texts, ranging from the late Tang to Yuan-dynasty works on internal alchemy.[8]

An essential part of this text, moreover, consists of a comprehensive outline of five phases leading to mental concentration and seven stages of bodily transformation to immortality. These also appear in the *Cunshen lianqi ming* 存神鍊氣銘 (Inscription on Visualizing Spirit and Refining *Qi*, DZ 834, YQ 33.12a-14b; see Lévi in Schipper and Verellen 2004, 375-76), a text closely associated with Sun Simiao 孫思邈 (581-682) of the seventh century. A yet different system of stages to the Dao appears in the *Tianyinzi* 天隱子 (Book of the Master of Heavenly Seclusion, DZ 1026; Robinet in Schipper and Verellen 2004, 303), allegedly transmitted by Wu Yun 吳筠 (d. 778) and edited by Sima Chengzhen. It is more comprehensive than the other texts, beginning with preparatory measures such as fasting and abstention as well as the establishment of the meditation chamber. The *Tianyinzi* has been published many times also in non-Daoist collections and is still a core work among qigong practitioners today.

Further supplementary materials include first the *Neiguan jing* 內觀經 (Scripture of Inner Observation, DZ 641, YQ 17.1a-6b; trl. Kohn 1989b; see Schipper in Schipper and Verellen 2004, 500), extensively cited by Zhang Wanfu 張萬福 in the early eighth century and thus probably another seventh-century document. Revealed by Lord Lao, it outlines various ways of observing the internal work-

---

[7] This is a major collection of materials on internal alchemy in 42 *juan*, dated to around 1151, however, materials tend to be copied erroneously or in fragments. See Boltz 1987, 231-34; Baldrian-Hussein in Schipper and Verellen 2004, 780-81.

[8] Unlike in the 1987 book, I render *ding* here as "stability" to distinguish its Daoist from its Buddhist in *samādhi or samatha*: there is a more physical dimension to the Daoist practice beyond the mere focus or concentration of mind. I also stick to the rather literal translation of "observation" for *guan*, which also can be (and has been) expressed with terms like "contemplation," "discernment," "insight," and "mindfulness."

ings of body and mind, adding detailed definitions of mental aspects. Next, the
Wuchu jing 五廚經 (Scripture of the Five Kitchens, DZ 763; see Verellen in
Schipper and Verellen 2004, 351-52; Mollier 2000), by Yin Yin 尹愔 of the
early eighth century adds an advanced cosmological dimensions to the picture.
Also being transmitted in a Buddhist version, it yet again confirms the close
interrelation between the traditions. Last but not least, Wu Yun's *Xinmu lun* 心
目論 (On Mind and Eyes, DZ 1038; see Baldrian-Hussein in Schipper and
Verellen 2004, 308) provides an imaginary dialogue between the eyes and the
mind on who carries more responsibility and has which precise tasks in the
quest for oneness with Dao.

Further Dimensions

"Sitting in oblivion" is much discussed in the classics and in the Tang—but
what about the early middle ages and the period since the Song? Only very few
passages use the term *zuowang*, but Daoists still strove to attain Dao and entered
deep absorptive states. Looking at the sources, it becomes clear that the emphasis on what it meant to "attain Dao" was different—visualizing deities and
reaching a spirit-like state to communicate with divine beings and travel to the
otherworld in ecstatic excursions in Highest Clarity in the early middle ages;
and transforming internal energies and creating an immortal embryo to ascend
to the celestial realms in internal alchemy (*neidan* 內丹) since the Song.[9] In both
contexts, when the term *zuowang* is used, it indicates a preparatory or secondary
form of practice.

Thus the *Sandong zhunang* 三洞珠囊 (A Bag of Pearls from the Three Caverns,
DZ 1139), by Wang Xuanhe 王懸和 (fl. 683),[10] lists many different techniques
and experiences under the heading of "sitting in oblivion and focusing one's
thinking" (*jingsi* 精思; 5.1a-2a). These techniques are in each case exemplified
by a specific text and personage. Whereas the text links *zuowang* with *Zhuangzi*
passages (chs. 2, 4,6), it describes *jingsi* as the practice of the first Celestial Master Zhang Daoling 張道陵 and claims that it led to his revelation of Dao.

The *Sandong zhunang* explains *jingsi* further by citing Ge Xuan's 葛玄 *Wuqian wen
jingxu* 五千文精序 (Essential Explanation of the Text in Five Thousand Words;
lost), presumably of the third century. This states that through focusing one's
thinking "the manifold wonders will duly come together. Looking inside one's
body . . . one can cause *qi* and [inner] deities to live forever" (5.2a). It then ex-

---

[9] On Highest Clarity meditation, see Robinet 1993; Miller 2008. For practices of internal alchemy, see Baldrian-Hussein 1984; Kohn and Wang 2009.

[10] On the text, see Reiter 1990. For further discussions, see Benn in Pregadio 2008,
832-33; Kohn and Kirkland 2000, 535; Reiter in Schipper and Verellen, 440-41.

pands the definition to include visualization of the body gods as prescribed in the *Huangting jing* 黃庭經 (Yellow Court Scripture, in DZ 263 [chs. 55-57], 402-403, YQ 11-12), one of the classics of Highest Clarity, and further links it with ecstatic journeys to the stars—moving into the realm of intentional visualizations and thus further away from oblivion. In other words, in Highest Clarity as reflected in the encyclopedia, *zuowang* was a meditation practice seen largely as a preparation for a level of mental focus necessary to attain communication with deities and go on ecstatic excursions.

The Song encyclopedia *Yunji qiqian* 雲笈七籤 (Seven Tablets in a Cloudy Satchel, DZ 1032; dat. 1019; see Boltz in Pregadio 2008, 1203-06; Schipper in Schipper and Verellen 2004, 943-45) presents a similar perspective. It, too, sees *zuowang* as preparatory, then links it with "transforming the body-self" (*huashen* 化身) and provides instructions that also involve physical movements and breathing:

> Every night after bedtime, lie down flat on your back and close your eyes, then calm your spirit and stabilize your spirit souls, reaching a state of oblivion ready for creative imagination. Next, exhale deeply two or three times, then twist quickly to the right and left and raise [and lower] the hips. Focus your mind on the navel to create a shadow personage three or four *cun* tall. Next, let the shadow figure divide into several million and see them exit from your head. Allow them to penetrate the room and rise up, moving into the heavens and filling all the dharma worlds, thinking: "All these are my body-self." (35.4ab; see also Eskildsen 2007)

Here the main focus is visualization and traveling ecstatically through the "dharma worlds." Oblivion is a state that prepares the practitioner for "creative imagination" and not, as in the *Tianyinzi*, the culmination of "imagination and visualization."

In internal alchemy, too, *zuowang* appears in a supportive function. A system that integrated previous techniques and specifically used the *Yijing* 易經 (Book of Changes) and alchemical metaphors, it focused on the transformation of bodily energies with the goal of creating an immortal embryo. Rather than a central focus, "oblivion" here appears as one form of practice among many, typically associated with inner observation (*neiguan* 內觀) and frequently interpreted in Buddhist terms as comparable to wall-gazing (*biguan* 壁觀) or sitting in absorption (*zuochan* 坐禪).[11]

---

[11] I render *chan* as "absorption" because the word originally transliterated the Sanskrit term *dhyāna*, which means "absorption." Another meditative *zuo* practice is "sitting in enclosure" (*zuoguan* 坐關), a form of long-term isolation in a sealed structure or cage, which be-

For example, the "Discourse on Inner Observation" in the *Zhong Lü chuandao ji* 鍾呂傳道集 (Zhongli Quan's Transmissions of the Dao to Lü Dongbin),[12] describes both *zuowang* and visualization (*cunxiang* 存想) as forms of inner observation that lead from a state of elementary wisdom to profound sageliness.

> Whether acquiring or rejecting, in all cases remain aware just how much the mind is like a monkey and the intention like a wild horse: never stopping, never staying but constantly afraid of pursuing things and losing them, willing [things] and not hitting the target. Instead, establish yourself firmly in the mental image [of observation] to find a state where the ears do not hear and the eyes do not see, the mind is not wild and the intention is not confused. Seeing affairs and things clearly, you cannot fail to practice inner observation and reach complete oblivion. (16.16ab)

Along similar lines Master Wenyuan 文元公, cited in the "Collected Essentials" section of the *Daoshu* explains that ordinary perception is like living under the seal of illusion and magic and that, in order to escape from that state, "students of the Dao must first learn to stop all thoughts and, if ever a thought should arise, be immediately aware of it" (3.1b). As long as they are "unable to be completely without thoughts, use the observation of emptiness" (*guankong* 觀空) to cleanse the mind; "if not yet able to rest in emptiness, use matching response," thus moving from immediate response to a sense of emptiness and eventually to complete freedom from thoughts. This, then is what "Zhuangzi did when sitting in oblivion and Bodhidharma practiced in wall-gazing; it is quite beyond the reach of beginning students" (2ab).

---

came popular in the nineteenth century (see Goossaert 2002). *Zuowang* was not connnected to this.

   [12] The text is contained in the collection *Xiuzhen shishu* 修真十書 (Ten Works on the Cultivation of Perfection, DZ 263, chs. 14-16). Another complete version being contained in the *Daoshu*, it probably dates from the twelfh century. See Boltz 1987, 139-41; Baldrian Hussein in Schipper and Verellen 2004, 801; Eskildsen 2009, 88-89.

Zuowang Today

Inheriting the tradition, twentieth-century Daoists, as reported by Erwin Rousselle who practiced in Peking in the 1920s, often use a combination of concentration, oblivion, and internal alchemy. Roussell's instruction began with a concentration exercise that tied all thoughts and conscious activities to the lower abdominal area, called in traditional literature the cinnabar or elixir field (*dantian* 丹田), in medicine the Ocean of *Qi* (*qihai* 氣海), and in the modern context "fixation spot."[13] The result was called "relaxation" and led to "peace of mind" in a state of formless absorption (Rousselle 1933, 178). Then "the technique of meditation is changed" and adepts learn a practice closely resembling internal alchemy: they bring internal *qi* into awareness and move it through the body in different ways, reflecting ancient methods of *qi*-guiding as much as observation or mindfulness practice (1933, 184).

Today Daoists use *zuowang* to denote a specific form of practice, describing it as a loss of self and conscious mentation. For example, Liu Xingdi of the Leigu tai Temple in Shaanxi says:

> *Zuowang* is allowing everything to slip from the mind, not dwelling on thoughts, allowing them to come and go, simply being at rest. It is important to take a good posture to still the body and calm the mind. Otherwise *qi* disperses, attention wanders, and the natural process is disturbed. Just remain empty and there is no separation from Dao. Then wisdom will arise and bring forth light, with is the clear *qi* of the person. Do not think too much about the theory of this, otherwise you are sure to disturb the mind. It is like the sun rising in the east and setting in the west. To think about stopping it halfway is a futile exercise. Just trust the inherent natural process. (Shi 2005, 6)

While this sees oblivion more of a state that is natural and not separated from Dao, reflecting the ancient *Zhuangzi*, Eva Wong, renowned author and long-term practitioner of Complete Perfection (Quanzhen 全真) Daoism, finds *zuowang* more of an actual method, but then also goes back to the ancients:

> *Zuowang* is a dropping of conceptions. When we drop conceptions, what we have is the natural emergence of the natural self, the natural celestial mind, which has been with us all the time. It is only because of our conceptions that we can't experience it. So when we practice *zuowang*, we are

---

[13] Jiang Weiqiao 蔣維喬 (1872-1955), also known as Master Yinshi, and author of the *Yinshizi jingzuo fa* 因是子靜坐法 (Quiet Sitting with Master Yinshi), was similarly inclined toward renaming and called it the "center of gravity." He, too, moved from here into the circulation of *qi* in inner alchemical fashion, establishing the microcosmic orbit. See Lu 1964; Kohn 1993b.

simply saying that here is a method where we can begin to drop conceptions. . . .

[For this] there are specific methods of meditation—*zuowang* is one of
them and *zazen* is another. Then, of course, there is Highest Clarity visualization, merging with the deities, that's another form of meditation. But
if we go back and look at originally what is taught in the *Laozi* and
Zhuangzi, everything is meditation—walking, sitting, standing—and when
we begin to realize this, then that is true meditation. There is no longer a
distinction between non-meditation and meditation. (Shi 2007, 8).

Actively taught in the West today both by the British Taoist Association (BTA)
under their leader Shi Jing, in Da Yuan Circle (formerly Orthodox Daoism of
America, ODA) guided by Liu Ming,[14] and in the Qigong and Daoist Training
Center by Michael Rinaldini (an initiate of the Longmen lineage of Complete
Perfection), *zuowang* is a formless, non-conceptual meditation that releases the
hold of the self. As Shi Jing says:

Zuowang is to sit and forget. What we forget is the thing we hold most
dearly: self, with all its opinions, beliefs, and ideals. We can be so caught
up in the concept of self that we only see the world as a place to fulfill
personal ambition and desire. (2006, 11; see also Rinaldini 2009, 187)

The practice releases this through just being with the natural process (*ziran* 自
然), in a mental state that is, according to Shi Jing, characterized by "choiceless
awareness," a "detached observation" of reality. Both these terms come directly
from Buddhist insight meditation and indicate the creation of a conscious observer as the agent of detachment and observation. It represents the modern
interpretation of *zuowang* following the increased Buddhist influence already
visible in internal alchemy and not supported in earlier materials, which describe the ultimate state in terms of the *Zhuangzi* as the "falling away of body
and doing away with perception."

While emphasizing that *zuowang* is without special techniques or methods and
means just being in the present, both Shi Jing and Liu Ming provide technical
instruction—just as the Tang texts give details on breathing awareness, mind
control, and proper attitudes.

Shi Jing, in a lecture at the beginning of a *zuowang* retreat, points out that one
should always "reaffirm one's intention at the beginning of every meditation

---

[14] The leaders of the BTA were initiated at the Leigu tai in Shaanxi and follow authentic Chinese teachings. Liu Ming (formerly Charles Belyea) claimed to have received the
transmission of the Liu family in Taiwan, but in effect cannot show an authentic Daoist
lineage. Still, his teachings reflect much of what is going on in China and are representative
for American practice. For details on his life and work, see Phillips 2008. Both show a fair
amount of Buddhist influence, BTA more of the vipassana type, ODA more Zen.

period," develop confidence in the practice (rather than enthusiasm which exhausts the *qi*) and make sure that the body is aligned and stable (2006, 13)

Liu Ming, moreover, specifies just how to achieve this stable alignment:

—base like a mountain, legs crossed or folded
—back straight but light, stomach empty
—head drawn upward, eyes holding a relaxed gaze
—tongue touching the roof of the mouth to connect the *qi* channels
—hands resting comfortable in lap
—breath flowing gently and in complete silence (Da Yuan Circle pamphlet)

Just as this is essentially the posture for zazen—with eyes open rather than closed as the Tang texts note—so the beginning method is essentially Buddhist: one should create stability of mind by following the breath and counting the exhalations (see Sekida 1975). From here, Liu Ming notes, one reaches a point of "embracing the One," a term borrowed from the *Daode jing*, which he interprets to mean being "relaxed" and "calm," sitting with "that which is naturally arising." There should then be no more effort, which is "a hazard to complete fruition," but one should naturally come to "returning to the source," a state best achieved in complete isolation for one year. As Liu says:

This is liberating our practice from all duality—it is the end of preciousness. Formality and informality, of course, blend seamlessly. Fruition is neither precious nor mundane. Some say this is letting personal practice gain universal dimensions, but there has never been a difference between these two. . . . It is also called "the body of light." In death we do not survive or become extinct. Submerged in the Nameless Dao, there is no death and no birth; there is neither here nor there.

This moves even the ultimate goal into a Buddhist sphere, replacing immortality with the complete cessation of birth and death, here and there (*nirvāna*), while also using Western alchemical terminology, "the body of light" to explain the new dimension.

To sum up, *zuowang* has meant a number of different things in the course of Chinese history. While both Chinese and Western Daoists still actively pursue its practice today, it has once again undergone quite a few transformations, retaining traces of the state outlined in the *Zhuangzi*, using various methods described in the middle ages, and evolving into the complex system of the Tang. Leading masters, and certainly those cited here, work with the traditional model and are familiar with the classical texts, using the *Zuowang lun* to inspire students and encouraging them with citations from the *Dingguan jing*. Yet they do not hesitate to put their own, new visions and practice methods on the old materials, thus keeping the tradition alive through change.

Chapter One

The Classic Core

The earliest description of sitting in oblivion, and first occurrence of the term *zuowang*, is in the ancient Daoist classic *Zhuangzi*, a composite work of thirty-three chapters that was compiled around 250 B.C.E. It contains the teachings of various early Daoist schools, such as the primitivists who wished to abolish all government and culture; the hedonists who found perfection in fulfilling all whims and pleasures; and the syncretists who combined classical Daoist thought with yin-yang cosmology and *Yijing* speculation (see Graham 1980).[1] A large portion of the text, most prominently the first seven or "inner" chapters, represent the thought of Master Zhuang himself. Originally called Zhuang Zhou 莊周, he was of lower aristocratic background, highly erudite, and a minor government servant. He worked for a local southern Chinese state, then withdrew to dedicate himself to his speculations, teaching his ideas to disciples and inspiring them to commit them to writing.

Especially chapters 6 and 19 contain passages that describe not only the state of oblivion, but also the stages leading to it and the ultimate personality characteristics achieved. Although vague and couched in rather obscure language and fictional presentations—the *Zhuangzi* is also considered the first book of traditional Chinese fiction—the descriptions provide a first glimpse of what was so inspiring about this state and its related methods. Explained by the text's main editor and commentator Guo Xiang, they show a vision of the ultimate overcoming of consciousness and identity, in favor of the functioning of the pure mind or spirit through person, leading to an ecstatic state called wandering, roaming, or utmost happiness and associated with an active consecutive di-

---

[1] The main translations used in this study are Watson 1968; Mair 1994; Graham 1981; and Ziporyn 2009. For an overview of both full and partial translations, see Wilhelm 2010.

vestment of outer strive and inner tension, not unlike the purifications under-gone by officiants in preparation for ancestral rituals.

Similar outlines of meditative states and related methods also appear in two further Daoist classics that are dated slightly earlier than the *Zhuangzi*: the *Daode jing* and the "Inward Training" chapter of the *Guanzi*. While the former empha-sizes the reduction of desires and sensory input in favor of a connection with Dao, the wondrous and the mysterious, the latter has detailed practice instruc-tions and focuses on the guiding of *qi* to benefit body and mind. Together the three ancient texts provide a basic, if ultimately sketchy, outline of what medita-tion in pre-Han proto-Daoist circles was like, lending themselves time and again as sources and inspiration and continuing to influence the unfolding of *zuowang* in later ages.

Sitting in Oblivion

"I let my limbs and physical structure fall away, do away with perception and intellect, separate myself from body-form and let go of all knowledge, thus joining Great Pervasion. This is what I mean by 'sitting in oblivion'." So runs the classic passage in *Zhuangzi* 6. Also explained with the phrase "making one's body like dried wood and one's mind like dead ashes" (chs. 2, 22), it describes a state where all visceral awareness of emotions and desires is lost and all sense perception is cut off. Completely free from dualistic thinking or bodily self-consciousness, it represents a state of no-mind where there are no boundaries between things and where the person as person has "lost himself," as the sage says (ch. 2; Watson 1968, 36; Santee 2008, 111-13). It matches the highest level of the meditative stages as found in pre-Han sources, usually described as "emptiness" (Roth 1997, 306).

A better understanding of what it entails is offered by Guo Xiang's commen-tary as recorded in the *Nanhua zhenjing zhushu* 南華真經註疏 (Commentary and Subcommentary to the Perfect Scripture of Southern Florescence, DZ 745; see Robinet in Schipper and Verellen 2004, 294-96):

> Sitting in oblivion—what could one not be oblivious of? First one aban-dons outward manifestations, then one becomes oblivious of that which causes these manifestations. On the inside one is unaware that there is a body-self; on the outside one never knows there are Heaven and Earth. Only thus can one become fully vacant and unify with the changes, and there will be nothing that is not pervaded. (7.39b; Kohn 1987a, 41; Robinet 1983a, 92)

Emphasizing the totality of oblivion, Guo Xiang describes it as occurring in two levels or stages, moving from manifest things, literally the "traces" (*ji* 跡),

to that which left the traces (*suoyi ji* 所以跡), the cause behind all existence, the underlying patterns that shape the world. The concept goes back to the *Zhuangzi*, which like the *Daode jing* (ch. 27) variously describes the perfected as being free from all kinds of tracks or traces, at one with the flow of Dao and the community of life (chs. 7, 11). Later applied in Chinese Buddhist thinking, the "traces" come to indicate the visible result of an action that is not the same as the original intention or feeling which caused it.

Guo Xiang also connects the underlying cause with Heaven and Earth, the movers of the cosmic patterns. He sees the resulting effect, the traces of their movements, in the individual's body-self (*shen* 身), the personal body and conscious identity, the familial and social personhood located within one's physical frame, the site of the personality constructed through self-cultivation, education, and social status (Sommer 2010, 216). This is quite distinct, already in the *Zhuangzi* and even more so in later Daoist literature, from the body-form (*xing* 形), the physical body which the *Zhuangzi* claims one is separated from in the state of oblivion: the discrete, visible shape that toils and needs to be fed, can be mutilated or made whole (2010, 218-19).

For Zhuangzi, in this passage the body-self is already obliterated in the two stages preceding the actual sitting in oblivion, when Yan Hui reports to Confucius—in his role as right-thinking student (Littlejohn 2010, 184)—that he is getting there: first he manages to become oblivious of benevolence and righteousness, next he abandons rites and music. These four are central virtues in the Confucian system that keep society together but, according to the *Daode jing* (ch. 18), signal the loss of Dao since they formalize something that should come naturally to people. Each time Confucius encourages him but notes that it is not good enough, that he still has a way to go. Guo Xiang explains:

> Benevolence is the trace of unbiased love. Righteousness is the effect of completing things. Love is not benevolence, but the trace of its activation. Completing things is not righteousness, but the effect of its manifestation. Maintaining benevolence and righteousness is not enough to understand the source of love and benefit, which is no-mind. Thus they must be abandoned. But this is merely the oblivion of the traces and effects, not penetration of the mystery. (8.38a; see Ziporyn 2009, 204)

Following this, he comments that rites are the outward functioning of the body-form, while music is the instrument of enjoying life; he again stresses that these are just traces and not the real thing (8.38b), which comes only when everything is let go completely and identity is dissolved fully in Dao, the mystery, the Great Pervasion. Still, the passage both clarifies the ultimate state to be attained and indicates the process of attainment, a step-by-step removal from outward traces and focus on the ultimate patterns and inner workings of the cosmos.

A related passage outlines a series of practices that lead to a state of complete oblivion where "nothing is unforgotten," describing the state as the Dao of Heaven and Earth:

> Finding loftiness without controlling intention, cultivating the self without benevolence and righteousness, ordering one's life without pursuing merit and fame, relaxing without retiring to rivers and oceans, living long without practicing healing exercises—nothing unforgotten, nothing not possessed: one rests serenely in the non-ultimate and the host of beautiful things naturally follows along. Such is the Dao of Heaven and Earth, the inherent potency [virtue, *de*] of the sage. (ch. 15; Mair 1994, 145; Watson 1986, 168)

Here the pursuit of loftiness (*gao* 高), self-cultivation (*xiu* 修), an ordered life (*zhi* 治), relaxation or leisure (*xian* 閑), and extended longevity (*shou* 壽) are all part of the process of reorganizing oneself along the lines of oblivion—yet without engaging in any of the virtues and practices commonly associated with these activities. As a result, one will rest calmly in the state before creation, the non-ultimate (*wuji* 無極) and have nothing to worry about as things develop perfectly of themselves.

In addition, the passage characterizes the mental state with a series of terms that continue to appear in the later tradition: quietude (*tian* 恬), calmness (*tan* 淡), serenity (*ji* 寂), and indifference (*mo* 漠) as well as "emptiness and nonbeing" (*xuwu* 虛無) and "nonaction" (*wuwei* 無偽). It emphasizes that "these maintain the balance of Heaven and Earth, are the manifestation of Dao and inherent potency," thus connecting the individual to the greater powers and deeper levels of the cosmos.

Chaos

A powerful early metaphor for the state of complete oblivion that is also used in later literature appears in the figure of Hundun 混沌, "Chaos," a cosmic being at the root of creation who does not have any senses. The *Zhuangzi* has the following story:

> The ruler over the southern sea was Shu [Tight]. The ruler over the northern sea was Hu [Abrupt]. The ruler over the center was Hundun [Chaos]. On occasion Shu and Hu would meet in the realm of Hundun who received them with great hospitality. The two then started to plan how they could possibly pay back Hundun's kindness. They said: "All people have seven orifices so they can see, hear, eat, and breathe. He alone has none of them. Let us try boring him some." So they bored a

hole every day, and on the seventh day Hundun died. (ch. 7; see Girardot 2009, 64).

Hundun is thus a cosmic entity before and beyond sensory perception and as such an image of the ideal state of oneness with Dao. Chapter 12, in addition, describes someone versed in the "arts of Mr. Hundun" as " a person who understands returning to simplicity and in nonaction has reached the uncarved state [pu 朴]. He fully embodies his essential nature and embraces the spirit, wandering freely in the midst of the world" (Girardot 2009, 79).

Nonaction, moreover, the essential attitude of someone in a state of oblivion, is described in images connected to the chaos theme:

> Nonaction in Heaven is purity; on Earth it is peace—
> The two combine and all things transform.
> Vast and vague, chaotic and obscure: they emerge from nowhere.
> Vast and vague, nebulous and hazy: they have no sign.
> (ch. 18; Watson 1968, 191; Mair 1994, 168; Girardot 2009, 84)

A clear relationship of sitting in oblivion with Hundun, moreover, appears in a speech by Vast Concealment (Hongmeng 鴻蒙) in chapter 11. Hongmeng is a figure connected with the Hundun mythology—hongmeng hongdong 鴻濛鴻洞 being another expression describing the creation time (Girardot 2009, 48)—but he is here presented as a master who gives instruction in the art of returning to the beginning. Like Hundun in the *Shanhai jing* 山海經 (Book of Mountains and Seas), he is shamanically "slapping his thighs" and "hopping and dancing like a bird," a technique of "aimless wandering" (fuyou 浮游) and "madness" (chang-kuang 猖狂)—the latter also characterizing the unified mind in *Zhuangzi* 4 and 7 (Girardot 2009, 88).

In his speech, he addresses Cloud Chief (Yunjiang 雲將), explaining methods of "mind nourishing" (xinyang 心養). He uses similar phrases as the classic passage on sitting in oblivion and links the oblivious mind with chaos:

> Just take the position of nonaction and all things unfold naturally. Let your body and limbs fall away, expel perception and intellect, leave relations and things behind in oblivion. Become mystically one with the immense and boundless, release your mind and free your spirit.
>
> Be silent and without an active spirit soul [that interacts with the world], and the ten thousand things will each return to their root. Each return to their root and rest in unknowing—dark, obscure, chaotic: they remain like this for the rest of their days.

However, the moment you try to know this state, you have already effected a separation from it. Don't ask its name, don't measure its foundation—it's the spontaneous life of each being. (ch. 11; Mair 1994, 99; Watson 1968, 122

This is further explained in the passage immediately following the Hongmeng story (Watson 1968, 123-24). Here, in contrast to the "common man" who in valuing face "welcomes those who are like him and scorns those who differ from him," the Daoist's "face and form have blended with Great Unity." He sees only "nonbeing" and, like Emperor Hundun, stands alone at the center as "the true friend of Heaven and Earth" (Girardot 2009, 88).

The state of chaos and nonbeing as the ultimate state of Daoist cultivation is also the end point of a reversal of the stages of decline which humanity went through historically from the golden age to the present—interpreted also psychologically as the fall from childhood innocence to adult self-consciousness. The *Zhuangzi* has:

> The knowledge of the people in antiquity was perfect. How was this so? They didn't even begin to perceive that things existed—thus it was perfect. It was complete. Nothing could be added to this! Next they thought that things existed but did not recognize any distinctions. After that, they saw distinctions but did not recognize right and wrong. The emergence of right and wrong was the destruction of Dao. (ch. 2; see Watson 1968, 41; Graham 1981, 54; Mair 1994, 17)

Guo Xiang names these four stages and explains them in terms of oblivion, making it clear that he sees the attainment of *zuowang* as an intrapersonal recovery of a cosmic state lost in human development. The first stage of original oneness he calls "Chaos Complete" (*huncheng* 混成) and says:

> This means being oblivious of Heaven and Earth, doing away with beings. On the outside not examining time and space, on the inside never conscious of one's body-self. Thus one can be boundless and unattached, going along with beings and fully according with all. (3.1b)

The next stage of beings (*wu* 物) means that oblivion is "no longer complete," but it is still free from distinctions (*feng* 封), which make up the third level of decline. The final stage is the perception of right and wrong (*shifei* 是非)—a central pair in the *Zhuangzi* and the core of its analysis of conceptual fallacies and exposition of relativism (see Hansen 2010; Roth 2010; see also Kjellberg and Ivanhoe 1996). This is the destruction of Dao, when "emotions begin to be partial and love develops fully" (3.2b; Knaul 1985a, 25). It is from this alienated and unpleasant level that practitioners return to full oblivion, their birthright and the best way of living in the world.

Another recovery of primordial oblivion, a gradated progress toward mystical attainment, is outlined in a passage that describes Buliang Yi' 卜梁倚 progress under the guidance of Nüyu 女偊 (Woman Hunchback):

> After three days, he was able to put the world outside himself Once he could do this, I continued my support and after seven days, he was able to put beings outside himself. Once he could do this, I continued my support, and after nine days, he was able to put life outside himself. Once he could do this, he achieved the brightness of dawn, and after this, he could see his own aloneness. After he had managed to see his own aloneness, he could do away with past and present, and after that, he was able to enter [a state of] no life and no death (ch. 6; see Watson 1968, 83; Graham 1981, 87; Mair 1994, 57).

This outlines the progress to complete oblivion and oneness with Dao in seven steps: the adept puts the world (1), beings (2), and life (3) outside himself—an activity interpreted by Guo Xiang as becoming "oblivious" (8.3a). From here he goes on to attain the brightness of dawn (4) and the ability to see his own aloneness (5). That is to say, he finds an inner clarity or radiance, possibly like the bright light within that in many meditation traditions signals the opening to pure consciousness. In "aloneness," moreover, he attains a state of nonduality which, according to Guo Xiang, means being free from all feelings about death. "Not hating death," he says, "means that one can be at peace with whatever one encounters; one is vast and open and without obstruction, seeing the cosmic pivot and acting with it" (8.3b). "Seeing one's aloneness" in his terms thus means "letting go of whatever one comes in contact with" (8.4a).

From here Buliang Yi abandons past and present (6) and finally enters a state completely beyond life and death (7), interpreted by Guo Xiang as "giving up all attachment to life and death" (8.4a), going beyond time and all existence and reaching oneness with Dao.

The Ideal State

What, then, is it like to be in a state of chaotic oblivion? The *Zhuangzi* uses the metaphor of drunkenness to describe it:

> When a drunken man falls from a carriage, though the carriage may be going very fast, he won't be killed. He has bones and joints the same as other men, but he is not injured as they would be, because his spirit is whole. He didn't know he was riding, and he doesn't know he has fallen out. Life and death, alarm and terror do not enter his breast. (ch. 19; Watson 1968, 198-99; Graham 1981, 137; Mair 1994, 176)

Here oblivion is a state of complete unknowing, an utter lack of awareness of where one is or what one does. There are no thoughts of disaster or alarm, or even of life and death, that might come into the mind. This, in turn, creates a safety net, preventing any kind of injury to the person. The spirit being whole, so is the person.

The *Liezi* 列子 (Book of Master Lie, DZ 668), lost in antiquity then reconstituted in the early centuries C.E. (see Graham 1961), which recounts many stories also told in the *Zhuangzi*, gives a more concrete example. It tells the story of Master Hua 華子 from the state of Song who was in oblivion to the point that he could no longer quite function in daily life:

> He would receive a present in the morning and forget it by evening, give a present in the evening and forget it by morning. On the road, he would forget to walk; in the house he would forget to sit down. Today he would not remember yesterday; tomorrow he would not remember today. (Graham 1960, 70)

This case of ancient Chinese Alzheimer's was naturally quite upsetting to his family who consulted various specialists, all to no avail, until a Confucian of Lu came and offered to do an early version of psychotherapy: "He tried stripping Hua, and he looked for clothes. He tried starving him, and he looked for food. He tried shutting him up in the dark, and he looked for light." Encouraged by these signs that there was a survival instinct still at work, the Confucian asked to be left alone with Hua and, literally overnight, jerked him out of his oblivious state—to the latter's great regret:

> Formerly, when I was in oblivion, I was boundless. I did not notice whether Heaven and Earth existed or not. Now suddenly I remember: all the disasters and recoveries, gains and losses, joys and sorrows, loves and hates of twenty or thirty years rise up in a thousand tangled threads. . . . Shall I never again find a moment of oblivion? (Graham 1960, 71)

In other words, the ideal state of oblivion creates a sense of inner peace and openness, a freedom from emotions and evaluations, success and failure, and any sort of strife. It is a state of inner wholeness where one flows along with Dao and just is—without memories or expectations, free from urges, pushes, or endeavors. Yet to maintain it one must be completely beyond any form of survival instincts: looking for light, food, and clothes when deprived of them is an indication that "perception and intellect" have not been "driven out completely."

Another way of describing this state is in terms of naturalness (*ziran* 自然), a term also translated as "spontaneity" or "immediacy." People are naturally and spontaneously at home in Dao as fish are in water (ch. 6). This feeling of being completely at home, in one's natural element, is further clarified with the metaphor of "perfect alignment" (*shi* 適) or comfort:

> One is oblivious of the feet when the shoes are comfortable; one is oblivious of the waist when the belt fits perfectly. Knowledge obliterates all right and wrong when the mind is in perfect alignment with all. (ch. 19; Watson 1968, 206-07; Mair 1994, 184)

This means oblivion is a state where one is naturally at home in the greater universe, as comfortable in one's mind and spirit as one is in clothes that fit well. Since the match is perfect, there is no need to evaluate it or develop feelings about anything. Since one is the only way one could be as determined by Dao, there is no urgency to change or develop regrets about not changing.

In terms of actual living experience, the *Zhuangzi* describes the "perfected of old" who "slept without dreaming and woke without worrying, ate without savoring and breathed deep inside. . . ; they knew nothing of loving life and hating death, came into the world without delight and left it without making a fuss" (ch. 6; Watson 1968, 78; Graham 1981, 84). In a state of oblivion, they were not interested in profit and loss, fame and gain, but "went along with what is right for things." Following in this line, the text emphasizes that those in harmony with Dao would naturally not encounter anything untoward and remained completely at peace when faced with death or disease, always accepting the changes and going along with the flow of life.

One example is Master Sang who has fallen into a state of poverty and reflects on why this should be so: "My father and mother surely wouldn't wish this poverty on me. Heaven covers all without partiality; Earth bears up all without bent: they surely would not single *me* out to become poor!" (ch. 6; Watson 1968, 91; Graham 1981, 93; Mair 1994, 64). The conclusion he reaches is that it must be "destiny" (*ming* 命), the life he is commanded (*ming*) to have by Heaven, something that is beyond human control and cannot be changed. By the same token, the *Zhuangzi* emphasizes that "there is no true master" of body and mind: we have no real possession of our bodies, which go on to change as they do, following cosmic laws far beyond the human sphere (ch. 2).

This means that, as Guo Xiang says, "we must understand that things are what they are spontaneously" and transform of themselves (Knaul 1985a, 19). The attitude to develop, according to him, is one of fluid adjustment—best achieved with little or no conscious evaluation. He uses a wide variety of terms for this, ranging from "align with" (*shi* 適) through "correspond to" (*dang* 當), "adapt to" (*ying* 應), "comply with" (*fu* 付), "rely on" (*yin* 因), "avail oneself of" (*dai* 待), "go along with" (*shun* 順), "let go" (*ren* 任), "follow" (*cheng* 椉), and "obey" (*zhi* 致), to "be content with" (*an* 安) and "resign oneself to" (*tuo* 託) (Knaul 1985a, 23; 1985b, 439). This large selection shows just how important adjustment to cosmic patterns and letting go of personal goals and strife is in this vision, and how hard the attainment of complete oblivion. If fully attained, however, it means an ecstatic freedom both from and within the world, a way of being which the *Zhuangzi* describes as "free and easy wandering" (*xiaoyao you* 逍遙遊) or "utmost happiness" (*zhile* 至樂) and which Guo Xiang calls "spontaneous attainment" (*zide* 自得).

A more poetic formulation of the same idea appears in Ruan Ji's 阮籍 (210-263) *Daren xiansheng zhuan* 大人先生傳 (Biography of Master Great Man), speaking as one who has reached the ecstatic freedom of oneness with Dao:

> Heat and cold don't harm me; nothing stirs me up.
> Sadness and worry have no hold on me; pure energy at rest.
> I float on mist, leap into heaven, pass through all with no restraint.
> To and fro, subtle and wondrous, the way never slants.
> My delights and happiness not of this world—
> How would I ever fight with it? (Holzman 1976, 202)

Mind Fasting

As regards specific practices that lead to the attainment of oblivion, the *Zhuangzi* describes a practice call "mind fasting" (*xinzhai* 心齋). Again, Confucius is talking to Yan Hui, but here he is the teacher who advises:

> Unify your will and don't listen with your ears but listen with your mind. No, don't listen with your mind, but listen with your *qi*. Listening stops with the ears, the mind stops with matching [perception], but *qi* is empty and waits on all things. Dao gathers in emptiness alone. Emptiness is the fasting of the mind.[2] (ch. 4; Watson 1968, 57; Graham 1981, 68; Mair 1994, 32)

To reach the inner emptiness of Dao, one thus begins with an act of will, turns one's attention inward, and withdraws the senses, using instead the mind, the flow of consciousness, to relate to things. Then one gives that up, too, and moves on to working with pure *qi*, the cosmic energy and material aspect of Dao that is impartial and open. In this contentless, non-conceptual meditation, both senses and mind are overcome—the former serving as the root of the emotions or "passions and desires," the latter creating mental classifications

---

[2] The word for "emptiness" used here is *xu* 虛, which usually describes a state of mind or inner sense of openness, an integral aspect of Dao. It is distinctly different from emptiness as a more abstract concept in the sense of the underlying nature of the world, which in Buddhism—and from there also in medieval Daoism—is expressed with the term *kong* 空. I supplement characters when needed to mark this distinction.

such as "right and wrong." The state to be achieved is one of emptiness and no-mind, characterized by the complete absence of conscious evaluation and an utter lack of feelings (Santee 2008, 114-15). As the *Zhuangzi* says: "Dao gave him a human face and Heaven gave him a human body, yet he does not let [feelings of] likes and dislikes enter and harm himself" (ch. 5). Instead, the perfected preserves his essence (*jing* 精), attains long life, and finds a peace of mind that matches Heaven and Earth.

The mind in this context appears in two forms: as the ordinary, evaluative mind which matches perception; and as the purified mind of *qi* which goes along with all. The *Zhuangzi* discusses these types of mind variously, calling the ordinary mind by different names, such as "human mind" (*renxin* 人心), "mechanical mind" (*jixin* 機心), and "the mind of life" (*sheng zhi xin* 生之心). This kind of mind is very limited in its reach and tends to keep people in a state of delusion (Tang 1966, 101). It is the mind which harbors all the dangers on the way toward Dao; it has to be subdued, controlled, and tamed, and eventually made into no-mind (Fukunaga 1969, 9; Jan 1981, 467).

From this average impure mind, then, another type of mind arises: as the *Guanzi* says, "Within the mind there is yet another mind" (13.11b). *Zhuangzi* 2 calls this "Heaven's storehouse—one fills it, yet it is never full; one drains it, yet it is never empty" (Watson, 1968, 45). Like the ocean, like Dao, like pure spirit, this mind never dies, it is called "one-with-Heaven" (ch. 15) and the "spirit tower." Being one with this mind gives people magical powers, "fire can't burn him, water can't drown him, beasts can't injure him" (ch. 17; Watson 1968, 182). A person of this mind can see in the dark, he can hear the inaudible, and discover the spirit within. This realized mind is given to everyone, the *Zhuangzi* asserts, and if everyone made it his teacher, then "who would be without a teacher?" (ch. 2).

Another way of distinguishing the two kinds of mind is by language. Words referring to ordinary mentation in the *Zhuangzi* tend to be written with the "heart" radical, while those expressing the workings of the perfect mind use that meaning "water." Thus all the various emotions, whether fear (*ju* 懼), anger (*nu* 怒), joy (*xi* 喜), even love (*ai* 愛) are expressions of "heart-mind" as much as the word for feeling or emotion itself (*qing* 情).

The calm mind of Dao, in contrast, is clear (*qing* 清) and pure (*chun* 淳), deep (*shen* 沈) and pervasive (*chong* 沖), bottomless like the abyss (*yuan* 淵) and translucent like "water that stops waving and becomes clear all the way [*zhan* 湛]" (Ching 1983, 238). The *locus classicus* in the *Zhuangzi* is a story where the Gourd Master lets himself be analyzed by a physiognomist shaman and shows him different aspects of the perfected mind, including death-like patterns of earth and three variations of the abyss (ch. 7; Watson 1968, 96; Graham 1981, 97;

Saso 2010, 149-50). This, he says, "has nine names," which are supplied in the *Liezi* and show the intensity of the water imagery:

> Whirlpools, still waters, currents, water bubbling up from the ground, water dripping from above, water slanting from the side, water dammed and turned back, water draining away in a marsh, several streams coming from one source, and the all hollowed-out abyss. (ch. 2; Graham 1960, 51)

Each of these, then, stands for a particular state of the primordial mind, the pure mystical spirit: from the water that has not yet emerged from the source, through the vastness of the primeval ocean, the beginning stages of Heaven and Earth without name or substance, to the pattern of Earth which is "still and silent, nothing moving, nothing standing up." In addition, water also expresses the activities of the pure mind in real life: it moves by running, gurgling, springing, and whirling, and may be defiled through the senses to become confused, muddled, turbid, and agitated. Another metaphor that is closely related to the water imagery is the mirror—often also expressed in the notion of the water mirror—which can be bright and shining or dull and obscured.[3]

Progress in mind fasting thus works backward from the ordinary heart-based mind through turbidity and agitation of the pure mind to its original form, eventually reaching its source in the abyss that is as deep and open as Dao itself. It is a process of stilling, calming, and purifying, which leads to a state of clarity and stillness, typically linked with intermediate stages of meditation in the early sources (Roth 1997, 306) and often associated with more enstatic states, reached through sensory withdrawal and a single-minded focus on the deep underlying root or source of the cosmos (see Eliade 1958).

Sensory Withdrawal

Fasting and the attainment of clarity and stillness are outlined in even more concrete terms in the story of Woodworker Qing. Charged with the task of making a bell stand, he starts by fasting:

> I always fast in order to quiet my mind. When I have fasted for three days, I no longer have any thought of congratulations or rewards, of titles or stipends. When I have fasted for five days, I no longer have any thought of praise or blame, of skill or clumsiness.

---

[3] On the notion of mind as mirror, especially also in the *Zhuangzi*, see Ching 1983; Cline 2010; Demiéville 1987; Lai 1979; Oshima 2010.

> When I have fasted for seven days, I am so still that I forget I have four limbs and a body-form or structure. By that time, the ruler and his court no longer exist for me. My skill is concentrated and all outside distractions fade away. (ch. 19; Watson 1968, 205; Graham 1981, 135; Mair 1994, 182)

Forgetting body form and structure, being completely oblivious of ruler, court, and audience, the woodworker brings oblivion into practical life and also demonstrates how fasting—physical and mental—is key to its attainment.

This process of fasting, moreover, is very much like the purification undertaken as preparation for ancestral and other rituals in Confucian circles (Sommer 2002, 99). Also called *zhai*, it could similarly last from one to seven days and involved abstention from all or specific foods as well as intoxicating substances, plus the avoidance of contact with blood and dirt, sexual abstinence, taking baths in fragrant waters, and withdrawal to solitude to concentrate the mind—all techniques also used in meditation (Roth 1997, 306). As the *Lüshi chunqiu* 呂氏春秋 (Mr. Lü's Spring and Autumn Annals, 3rd c. B.C.E.) describes it:

> A gentleman fasts and observes vigils, makes sure to stay deep inside his house, and keeps his body utterly still. He refrains from music and sex, eschews associations with his wife, maintains a sparse diet, and avoids the use of piquant condiments. He settles his mind's *qi*, maintains quietude in his organs, and engages in no rash undertaking. (5.42; Knoblock and Riegel 2000, 135; Lo 2005, 166)

The practice here, just as the technique reported by Woodworker Qing, entailed a reversal of ordinary states of perception by removal from the sensory world combined with a cognitive exercise of concentration and opening to the otherworld—the world of emptiness and Dao in the *Zhuangzi*, the world of the ancestors in Confucian ritual. In the latter, as outlined in the *Liji* 禮記 (Book of Rites) the sacrificer thought "about the deceased and remembered what they looked like, how they sighed and how they laughed;" he recalled those things that pleased the departed and became very involved in their emotional life (Sommer 2002, 99; 2003, 212). Occlusion, sensory deprivation, isolation, and starvation all served to allow entry into things otherwise beyond the senses, the opening of a sphere outside of ordinary perception (2002, 100).

In both the Confucian and Daoist environments, the practice enhanced the awareness that one was part of a larger network—of spirits and ancestors in one, of Dao and *qi* in the other. It also connected practitioners to their parents: the ancestral forbears in Confucianism (Sommer 2003, 210); Dao, Heaven and Earth in Daoism (Mugitani 2004). This similarity is not accidental. As Deborah Sommer points out, "the *Daode jing* shares the same vocabulary as the liminal experience of the spirit world in Confucian sacrificial offerings" (2003, 211).

The *Daode jing*, moreover, supplies further details on the classical idea of sensory withdrawal. It notes that one should control sensory input, since overindulgence will result in loss: "The five colors will cause the eyes to go blind, the five tones will cause the ears to be deaf, the five flavors will cause the palate to be spoiled" (ch. 12). The practice is one of "decreasing and again decreasing" (ch. 48), which matches the expression "mysterious and again mysterious" (ch. 1) as a description of Dao, and is interpreted by the Song scholar Chen Jingyuan 陳景元 as "abysmal and again abysmal" (*yuan* 淵)—once more evoking the abyss as an image for the pure mind at one with Dao (DZ 714; Fujiwara 1980, 666).

Like the sacrificer preparing in withdrawal, the practitioner of oblivion is to leave the outside world behind: "Cut off contacts, shut the doors, and to the end of life there will be peace without toil" (*Daode jing* 52, 56). He should reduce possessions, because "to have little is to possess, to have plenty is to be perplexed" (22), and make sure that "there always be no desires so that the wondrous may be observed" (1). The text also makes it clear that any sense of personality and social persona can only be harmful, causing nothing but trouble: "The body-self is the reason why I have terrible vexations. If I did not have a body-self, what trouble would I have? (13). It concludes that it is much better to be insignificant and "embrace the One" (22).

Doing so, one reaches oneness with Dao, which is a return to one's origin, an inward movement of withdrawal: "All things flourish, but each returns to its root. This return to the root means stillness, it is called recovering original destiny. Recovering original destiny is called the eternal, and to know the eternal is called brightness" (16). This establishes a connection between stillness and clarity—the idea that as the mind settles like standing water it will not only become unmoving but also clear and reflective, like the ideal mirroring mind of the sage.

Matching this theme of simplicity and return, the *Daode jing* encourages its followers to "abandon learning," to become like and infant and let the mind be ignorant and dull. It speaks of "achieving highest weakness by being like an infant" (10) and has the sage say: "The multitude are merry . . . I alone am inert, showing no sign [of desires]" (20). This sentence is explained in the *Laozi Xianger zhu* 老子想爾注 (Xianger Commentary) in terms of mental activity.[4] Ordinary people, it explains, have always plenty to plan for, to worry about, but the sage has "abandoned and forgotten all" (Rao 1992, 27). Again the same chapter reads: "Mine indeed is the mind of an ignorant man, indiscriminate and dull. . . . I alone seem to be in the dark." Here the *Xianger zhu* gives the explanation that "the adept of immortality closes his mind and never worries about

---

[4] The text is attributed to the third Celestial Master Zhang Lu 張魯 and dated to around 215 C.E.; it was lost but recovered in fragments from Dunhuang (ed. Rao 1992; trl. Bokenkamp 1997).

false and evil, profit or gain." The dullness of the sagely state of mind is thus explained as a form of oblivion, a way of maintaining emptiness and peace.

Dao in the *Daode jing* is an underlying cosmic oneness, the "root" of all existence, not as strongly described in terms of ever-changing flow of life as in the *Zhuangzi*. The goal of *Daode jing* practice is accordingly the recovery and preservation of this underlying source, the complete merging with it in deep, dark, dull quietude and firm stability. As it says: "Mysterious potency becomes deep and far-reaching, and with it all things return to their original natural state. Then complete harmony is reached" (65). Only when this is attained does movement again occur—very much like the fasting woodworker or sacrificer achieves complete stillness before going out and about his task. Then and only then one can find "long life and eternal vision" (59), live in such a way that "there is nothing that is not done" (48), and encounter good fortune in all one's undertakings—reach free and easy wandering and perfect happiness.

Energetic Practice

Yet another method leading to oblivion in the early texts is the alignment of the body and stabilization of *qi*, best described in the "Inward Training" chapter of the *Guanzi*. According to this, adepts refine their *qi* through physical control and moderation in lifestyle and diet, withdrawal from sensory stimulation, and sitting in meditation. They pursue the fourfold alignment of body, limbs, breath, and mind. First they take a proper upright posture and align their limbs, then they breathe deeply and consciously, regulating the breath and creating a sense of quietude within. From there they practice single-minded focus for the attainment of a tranquil mind, also described as the "cultivated," "stable," "excellent", and "well-ordered" mind. This well-ordered mind then creates an open space within, a lodging place (*she* 舍) for vital energy.

Once filled with the potency of *qi*, adepts achieve complete balance in body and mind. They reach a level of simplicity that allows them to let go of things and be free from sensory overloads. Finding a state of serenity and repose in detachment from emotions that resembles the state of clarity and stillness proposed in the *Daode jing*, they walk through life in harmony with all, free from danger and harm. At peace within and in alignment with the world, they attain a level of physical health that keeps them fit and active well into old age. Reaching beyond ordinary life, they gain a sense of cosmic freedom that allows them to "hold up the Great Circle [of the heavens] and tread firmly over the Great Square [of the earth]" (Roth 1999, 112-13).

Another set of early practice instructions appears in an inscription on a dodecagonal jade block—possibly a knob on a staff (Chen 1982)—of the Zhou dynasty from the fourth century B.C.E and thus slightly predates both *Daode jing* and "Inward Training." Its inscription in forty-five characters has been studied variously (Wilhelm 1948; Engelhardt 1996, 19; Li 1993, 320-23). It reads:

> To *guide* the *qi*, allow it to enter deeply and collect it. As it collects, it will expand. Once expanded, it will sink down. When it sinks down, it comes to rest. After it has come to rest, it becomes stable.

> When the *qi* is stable, it begins to sprout. From sprouting, it begins to grow. As it grows, it can be pulled back upwards. When it is pulled upwards, it reaches the crown of the head.

> It then touches above at the crown of the head and below at the base of the spine. Who practices like this will attain long life. Who goes against this will die. (Harper 1998, 126; see also Roth 1997, 297-98)

This describes a *qi* practice still part of Daoist meditation and well documented from the middle ages onward. In a position of quietude and sensory withdrawal, practitioners inhale deeply, allow the breath to enter both the chest and the mouth, and in the latter mix it with saliva, another potent form of *qi* in the body. Moving their tongue around their mouth, they gather the saliva and gain a sense of fullness, then swallow, allowing the *qi* to sink down. They feel it moving deep into their abdomen, where they let it settle in the central area of gravity, known in Chinese medicine as the Ocean of *Qi* and in Daoism as the elixir field. There the *qi* rests and becomes stable. This may well be the point of inner strength, stability, and even enstasy featured in the *Daode jing*.

As adepts repeat this practice, however, the *qi* first accumulates and becomes stronger, then begins to move from stillness into movement, from clarity into radiance. It does not remain in the lower abdomen but spreads through the body or, as the text says, it "sprouts." Once this is felt, adepts can consciously guide it upwards—a technique that usually involves pushing it down to the pelvic floor and then moving it gradually up along the spine, both in close co-ordination with deep breathing. Eventually a sense of connection to the flow of cosmic energy develops (Kohn 2008b, 14-15).

In other words, some sections of the *Zhuangzi* emphasize the complete aboli-tion of self, perception, and consciousness in something called "sitting in obliv-ion," a state beyond life and death that allows the person to flow along with the changes in ecstatic freedom—expressed also in numerous examples of playful and exceedingly competent people, who have an uncanny knack for certain things (such as Butcher Ding in ch. 3, or the swimmer in ch. 22) (see Crandell 2010). Other sections as well as the *Daode jing* match traditional Confucian prac-tices of fasting in preparation for ancestral sacrifices and focus more on sensory withdrawal and the attainment of internal stability. This stability, which comes with a change in perception from the senses to the mind and eventually to *qi*, is expressed as "clarity and stillness"—a dominant term in later Daoist literature.

Yet other pre-Han sources, such as the "Inward Training" chapter of the *Guan-zii* and the jade block inscription link meditation with physiological practices of internal *qi* manipulation: collecting, visualizing, and guiding it through the body in an effort to attain a stable, excellent, and well-ordered mind as well as health, vigor, and long life.

The variety of practices can be roughly linked with stages of meditation in early texts as described by Harold Roth (1997), which lead from alignment (*zheng* 正) through stillness (*jing* 靜) and clarity (*qing* 清) or radiance/brightness (*ming* 明) to emptiness (*xu* 虛). Yet the texts are not rigid about them: breathing practice may also lead to cosmic freedom, there is a fallling away of the self in fasting, and sensory withdrawal plays a role in the progress to oblivion. This apparent confusion has two effects: for one, it reveals the subtle interconnection between physical manipulation of *qi*, sacrificial methods of fasting and purification, mental exercises in concentration and calmness, and the pursuit of an ultimate way of being in the world; for another it allows adepts to tailor the methods to their needs and unique abilities—another feature that became dominant in later centuries. Ever since have Daoists been well aware of the complexity and inherent power of their tradition and used all these techniques in a multiplicity of ways. Under the heading "sitting in oblivion" they have, moreover, integrated them into an organized system, expanded and well documented in Tang-dynasty sources.

Chapter Two

Twofold Mystery

The first appearance of "oblivion" in the Tang dynasty occurred in the seventh century in a teaching called Twofold Mystery (*chongxuan* 重玄) after the phrase "mysterious and again mysterious" in *Daode jing* 1. Named as such by the court ritualist Du Guangting 杜光庭 (850-933) in his extensive commentary collection called *Daode zhenjing guangsheng yi* 道德真經廣聖義 (Extensive Sagely Meaning of the *Daode jing*, DZ 725; see Verellen in Schipper and Verellen 2004, 293-94), it was prominent among the Daoist elite at the time and served as a theoretical framework for integrating complex Daoist teachings. These had grown exponentially in the early middle ages not only due to the many varied revelations of new scriptures, heavens, and practice methods, especially in the Great Clarity (Taiqing 太清), Highest Clarity (Shangqing), and Numinous Treasure (Lingbao 靈寶) schools, but also in response to advanced Buddhist worldview.[1]

The school inherited the teachings of the Northern Celestial Masters centered at Louguan 樓觀 (in the Zhongnan mountains, southwest of modern Xi'an), including their veneration of Lord Lao and their exegesis of the *Daode jing* in the *Xisheng jing* 西昇經 (Scripture of Western Ascension, DZ 726; trl. Kohn 2007; see Schmidt in Schipper and Verellen 2004, 685-86). Its thinkers were court Daoists involved in politics and debates with Buddhists whose main interest was to present Daoist teachings in a comprehensive and competitive way (see Assandri 2009). Heavily relying on the so-called *tetralemma*, a formation of logic, and the two truths theory, adapted from the Buddhist Madhyamaka

---

[1] For a survey of Daoist schools, see Kohn 2001; Robinet 1997. On Great Clarity, see Pregadio 2006; on Highest Clarity, see Miller 2008; on Numinous Treasure, see Bokenkamp 2007. For the interaction with Buddhism, see Mollier 2008 and also ch. 7 below.

school, they expressed their ideas largely in commentaries to the classics and set the stage for the theoretical understanding of meditation in the main *zuowang* system of the eighth century.

Their concepts, moreover, formed the foundation of the scholastic interpretation of Daoist concepts, contained in encyclopedias and technical treatises both of the early and the late Tang, which strove to classify, structure, and analyze different forms of meditation, formalizing the distinction of enstasy and ecstasy already visible in the core classics.

The Xisheng jing

The *Xisheng jing* is an important conceptual text of medieval Daoism that is cited numerous times in *zuowang* literature and has merited several Tang commentaries associated with Twofold Mystery. First mentioned in connection with the conversion of the barbarians and as such quoted in Buddhist polemics (Zürcher 1959, 311), the text is set at the transmission of the *Daode jing* to Yin Xi 尹喜, the Guardian of the Pass, and claims to contain Laozi's oral explanations of Daoist doctrinal intricacies. It consists of thirty-nine sections, which can be divided into five cycles of progressive teaching: Dao Knowledge, Dao Practice, Cosmization, The Sage, and The Return. They describe in a rather theoretical way how practitioners are to overcome deliberate, classificatory thinking and become one with the Dao in no-mind, no-body, and no-intention.

After first outlining Yin Xi's practice, the text begins by expostulating on the fundamental problem of speaking about the ineffable. Next it explains how Dao is immanent in the world and outlines a way of accessing it. Third, a more concrete explanation of theory and practice of Dao is given, with reference to the practice of meditation, largely in terms of reaching emptiness and nonbeing, peace and tranquility. The fourth cycle deals with the life of the sage, a true person of Dao yet active in the world as teacher, helper, ruler. The final goal, however, goes beyond even that and is the complete return to Dao, the joining of body, mind, and self with cosmic flow. The text ends with a recovery of the beginning, describing Laozi's ascension and his key advice to Yin Xi: "When all impurities are gone, the myriad affairs are done" (Kohn 2007, 48-49).

In historical terms the text can be placed in the environment of Louguan, the first Daoist monastery and center of the Northern Celestial Masters located in the Zhongnan mountains west of modern Xi'an. It was probably founded by Yin Tong 尹通 (398-499?), an alleged relative of Yin Xi who received the Dao in 424, then embarked on a course in dietetics, nourishing on "yellow essence" or deer-bamboo and asparagus (Needham 1976, 112), to become an accomplished Daoist and assemble a number of disciples. Changing the earlier legend, which placed the transmission of the *Daode jing* to the Hangu Pass 函谷關 east of modern Xi'an, he claimed that Louguan was where Laozi spoke the sacred words, thus making it into one of the most holy places of the religion (Qing 1988, 434). The center rose to prominence after the end of the Daoist theocracy in the mid-fifth century, when numerous Daoists had to leave court and needed a center to continue their community (see Kohn 1997).

By the late 470s, it had about forty Daoists in residence. At this time, Wang Daoyi 王道一 arrived and initiated a new phase of development. Not only were the buildings repaired and greatly expanded, but a major collection of Daoist scriptures and ritual manuals was undertaken, including not only northern but also southern materials (Qing 1988, 435; Ren 1990, 222; Kohn 1997). Louguan with this became a center of Daoist knowledge and served as an important location for the integration of the religion.

Still rather nebulous in the fifth century, Louguan became more historically visible in the sixth, when its masters played an active role in both religion and state. Wei Jie 韋節 (496-569), for example, a resident of Mount Hua and the first commentator of the *Xisheng jing* (Kohn 2007, 161), not only participated in various minor debates but also served as the Daoist master who initiated Emperor Wu in 567 (Lagerwey 1981, 19). Wang Yan 王延 (519-604), in 572-578, was the leading scholar in the imperially sponsored compilation of a Daoist catalog, known as the *Zhunang jingmu* 珠囊經目 (Catalog of the Bag of Pearls; lost; see Kohn 1995, 219). Yan Da 嚴達 (514-609), was a senior Daoist at Emperor Wu's Tongdao guan 通道觀 (Monastery of Pervading Dao) and staunch supporter of his policies and Daoist visions (Lagerwey 1981, 13). In the seventh century, moreover, Louguan masters included influential figures such as Li Rong 李榮 and Cheng Xuanying 成玄英 (fl. 650), both respected at court, participants in debates with Buddhists, commentators on the classics, and exponents of Twofold Mystery (Kohn 2007, 188-91; Assandri 2009, 39-46).[2]

In their *Xisheng jing* commentaries, Louguan thinkers paved the way for the newly developing understanding of Daoist meditation. Thus, Wei Jie says:

> The more advanced religious practice leading toward Dao is meditation. The practitioner concentrates his internal *qi* and visualizes the body divinities. Sensory impressions cease. Cravings for outer things diminish. The result is complete oblivion.

> On the outside become oblivious of all seeing and hearing and in due course all desires to see and hear will cease. On the inside become completely oblivious of thinking and tasting, and in due course all craving for language and food will end. When all without and within has ceased, one

---

[2] They also included the abbot Yin Wencao 尹文操 (622-688), a possible elder relative of one of the main *zuowang* authors in the eighth century. See ch. 3.

can be serene and obscure. In such a state one will return to the state when there were no beings. (20.13; Kohn 2007, 176)

The "state when there were no beings," then, in adaptation of the *Zhuangzi* sequence of decline, is the time when one was utterly unconscious of the existence of anything at all. This is associated with the complete loss of selfhood: "Originally I am free from self, yet suddenly there it is. Always remain oblivious of this self, then you are like you were before birth" (12.15).

Li Rong echoes this when he says in his *Xisheng jing* commentary:

When the One does not leave the body, one naturally attains Dao. Then the Three Ones come to be permanently present in the three palaces [elixir fields] of the human body. Concentrate on them and never let them go; then the gods will naturally descend. Once the gods have descended, Dao of perfection is complete. (12.2)

While encouraging the visualization of deities along the lines of Highest Clarity practice dominant at the time, he also repeatedly describes how one decreases and again decreases, reduces conscious evaluations, enters a state of oblivion, and then goes on to become oblivious of this. All conceptual hold on existence is abandoned in favor of a growing attainment of Dao, all constructed mental states are given up in favor of practical experience, the traces left behind for that which left the traces. A key passage is in his commentary to *Daode jing* 14:

One goes beyond beings and returns to where there are no beings. In a state without beings there are no forms to be seen or sounds to be heard. Thus one joins with the invisible and the inaudible. With these, one reverts to complete serenity. (Yan 1983, 777)

This closely matches Cheng Xuanying's explanation of *zuowang*. He says:

Even though auditory perception belongs to the ears and visual power is a function of the eyes, they ultimately depend on the mind. Once one has awakened to the fact that the body does not really exist, that the myriad states of the mind are empty, then one can smash up one's body, drive out intellect and do away with understanding. (DZ 745, 7.39b)

Like Guo Xiang, Cheng sees the two aspects of sitting in oblivion as "a separation from one's bodily form on the outside" and "a dismissal of all mental knowledge on the inside." As the sage has thus given up any personal ego-identity in either mind or body, his wisdom is characterized as "perfect and oblivious" (Robinet 1977, 245). While continuing the traditional pattern, these thinkers thus also advanced its understanding, integrating alternative meditation methods and new conceptual structures to bring it to an entirely new level.

Levels of Truth

The name Twofold Mystery goes back to the expression "mysterious and again mysterious" in *Daode jing* 1. The word "mysterious" (*xuan* 玄) is explained by Cheng Xuanying in his commentary.

> Mysterious means deep and profound. It is also an expression for being without obstructions. The two minds of being and nonbeing, the two visions of outcome and subtlety all spring from the one Dao. They arise together, but have different names, but despite their different names they belong to the one Dao. This is called deep and profound.

> The mysterious nature of depth and profundity is realized in the return of principle to no obstruction. Being neither obstructed by being nor obstructed by nonbeing—this is what we mean by mysterious. (ch. 1; Yan 1983, 303; Robinet 1977, 108)

Twofold Mystery thus envisions the mystical process in two steps, described as double forgetting (*jianwang* 兼忘). Practitioners must first discard all concepts of being, then proceed to discard all ideas of nonbeing. These two are, moreover, identified as mental projections (*jing* 境), i.e., illusory mental imaginations that are projected outward and create an apparent reality of "being;" and active wisdom (*zhi* 智) or mind as such (*xin* 心), the inherent function of active consciousness which signifies "nonbeing" (Robinet 1977, 245). "Forgetting" both means the reorganization of ordinary consciousness to absolute consciousness and again from absolute consciousness to no consciousness at all in complete oblivion. Yet the sagely state is not nothingness but the "embodiment of the Dao of Middle Oneness," a state of radiance and surging activity. Cheng says:

> On the outside the sage has no mental projections that would be desirable. On the inside he has no mind that could do any desiring. Mind and mental projections both obliterated, mind becomes no-mind. Where there were mental projections and illusions before, there is now only the emptiness of mind. Yet even though the mind is no-mind, it shines forth in numinous radiance. (ch. 3; Yan 1983, 313)

The division of mentation into projections and mind, the perception of being and nonbeing, goes back to Buddhist Madhyamaka. Founded in the second century by the Indian thinker Nāgārjuna, it made a strong impact on Chinese Buddhism in the fifth and sixth centuries. [3] Its main Chinese exponent was Jizang 吉藏 (549-623) whose works *Erdi zhang* 二諦章 (On the Two Levels of

---

[3] For discussions of Chinese Mādhyamika, see Fung 1952, 2:11, 293; Robinson 1967. On Jizang's impact on Daoist thought, see Kamata 1966, 84; Assandri 2009, 91-97.

Truth) and *Sanlun xuanyi* 三論玄義 (Mysterious Meaning of the Three Treatises) formulated concepts of central importance for Twofold Mystery.

Here he assumes a basic dichotomy of two levels of truth, the worldly and the absolute, being and nonbeing, projections and mind, which are realized in three stages. First one moves from seeing reality or "all dharmas" as existent to understanding that they are ultimately emptiness and nonbeing. Then one sees that nonbeing, too, is a way of conceptualizing the world and moves into the realm of nonduality by affirming both being and nonbeing as states of mind. Third, one realizes that "both duality and nonduality are worldly truth, whereas neither duality nor nonduality is the highest truth. . . . This is the Middle Path without duality" (Chan 1963, 360; see also Ng 1993, 25-26).

The structure of the two levels of truth as applied to the three stages leads logically to the analytical method of the "Four Propositions," technically known as the *tetralemma* and the hallmark of Madhyamaka as much as of Twofold Mystery:

> affirmation of being;
> affirmation of nonbeing;
> affirmation of both, being and nonbeing;
> negation of both, being and nonbeing.
> (Robinson 1967, 57; Robinet 1977, 117; Assandri 2009, 1)

In practice, meditators proceed from the ordinary worldly assumption that everything exists to the enlightened vision that all is empty. This is the first stage of mystery, decreasing, and oblivion. Once this state is reached, the conviction that all is empty becomes in itself a form of attachment. Emptiness becomes an established way of looking at the world, a kind of mental state, a created illusion. It is therefore necessary to proceed further and go beyond emptiness. Practitioners have to discard even nonbeing in order to realize that all and everything is both being and nonbeing at the same time. This in turn leads to the insight that, since all is being and nonbeing at the same time, things ultimately neither exist nor not exist. As Cheng Xuanying says:

> Adepts must first discard all desires, then proceed to discard the level of no-desires. Only then can they truly accomplish twofold discarding of the two sides and wondrously merge with the Dao of Middle Oneness. Beings and ego looked upon in equalized fashion, mental states and wisdom both forgotten—when someone makes such a state his principle of government, then everything will be well ordered. (ch. 3; Kohn 2007, 183)

Daoists thus not only wish to attain the personal state of unlimited freedom in oblivion but see its attainment as a way to cosmic and political order, still pursuing the age-old dream of Great Peace.

Observation

Another dimension of meditation that developed under the impact of Twofold Mystery is the scholastic definition and classification of different types, which further enhances the difference between the enstatic and ecstatic modes and paves the way for the systematization of *zuowang* in the eighth century. The main source here is the encyclopedia *Daojiao yishu* 道教義樞 (The Pivotal Meaning of Daoist Teaching, DZ 1129), by Meng Anpai 孟安排 (fl. 699).[4] Written to demonstrate the depth and sophistication of Daoist thought in the face of Buddhist criticism, the text adopts and reconceptualizes many Buddhist concepts, integrating them successfully into a Daoist worldview. For example, it speaks of "the three vehicles" (*sancheng* 三乘), but rather than using the term to designate distinct traditions of Daoism, it applies it as a generic device for acknowledging the mutual validity of different Daoist goals or sensibilities. Similarly it adopts the term "body of the law" (*fashen* 法身, *dharmakāya*), which in Buddhism refers to the spiritual or true body of the Buddha, and uses it to denote the cosmic nature of the human body (see Assandri 2009, 179-83).

The ten *juan* of the text divide into thirty-seven sections, five of which are lost. Within each section the material is first presented according to "Definition" (*yi* 義) and "Explanation" (*shi* 釋), then supplemented with further references and interpretations.

Section 7 on "The Twelve Classes" of scriptures, provides a list of different methods used for spiritual attainment. It has:

1. Meditation on deities and visualization of perfected;
2. Mind fasting and sitting in oblivion;
3. Pacing the void and flying through emptiness;
4. Nourishing by inhaling the six *qi*;
5. Practicing healing exercises [*daoyin* 導引] according to the three luminants. (2.22b)

All of these, it asserts, "work with mind and *qi* in mutual support and lead to a mystical pervasion of spirit and Dao." Presenting thus physical and longevity techniques in direct connection with the guiding of *qi* and more meditative practices, the text shows the way toward integrating the different Daoist systems of practice—a challenge taken up successfully by later Tang masters.

---

[4] The text is the sole subject of Wang 2001. It has been indexed in Nakajima 1984a. Discussions appear in Assandri 2009, 72-76; Bokenkamp 1986, 141; Kamata 1966, 202; Kohn 1992, 149-54; Kohn and Kirkland 2000, 352; Ren and Zhong 1991, 878-79; Robinet 1997, 191-92; Schmidt in Schipper and Verellen 2004, 442; Sharf 1991, 56-60; Sunayama 1980, 43; Yoshioka 1959, 309-68.

In section 17, next, it focuses specifically on "observation" the technical term used for both Daoist visualization and Buddhist insight practices. It distinguishes stability and insight (*dinghui* 定慧), matching states achieved through cessation and observation (*śamathā-vipaśyanā*; *zhiguan* 止觀; "stop and look") as outlined in the texts of the Tiantai 天台 school. It describes them as the "wondrous gates of emptiness and existence" which lead to the attainment of the "field of Twofold Mystery" and the "ford of double relinquishing," thereby finding access to ultimate perfection and "liberation from all dharmas" (5.3b).

In its "Explanation," the text next renames the two types as "observation of *qi*" and "observation of spirit," then identifies the terms *qi* and spirit as body-self and mind. In other words, it sees the two fundamental kinds of meditation practice described here as focus on physical phenomena and on mental occurrences—what later adepts of internal alchemy speak about in terms of essential inner nature and original destiny (*xingming* 性命). The goal of the practice, then, is to create mental stability by focusing on the "form and image" of the body-self and to open up to "empty insight" by allowing the stable mind to flow about freely "without obstructions or limits" (3b).

Next, the *Daojiao yishu* cites the *Benji jing* 本際經 (Scripture on Original Time; ed. Wu 1960, Wan 1998), another text used variously by the exponents of oblivion in the eighth century. Compiled in the beginning of the Tang, its authors were the *Daode jing* commentator Liu Jinxi 劉進喜 and Li Zhongqing 李仲卿, both residents of the Qingxu guan 清虛觀 (Clear Emptiness Temple) in Chang'an and active in the Buddho-Daoist controversies (Robinet 1977, 102-3; Sharf 1991, 36-37; Assandri 2009, 40-41).

The *Benji jing* presents itself in a Mahāyāna format, claiming to document the sermons of a variety of celestial beings, including traditional Daoist deities, such as the Heavenly Worthy, Lord Lao, Zhang Daoling, and the Sovereign of Heavenly Perfection, together with bodhisattva-like figures, such as Universal Virtue. The title phrase *benji* originates in Buddhist literature, where it occurs in the Chinese title of the *Saṃyuktāgama sūtra* (T. 99, 2.240b) and refers to the state before universal creation. The expression evokes an image found in an ancient Indian origin myth, according to which being develops from nonbeing through the formation of a cosmic egg that splits into Heaven and Earth. The various chapters of the text are not integrated perfectly but show a shift in the role and importance of Lord Lao (see Assandri 2008).

The *Benji jing*, like other texts of the era, focuses on the notion that all sentient beings have "Dao-nature" (*daoxing* 道性), an adaptation of Buddha-nature, which is their true so-being as it is "embodied in all conscious beings and even all animals, plants, trees and rocks" (*Daojiao yishu* 8.6b; Kamata 1969, 11-80). The goal of Daoist practice is the full realization of this Dao-nature through a variety of practices, including nonaction and various meditations, as well as by gaining full comprehension of the world according to this vision. Much of the argument of the *Benji jing* follows Buddhist models, making use of Mādhyamika dialectics.

The text was widely known in the Tang, as is documented by its survival in eighty-one Dunhuang manuscripts and its frequent citation in other Daoist works. In 741, Xuanzong had it copied in temples throughout the land so that it could be recited and lectured on during purgation rites. He credited a subsequent abundant harvest to those activities (Benn 1977, 248-49; Sharf 1991, 39).

The *Benji jing* as cited here confirms the analysis of the *Daojiao yishu*, adding the importance of visualizing deities in the process of merging with Dao. *Qi* in this context is "a flickering image, coming to match the individual body-self," while spirit is described as without bent or limit, thus "illuminating emptiness and existence." The text further identifies observation as the conscious activity of thinking and examining—thinking meaning "visualization of wondrous oneness," while "examining" is to "envision the shapeless" (3b). It also adds that "proper observation" (*zhengguan* 正觀) means to "not take in, not let go, not move, not rest—just entering oneness and the gate of the wondrous" (4a). This is the attainment of the first level which is also no level at all, since there is ultimately nothing to be attained (4a). From here, it expands further on the distinction between observation of *qi* and of spirit, linking them with the proper understanding of being and nonbeing, the apperception of "wondrous being" and "perfect emptiness," as well as with the cultivation of states beyond and within the world (4a).

Emptiness

Following this, the *Daojiao yishu* moves on to classify observation differently by distinguishing the three observations of "apparent dharmas" (*jiafa* 假法), "solid dharmas" (*shifa* 實法), and "partial emptiness" (*piankong* 偏空). It defines them as states before mysterious awakening (*xuanwu* 玄悟) and part of the "Lesser Vehicle," thus not signifying the full level of attainment. It has:

> As concerns the observation of apparent dharmas, "apparent" means having a temporary appearance, whereas "dharmas" refers to embodied reality. . . . For example, when it comes to understanding the fact that the five aggregates [matter, feeling, perception, reaction, and consciousness] make up oneself, how could one know which aggregate is oneself? Thus the *Zhuangzi* says, "The hundred joints, the nine openings, the six organs all come together and exist here. But which part should I feel closest to?" [ch. 2]. If you don't feel very close to any part as the one that constitutes yourself, you have begun to understand the emptiness of apparent dharmas. (4b-5a)

In other words, the first step is to see one's body as consisting of a variety of interrelated forces and activities, none of which can be truly defined as "I" and thus give rise to a permanent sense of ego-identity. Seeing this, one's attachment to projected reality and the shenanigans of the mind is first loosened. Then one can move on to the "observation of solid dharmas."

> [This] deals with the embodied substance of everything. Knowing already that all apparent dharmas are empty, you must now ask: What is embodied substance? Where does it come from? It must arise from something else. And if it comes from something else, that means that there is an endless chain of arising. And if there is no such endless chain, that means that it arises from emptiness. If we say, however, that it arises from emptiness, then we must again push on this emptiness. But emptiness is not anything—so how can we say it gives rise to anything? In this way we can understand that real dharmas cannot be accepted either. This is the observation of real dharmas. (5a)

This closely echoes the discussion in the chapter on "Making All Things Equal" (*Qiwulun* 齊物論) in the *Zhuangzi* which, too, searches for the "not yet beginning of not yet beginning of beginning," i.e., it poses the question of where human existence ultimately originates (Graham 1969, 155). As Guo Xiang reformulates:

> What came into existence before there were beings? If I say that yin and yang came first, then since yin and yang are themselves entities, what came before them? Suppose I say nature came first, but nature is only things being themselves. Suppose I say that Perfect Dao came first, but Perfect Dao is perfect nonbeing. Since it is non-being, how can it come before anything else? Then, what came before it? There must be another thing, and so ad infinitum. (24.3b; Chan 1963, 335).

Guo Xiang concludes, "We must understand that things are what they are spontaneously and not caused by anything else" (Knaul 1985b, 19). The *Daojiao yishu*, on the other hand, by the same reasoning reaches the realization that everything is empty, i.e., lacks substantial permanent existence. It moves on from there to the "observation of partial emptiness":

> "Partial" here means not yet proper, whereas "emptiness" refers to a vacuous, pervasive way of seeing. This is practiced in order to get rid of all the numerous diseases of attachment which all beings are suffering from. Thereby one comes to realize emptiness little by little. (5a)

The full attainment of emptiness, then, means that one takes emptiness as emptiness and nothing else (5b), which is realized in yet another set of three forms of observation, that "being" (*you* 有), "nonbeing" (*wu* 無), and "the Middle Way" (*zhongdao* 中道) (Kamata 1963, 211) This set most closely resembles the

Tiantai system which also classifies observation in three types of "apparent dharmas," "emptiness," and "the middle" (Ng 1993, 136). The first means coming to understand that one is obstructed (*ai* 礙) by substance and solidity as created in mental projections (5a). The second leads to the appreciation of nonbeing as freedom from obstructions, however, the notion itself of being free from obstructions turns out to be yet another obstruction (6a). Eventually, by observation of the Middle Way one sees that being and nonbeing also coincide with not being and not non-being and thus goes beyond all perception (6b). This is the ultimate attainment of emptiness, the vision of life from a perspective of oblivion.

Later Interpretations

Further formulations of Twofold Mystery thought and classifications of meditation appear in the late Tang and early Song, in a group of texts that present a comprehensive religious Daoist philosophy. They include first the *Sanlun yuanzhi* 三論元旨 (Primordial Pointers of the Three Theories, DZ 1039), which has three sections on "Dao as Ancestor" (*daozong* 道宗), "Vacuous Delusions" (*xuwang* 虛妄), and "The True Source" (*zhenyuan* 真源). The "three theories" of the title can also refer to the original unity of Dao, mind, and inner nature as well as to the subtle aspects of body energy: essence, *qi*, and spirit (De Meyer in Schipper and Verellen 2004, 308). Citing the *Zhuangzi* by its honorific title, which was bestowed in 742, it is probably of late Tang origin.

Next is the *Daoti lun* 道體論 (The Dao and Its Embodiment, DZ 1035; partial trl. Kohn 1993, 19-24), transmitted by a certain Tongxuan xiansheng 通玄先生 who could be Sima Chengzhen or Zhang Guo, but is most likely Zhang Jianming 張薦明 (d. 939) (De Meyer in Schipper and Verellen 2004, 306). The text is written in question-and-answer format like the recorded sayings (*yulu* 語錄) of Buddhist masters and divides into three parts, "On Laozi's *Daojing*," "Questions on Dao," and the "Meaning of Dao Embodiment." It is highly theoretical and scholastic, but makes some reference to stages of oblivion.

Third is the *Dadao lun* 大道論 (On the Great Dao, DZ 1037), ascribed to Zhou Gupu 周固樸, which cites Du Guangting's *Guangsheng yi* and observes Song-dynasty taboo characters—thus belonging to this period. It focuses on a logical, scholastic interpretation of Daoist thought and divides into eighteen sections, including "Utmost Dao," "Handing Down the Teaching," "Distinctions," "Mind Practice," and "Cultivating Dao" (see Sakauchi 1996; Schipper and Yuan in Schipper and Verellen 2004, 738-39).

The texts contain highly speculative analyses of Dao and its role in the world. Thus the *Daoti lun* begins by defining it as beyond all, neither being nor nonbe-

ing, neither formless nor formed, neither right nor wrong. The text then uses
Mādhyamika logic to affirm the double and yet nondual nature of Dao, con-
trasting it with inherent potency and offering various similar pairs, including
Dao and beings, principle and affairs, emptiness and existence, and names and
reality. In all cases the two are two yet not-two, the same yet different, born yet
unborn, nameless yet named. Both are part of the same ultimate mystery, and
so appear in different ways under different conditions. To realize them, one
must practice double forgetting and sit in oblivion to reach the state of naturalness or so-being in the totality of Dao. As the text has:

> As Dao pervades and transforms all things, known and named, only by
> becoming oblivious this pervasion can one truly encounter its inherent
> potency. Then one can go along completely with all names and standards,
> dissolve all traces and allow potency to complete both. From there, one
> can go on to obliterate once more, even giving up on the ancestor [Dao]
> and the ultimate [root of creation]. Then one can be free from all rules
> and control. Should at that point any desires appear, they can be guided
> back to the mysterious origin. They will duly weaken and perish. (pref. 1a)

Outlining the cosmology of Dao, the text explains how it underlies all existence
and brings forth beings in a mutual productive relationship: "Beings need Dao
to embody themselves. At the same time, Dao needs beings to embody itself,"
like fish depending on water (2a). Yet, however much the multitude of beings
are essentially only manifestations of eternal Dao, they still begin to become
separate and have names. These names signify a projection of mental states,
which need to be overcome to find one's true birthright as part of Dao:

> Diminish and again diminish, and there will be no fetter that does not
> dissolve. Dao and its inherent potency both obliterated, one mysteriously
> joins beings and oneself in pervasive oneness. Thus one can be great and
> overflowing [like Dao]. (3a)

The *Dadao lun*, in its last section on "Observation and Cultivation," too, emphasizes the distinction between projections and the pure mind, saying that "all
deluded imaginings and upside-down perception originate from the mind
which brings forth distinctions and classifications, is attached by thoughts to
the body-self identified as "I," hangs on to projected reality, and gives rise to
delusion" (23a). Echoing the *Daode jing* and citing the *Yebao jing* 業報經 (Scripture of Karmic Retribution, DZ 336),[5] it notes that "the reason why we are
troubled by a host of sufferings is that we have a body-self. Once immersed in
the cycle of life and death, we cannot get free from it by ourselves" (23a).

---

[5] Dated to the late sixth century, this text details rules of karmic cause and effect. See
Nakajima 1984b; Kohn 1998c; Lagerwey in Schipper and Verellen 2004, 518-20.

But there is a way out, through attaining clarity and stillness and moving into complete oblivion. The text has:

> All we need to do is stabilize the will and observe the body-self. In effect all perception is vacuous and lop-sided. Once we come to know that all is vacuous and lop-sided, deluded imaginings gradually dissolve. When deluded imaginings are dissolved, one will rest in clarity and stillness both within and without and spontaneously reach awakening.

> The path that leads to this is called oblivion of the body-self. Once one has obliterated the body-self, all delusion and entanglements vanish automatically. Zhuangzi says: "At peace with the times and going along with all situations, sorrow and happiness have no way to enter in" [ch. 3]. This is the state of self-oblivion of the accomplished person. (23b)

More specifically, it defines observation as wisdom and the detached regard of universal order. It also cites the *Benji jing* which defines it on three different levels that match the mind-fasting of the *Zhuangzi*: as organically seeing outside objects with ones eyes; as evenly mirroring all objects with pure spirit; and as going beyond both by "abandoning the myriad phenomena on the outside and intercepting the host of karmic conditions on the inside." Once competent in doing this, "one enters the mysterious and there are gradual steps—there is only the straight path of behaving in a sagely manner" (23a).

The *Benji jing* also appears in the *Sanlun yuanzhi*, where it is cited with a passage that compares the pollution of the pure mind by even a single deluded thought to the lighting of even a single spark in a dark room: it takes very little to dispel the original ambiance. Thus "the sages say: Guard the One and find a thousand certainties; err in the One and get entangled in a myriad doubts" (2b). Continuing with the light imagery, the text next says that mental projections hide the true mind like mist and clouds obscure the light of the sun and that one only needs to purify oneself to emptiness and reach a state of oblivion: not knowing why or what one is forgetting (3a).

Still, there is perception, described in a way that merges Daoist and Buddhist terms and is reminiscent of Zen: before oblivion and enlightenment, we know and see things as being so. Becoming oblivious of knowledge and vision, we enter an altered state that is not yet complete. Once completely oblivious of self and others, there is complete awakening, and once again we know and see things as being so but on a new and refined level. Once perfect knowledge and perfect vision are attained, truly nothing is seen or understood any longer—the self has merged completely with the origin, "wisdom and inner nature become one, flowing everywhere in full pervasion" (3a).

The text also establishes several levels of attainment, describing a sequence that reaches from purity (*cheng* 澄) through quietude (*jing* 靜), oblivion (*wang* 忘),

enlightenment (*ming* 明), and open pervasion (*da* 達) to realizing awakening and completing perfection (*liaowu chengzhen* 了悟成真) (2b-3a). These go hand in hand with changes in the basic make-up of the mind, reaching from coarse through fine (*xi* 細) and subtle (*wei* 微) to wondrous (*miao* 妙). Through purification and cultivation one makes the mind extremely coarse, and its fine aspect emerges; one makes it extremely fine—i.e., clear and soft, pure and plain—and its subtle dimension comes to the fore; one makes it extremely subtle—defined as spirited and lustrous, empty and serene—and its wondrous nature is activated; one makes it extremely wondrous—utmost and profound, perfect and part of the source—and it merges with Dao (5b-6a).

Within this framework, then, the text further defines different modes of working with the mind to reach various levels of stability:

1. tame the mind and rest in oneness: stability in calmness 安定;
2. make the mind into ashes and forget oneness: stability in dissolution 滅定;
3. awaken the mind to perfect oneness: stability in cosmic peace 泰定.

From here, the different forms of body change into the major kinds of supernatural being:

1. body-self 身 rising up in transformation of wings: become an immortal 仙;
2. body-form 形 ascending in perfect spirit: become a perfected 真;
3. body-structure 體 merging with inner nature: become a sage 聖.

And at the same time, the mind attains different forms of perfection and awakening is guaranteed:

1. mind mirroring all with bright insight: one awakens to immortality;
2. mind pervading perfect spirit: one awakens to perfection;
3. mind harmonizing with inner nature: one awakens to sageliness. (5b)

Altogether the later documents of Twofold Mystery present various modes of the path to immortality, adapting various aspects of Buddhism and integrating the concepts and stages of eighth-century Daoists. Doing so, they establish a theoretical framework for internal alchemy which begins its rise to prominence at this time and set the stage for later interpretations and adaptations of oblivion.

Chapter Three

Tang Masters

The fully developed system of sitting in oblivion appears in the works of four leading Tang Daoist masters who were equally ensconced in the official religious hierarchies of the day, closely involved with the imperial court, and subject to the vision of unification and overall integration. They all also had some contact with Buddhism and were conscious of the medical and longevity dimensions of practice.

The earliest among them is Sun Simiao, today venerated as the King of Medicines who came to the Dao due to illness and, although initiated in the basic ranks of the integrated hierarchy, remained due to his calling as a physician and healer. Second is Yin Yin, the editor and commentator of the *Wuchu jing* and possibly a relative of Yin Wencao, abbot of Louguan and major player in the seventh century. The most important among them is Sima Chengzhen, patriarch of Highest Clarity and prolific author whose work is central to the system of oblivion. The last of the group, finally, is Wu Yun, initiated and dedicated Daoist as well as seeker for long life, who is particularly well known as a poet whose stanzas on ecstatic journeys have become famous far and wide.

Sun Simiao[1]

Sun Simiao 孫思邈, was born in 581 near the western capital of Chang'an. According to official biographies, which tend to stereotype masters as child prodigies and emphasize personal virtues, such as bone-deep honesty and a hesita-

---

[1] The next few sections are adapted from the extensive discussion of Sun's and Sima's lives and works on physical practices in Kohn 2008b, ch. 4.

tion to accept imperial honors, he was a precocious child who studied eagerly from an early age. By age twenty he supposedly not only had an extensive knowledge of the classics, but was also familiar with Buddhist and Daoist scriptures. Despite several invitations to serve at the imperial court under the Sui and early Tang dynasties, he went to live in seclusion on Mount Taibai 太白山 in the Zhongnan mountains, about a hundred miles from his ancestral home.[2]

In contrast to this shining and easy childhood that brought forth an upright and noble character, an autobiographical note in the preface to his *Qianjin yao-fang* 千金要方 (Essential Priceless Prescriptions) notes that he was a rather sickly boy who underwent all kinds of treatments, thus inspiring a great interest in medical matters and an inclination toward longevity practices and Daoist seclusion. The text says:

> In my childhood I suffered from a cold disorder due to winds and constantly consulted physicians. My family's finances were exhausted to pay for medicine. So it was that during my student years I held the medical classics in special regard, and that even in my old age I have not set them aside.
>
> As to the reading of pulses and other techniques of diagnosis, the gathering of herbs and their compounding, administration and dosage, hygiene and the various precautions associated with health—when I heard of any man who excelled me in any of these, no distance would keep me from him. I would learn what he had to teach and apply it. When I reached maturity, I became aware that I had attained some understanding. (Sivin 1967, 271; Engelhardt 1989, 279)

This documents Sun Simiao's early start in medical studies due to an intense personal need and the complete dedication of his efforts to being the best and knowing the most in this field. To this end he also traveled widely, collecting ancient books and recipes all over the country and, especially between 605 and 615, engaged in various alchemical experiments to find the medicine of immortality, thus entering the realm of religion and going beyond the goals of healing and long life.

As regards meditation, it is likely that—like Sima Chengzhen—he received instruction in basic Buddhist practice as based on the Tiantai 天台 school, i.e., in concentration through breath awareness (*śamatha*) and open awareness in insight (*vipaśyanā*) (Sakade 2007, 12). As a healer, he prescribed various medicinal formulas to support the practice, using, for example, the juice of the mulberry (leaves, seeds). If taken regularly over a period of ten days, he says,

---

[2] Details of Sun's early life are outlined in Sivin 1968, 82-96; Engelhardt 1989, 266; Sakade 2007a, 10; Chen 2000, 91-94.

> awareness will be broad and wisdom pervasive, leading to the first *dhyāna*
> [*chanding* 禪定; *samādhi*; stage of absorption]; taking it for twenty days,
> one reaches the second *dhyāna*; after one hundred days, one finds oneself
> in the fourth *dhyāna*; and after one entire year of consecutive use, the
> fourth *dhyāna* is reached. Then the myriad phenomena will all be seen for
> what they really are and one will be able to let go of the World of Desire,
> observing all the different worlds and mental projections like seeing the
> palm of one's hand, thus realizing Buddha-nature [*jian foxing* 見佛性; Jap:.
> *kenshō*]. (*Qianjin yifang* 12.2; Sakade 2007, 12)

Most of his recorded case histories, and therefore his main activities as a physician, date from 616 to 626. In 633, it seems, he was in Sichuan, where he con-
ducted various alchemical experiments and contracted "cinnabar poisoning"
(*dandu* 丹毒). He reports on the illness in his *Qianjin yifang* 千金翼方 (Supplementary Priceless Prescriptions):

> While asleep, I felt pain throughout the flesh and bones of my extremi-
> ties. By dawn, my head was aching and my vision unclear; there was a
> blister the size of a crossbow pellet on my left temple, which ached so
> badly I could not bring my hand near it. By noon the swelling had spread
> to my right temple, and by night it had become general. My eyes, once
> closed, could not be reopened. I came very close to death. The county
> magistrate, Squire Zhou, treated me with every sort of medication, but
> without remission. After seven days I myself worked out a prescription
> which was magical in its efficacy. (22.30a; Sivin 1968, 251)

The same text also contains several passages suggesting that Sun Simiao was an
ordained Daoist of the Celestial Masters level, i.e., the lowest and most popular
level of the Tang Daoist hierarchy (Kohn 2004b, 16). He refers to certain exor-
cistic formulas that were reserved for exclusive recital by Daoist masters and it
seems unlikely that someone uninitiated would have had access to them (Sivin
1978, 312; Engelhardt 1989, 267). Even in his medical function, moreover, he
applied Daoist recipes, using the same methods for herbal compounds as for
alchemical drugs and prescribing remedies that on occasion involved massive
doses of highly toxic ingredients such as mercury (Sivin 1968, 142).

Besides continuing to heal and pursue immortality, Sun apparently did his main
writing between 730 and 760. In 759, having become quite famous as a physician and master of long life, he joined the retinue of Emperor Gaozong in an
informal capacity. After about fifteen years, he requested permission to retire
from the court on account of illness and presumably died in 682, a good hundred years after his alleged birth in 581. These dates may well be an exaggera-
tion of the chroniclers, eager to show him successful in his quest for long life.
They also claimed that he attained immortality, insisting that for one month
after his death there was no change in his appearance or physical decomposi-

tion and that his corpse, when placed in the coffin, was as light as cloth—information that should be taken with a grain of salt (Sivin 1968, 130; Engelhardt 1989, 267). Still, the chroniclers made a strong case for Sun's extraordinary powers, leading to his wide-spread veneration as the King of Medicines in Daoist temples and popular shrines to the present day.

Sun Simiao was a prolific writer. The standard histories of the Tang list twenty-two works ascribed to him, a number that grew to about eighty over the centuries (Sivin 1968, 60; Engelhardt 1989, 277). Only a handful of these survive, the most important among them being the "Priceless Prescriptions" series, extensive collections of highly technical medical information that date from the 650s and are still actively used by physicians in China today (Sivin 1968, 132). As for more spiritual works, Sun is credited with two brief general outlines on how to best live one's life: the *Baosheng ming* 保生銘 (On Preserving Life, DZ 835; trl. Kohn 2008a, 134; see Despeux in Schipper and Verellen 2004, 353), a concise treatise extolling moderation, a regular life-style, and virtuous attitudes; and the *Fushou lun* 福壽論 (On Happiness and Long Life, DZ 1426), a presentation of the workings of fate and various ways to enhance it.[3]

Two further works on longevity techniques that are highly respected in Daoist circles include first the *Zhenzhong ji* 枕中記 (Pillowbook Record, DZ 837, YQ 33.1a-12a; see Engelhardt 1989), a collection in five sections that cover Prudence, Prohibitions, Exercises, *Qi*-Guiding, and Guarding the One—a visualization of deities in the three elixir fields (see Lévi in Schipper and Verellen 2004, 346-47). In addition, there is the *Yangxing yanming lu* 養性延命錄 (On Nourishing Inner Nature and Extending Life, DZ 838; YQ 32.1a-24b), a summary of nourishing life practices which is linked with various masters in the bibliographies but may well be a work of Sun or of his disciples. It contains six sections: General Observations, Dietary Precepts, Miscellaneous Taboos, Absorbing *Qi* to Cure Diseases, Exercises and Massages, and Controlling Sexual Activity.[4]

Beyond these, two texts are more specialized and religious in nature: the *Danjing yaojue* 丹經要訣 (Essential Formulas of Alchemical Classics, YQ 71; trl. Sivin 1968), which collects various formulas for preparing immortality elixirs; and the text translated below, the *Cunshen lianqi ming*, a concise outline of basic medita-

---

[3] This is probably the same as the *Fulu lun* 福錄論 (On Happiness and Prosperity), ascribed to Sun in the early bibliographies (Sivin 1968, 132). On these two texts, see Despeux in Schipper and Verellen 2004, 353 and 743.

[4] A Japanese translation of the entire text with extensive annotation is found in Mugitani 1987. Sections 2 and 3 appear in English in Switkin 1987. Section 4 is translated and analyzed in Jackowicz 2003. For a brief discussion as to authorship and provenance, see Despeux in Schipper and Verellen 2004, 345-46.

tion practice, followed by an outline five major stages of the mind and seven stages of the self as it transcends to immortality which also feature in the *Ding-guan jing*, appendix to the *Zuowang lun*.

Yin Yin

Yin Yin 尹愔 was the son of the scholar and *Chunqiu* 春秋 (Spring and Autumn Annals) specialist Yin Sizhen 尹思貞 (c. 716). Only little is known about him. According to the *Chang'an zhi* 長安志 (Record of Chang'an), he served as imperial counselor under Xuanzong and was the abbot of the Suming guan 肅明觀 (Monastery of Majestic Brightness) (8.5b; Mollier 2000, 62-63).

According to the *Tangshu* 唐書 (History of the Tang, ch. 34), he was the author not only of the commentary to the *Wuchu jing* translated below but also of a 15-*juan* explanatory work on the *Daode jing* entitled *Xinyi* 新義 (New Interpretation). Gaining fame from this work, he was summoned to court by Emperor Xuanzong and treated with great respect. The emperor appointed him as Grand Master of Remonstrance, Member of the Academy of Scholarly Worthies, and Historiographer. Yin at first refused to accept these positions but acceded to the imperial request in 737 and combined their related duties with those of Daoist abbot. After his death in the 740s, he posthumously received the rank of Policy Adviser in the Chancellery (De Meyer 2006, 48).

Yin's role in Tang Daoism is enhanced by the possibility that he was a descendant of Yin Wencao 尹文操 (622-688) (Benn 1977, 117), who served as abbot of the important institution of Louguan, which was renamed Zongsheng guan 宗聖觀 (Monastery of the Ancestral Sage) in the early Tang in response to the institution's support for the rising dynasty (Qing 1988, 436; Kohn 1997, 114-16; 1998a, 22; see also Bokenkamp 1994).

His life is recorded in the *Da Tang Yin zunshi bei* 大唐尹尊師碑 (Inscription for the Venerable Master Yin of the Great Tang Dynasty), a tomb memorial by Yuan Banqian 員半千, dated to 717 and contained in the Yuan collection *Gu Louguan ziyun yanqing jing* 古樓觀紫雲衍慶集 (The Abundant Blessings of the Purple Clouds at the Old Lookout-Tower, DZ 957, 1.4b-9b; also in Chen et al. 1988, 102-04). According to this, Yin Wencao was born in Tianshui 天水 in modern Gansu, in a family whose noble traces go back well into the Zhou dynasty. His birth was accompanied by supernatural auspices, and he could read immediately at birth.

From an early age, he was a great enthusiast of the Yin family and its noble forebears (notably Yin Xi, the Guardian of the Pass who received Laozi's *Daode jing*), studied the *Xisheng jing* and the Numinous Treasure scriptures and gradually moved closer to his Daoist career (1.5b). His goals clarified when he met

Zhou Fa 周法, an accomplished Daoist, who became his teacher. He was the first to introduce Yin to the arts of ecstatically flying through the universe and gave him his initial lessons in immortality techniques. With his help Yin Wencao was soon ready to join the illustrious ranks of the celestials (1.6a).

In 636, Yin renounced the householder's life and joined the monastic community at Louguan. Training seriously in the advanced meditation and visualization, he soon became an accomplished master (1.6b). To develop to greatest heights, he spent some time as a recluse in the Zhongnan mountains. In 649, a spiritual voice told him that his old teacher had ascended and he went into three years of mourning. After that, he went to Mount Taibai, where he had a major mystical experience—"seeing what he had never seen before, hearing what he had never heard before" (1.6b). At this time, he also had his first vision of the god Laozi, descending to him as a huge nine-colored statue through a thick layer of clouds and accompanied by the reverberation of heavenly drums.

In 656, Yin Wencao left his seclusion and moved to the capital, then spend over thirty years going back and forth and giving service to the empire. Emperor Gaozong valued his counsel and rewarded him with ranks and honors. In 668, after a divine comet blessed the empire, he had the defunct residence of the Prince of Jin restored and given over to Yin as the Haotian guan 昊天觀 (Monastery of Imperial Heaven) (1.7a). In 677, he made Yin abbot of the Zongsheng guan, and in 679, he ordered him to celebrate Daoist rites in Luoyang, during which the deity Laozi descended in front of the assembled court, surrounded by celestial officers and riding on a white horse (Kohn 1998a, 22). The emperor was so taken with this impressive sign of celestial goodwill that he asked Yin to write a formal account of the deity's exploits: the *Xuanyuan huangdi shengji* 玄元皇帝聖記 (Sage Record of the Emperor of Mystery Prime), a text in ten *juan* and 110 sections, each of which contained an encomium (1.7b). In addition, the emperor bestowed on him the formal title Great Officer of Silver-Green Radiance and offered him the position of chamberlain of ceremonies. Yin, however, refused the latter, preferring his Daoist career to more active state involvement (1.8a).

In 688, Yin Wencao announced his impending transformation and ascended to the empyrean. Besides his Laozi hagiography, he also wrote a supplementary section to the account of Louguan masters, the *Xiaomo lun* 消魔論 (On Dissolving Evil), and the *Quhuo lun* 祛惑論 (On Dispersing Doubts) (1.8b). He is also known for his catalog of Daoist scriptures, the *Yuwei zangjing* 玉緯藏經 (Collected Scriptures of the Jade Net; Yoshioka 1959, 261).

Yin Yin, following in his presumed forbear's footsteps, thus is another noble representative of the group responsible for advanced meditation material: Daoists, aristocrats, and active players at court.

Sima Chengzhen

Sima Chengzhen 司馬承禎 (647-735), *zi* Ziwei 子微 or Baiyun xiansheng 白雲
先生, was the twelfth patriarch of Highest Clarity Daoism (see Engelhardt 1987,
35-61; Chen 2000, 94-95). A native of Henan, he was a descendant of the imperial house of the Jin dynasty that ruled China in the third and fourth centuries.
Even after losing the throne, the family remained at the top of the official hierarchy, so that Sima's grandfather served as a senior governor under the Sui and
his father was a high-ranking officer under the Tang. Trained well in the classics and arts of the gentleman, such as calligraphy and poetry, Sima is described
in the sources as a highly precocious and very intelligent child. Some even claim
he was able to speak at birth.

Still, rather than dedicating himself to standard Confucian service, he opted for
a career in Daoism, which in the eighth century had risen to official status and
was the main religion supported by the state. He began his Daoist studies on
Mount Song 嵩山, the central of the five sacred mountains located near Luoyang in his native Henan. At the age of 21, in 669, he underwent Daoist ordination under Pan Shizheng 潘師正 (594-682), the eleventh patriarch of Highest
Clarity and direct successor of Tao Hongjing 陶弘景 (456-536), the first official
leader and main coordinator of the school.

Continuing his climb through the Daoist hierarchy and absorbing all the esoteric rites and scriptures of the different schools, Sima was chosen to succeed
his teacher as leader of the school in 684. In this role, he understood himself
very much as an heir to Tao Hongjing, whom he sincerely venerated and variously praised in his writings. Moving the headquarters of the school, he settled
on Mount Tongbo 桐柏山 in the Tiantai range in Zhejiang, returning to where
"at the beginning of the fifth century, the Highest Clarity texts were propagated
for the first time" (Strickmann 1981, 34) while also connecting to the flourish-
ing Buddhist center there.

Sima Chengzhen was invited to court four times: first by Empress Wu (r. 690-
705), then, in 711, by Emperor Ruizong (r. 710-711). This emperor built a
monastery for him in the Tiantai Mountains, and one of his daughters became
Sima Chengzhen's disciple. The remaining two invitations were issued by Emperor Xuanzong (r. 712-756): in 721, Sima initiated him as a priest of Highest
Clarity (De Meyer 2006, 23); in 727, he offered him a divine sword and mirror
cast and engraved by himself.[5] Following Sima's suggestion, in 734 the emperor
had shrines to the gods of the five sacred mountains erected on each summit

---

[5] This is documented in his *Shangqing hanxiang jianjian tu* 上清含象劍鑑圖 (Chart of a
Highest Clarity Sword and Mirror and Their Symbols, DZ 431), which describes the objects
and their inscriptions with explanatory comments. See Fukunaga 1973; Schafer 1979.

and soon after ordered him to take up residence on Mount Wangwu 王屋山, located north of Luoyang and thus closer to the capital. It was also one of the ten major grotto heavens of Daoism, thought to connect the world of the living with that of the immortals. The emperor had a large monastery erected there, the Yangtai guan 陽臺觀 (Sunlit Terrace Monastery), and Sima Chengzhen spent the later part of his life there (Schafer 1980, 45; Engelhardt 1987). This is also where the inscription of the *Zuowang lun* was engraved in 829, showing a continued presence of Sima's teachings and disciples.

Like Sun Simiao, Sima Chengzhen traveled widely, propagating Daoist teachings and seeking out learned masters. He was well versed in medical knowledge and engaged in the various longevity practices, abstaining from grains for extended periods, taking herbal medicines to enhance and transform his *qi*, and engaging in all sorts of Daoist practices. However, unlike Sun Simiao who had a predominantly medical focus, Sima's entire practice was steeped in the religious dimension of the teaching: connected at all times with the deities in the body and the heavens and closely interlinked with ritual practices, talismans, and incantations. Within this framework, he became known for his extraordinary powers. For example, a story in his biography in the tenth-century collection *Xuxian zhuan* 續仙傳 (Supplementary Immortals' Biographies, DZ 295; Penny 2000, 121; Verellen in Schipper and Verellen 2004, 429) tells how he and another Daoist celebrated the fall purgation rites and, after a round of lengthy rituals, went to sleep around midnight.

> Suddenly the Daoist heard a sound. It seemed as if a small child was reciting a classical text and as if bells of gold and jade were sounding. He collected his clothes and crept closer to examine the source of the sound. Then he saw a miniature sun on Sima's forehead. It was about the size of a coin and spread a bright radiance. He stepped closer and listened carefully. The sounds came from Sima's head. (1.2a; Engelhardt 1987, 41)

That is to say, Sima's Daoist powers were such that the deities were present within his body at all times, even during sleep. They were so prominent that their radiance issued from his head and their chanting could be heard even with ordinary senses.

Not only involved with rituals and devotion, Sima Chengzhen as patriarch of the leading Daoist school also engaged in frequent interactions with the imperial court and the aristocracy of the time and was mentioned variously in Tang poems (see Kroll 1978). He had many close friends with whom he exchanged poems and learned discussions, and went out of his way to make Daoist teachings available to lay adepts.

His extant works speak of this effort.[6] For example, he promoted knowledge of Daoist sacred geography in his *Tiandi gongfu tu* 天地宮府圖 (Chart of [Divine] Palaces and Provinces in Heaven and Earth, YQ 27). The text contains a list of the seventy-two auspicious places of Highest Clarity with short explanations of their whereabouts and probably had pictures in its original version. He also enhanced understanding of what it meant to be a serious Daoist master in his *Shangqing shidi chen Tongbo zhenren zhen tuzan* 上清侍帝晨桐柏真人真圖讚 (A True Pictures and Praises of the Perfected of Mount Tongbo in Service of the Imperial Radiance of Highest Clarity, DZ 612; see Verellen in Schipper and Verellen 2004, 424-26). This work is a collection of eleven short biographies of Highest Clarity saints connected with Mount Tongbo, in each case including an illustration and words of praise.

Besides the *Zuowang lun* and *Tianyinzi* which describe stages of meditation and map the path of Daoist cultivation, his most practical work is the *Fuqi jingyi lun* 服氣精義論 (How to Absorb *Qi* and Penetrate [Ultimate] Meaning, DZ 830, YQ 57), also extant in a variant version under the title *Xiusheng yangqi jue* 修生養氣訣 (Formulas on Cultivating Life and Nourishing *Qi*, DZ 277).[7] The text outlines the different aspects of physical cultivation in nine steps, placing the most advanced first. Reading it in reversed order, one should begin by establishing a clear diagnosis, defining one's physical condition and taking special care to spot latent diseases that may or may not erupt in the future. In a second step, one should treat these disease tendencies with various *qi*-balancing methods, then move on to energize the five inner organs, making sure they store ample *qi*, and take care to live in moderation, avoiding excessive strain or emotions.

Moving into the more refined level of practice and starting to engage with immortal dimensions, in step five one can gradually begin to replace ordinary food with herbal concoctions, allowing the body to cleanse and refine itself as it opens up to more subtle states. This, then, can be supplemented with "talisman water," i.e., the remnants of a burnt talisman mixed with water. Taking this, adepts align themselves with the higher energies of the cosmos. The last three steps involve healing exercises, the absorption of *qi*, and the ingestion of the five sprouts, the pure energies of the five directions of the universe, which firmly places the adept into the larger cosmic context of the Dao.

---

[6] Altogether Sima Chengzhen wrote or edited fifteen works (Chen 1975, 58). Judged from the titles, most of his lost works dealt with physical immortality practices, but they also included a commentary on the *Shengxuan jing* 昇玄經 (Scripture of Ascension to the Mystery; DZ 1122 plus Dunhuang manuscripts; see Yamada 1992). This played an important role in seventh-century Daoism and was frequently cited interchangeably with the *Xisheng jing*, one of the textual forerunners of the *Zuowang lun* which quotes it heavily.

[7] The text is translated and analyzed in Engelhardt 1987. For a survey, see Engelhardt 1989. For a discussion, see Baldrian-Hussein in Schipper and Verellen 2004, 373-74.

Sima Chengzhen himself engaged in these practices and lived a long and healthy life. What is more, according to the biographers, he bypassed death in a well-orchestrated ceremony of ascension. In June of 735, after announcing his imminent transformation for transfer to an official post in the celestial administration, he sat quietly in meditation and accompanied by white cranes, purple clouds, and celestial music, ascended to emptiness, vanishing before the astounded eyes of his disciples (Engelhardt 1987, 51). The Daoist master thus returned to his true home above the clouds. He was posthumously awarded the title Zhenyi xiansheng 禎一先生 (Master of Auspicious Oneness).

Wu Yun

Quan Deyu 權德輿 (759-818) notes that Wu Yun 吳筠 (d. 778) was born around the year 710 in Huayin 華陰 near the sacred mountain of the west.[8] Dedicated to the Dao from an early age—some sources speak of age fifteen— he studied first on Mount Yidi 倚帝山 near Nanyang in Henan. There he "extensively investigated the ancients and persistently pursued what is beyond this world. He cultivated the plant of immortality and rested among the clouds. Fame and profit were meaningless to him" (De Meyer 2006, 10-11).

In the early years of the Tianbao era (741-755), Wu Yun followed a summons by Emperor Xuanzong and left his seclusion to attend an audience at court. He then decided to pursue a more official career as a Daoist priest and went to study on Mount Song, the sacred mountain of the center, where Sima Chengzhen was also initiated. There he trained under Feng Qizheng 馮齊整, a disciple of Pan Shizheng, the eleventh patriarch of Highest Clarity (De Meyer 2006, 33).

Following this, he might possibly have moved to become a court official, but failed the *jinshi* 進士 examination. Still, he came to serve the empire:

---

[8] Quan wrote two biographies of Wu Yun, contained in *Quan Tangwen* 全唐文 (Complete Tang Literature), chs. 489 and 508. His more reliable account also appears as the preface of Wu's collected works in the Daoist canon (DZ 1051). They are translated in Kirkland 1986, 104-06; collated into one narrative in Schafer 1981, 378-81; and discussed extensively in De Meyer 2006, ch. 1. Quan's work formed the basis for the official account of Wu Yun's life in *Jiu Tangshu* 舊唐書 (Old History of the Tang), ch. 192, and for its hagiographic development in the preface of the *Nantong dajun neidan jiuzhang jing* 南統大君內丹九章經 (Scripture in Nine Stanzas on Inner Alchemy by the Great Lord of the Southern Lineage, DZ 1054), both rather untrustworthy (De Meyer 2006, 3-4). For an analysis of Wu's biography, see Schafer 1981, 381-84; for a discussion of the Confucian impact on his image, see Kirkland 1986, 96-103; for a careful historical description of his life, see Kamitsuka 1979, 33-36; for an extensive discussion of his vita, including much poeteic material, see De Meyer 2006, ch. 1.

In Tianbao 13 [754)], Wu Yun was summoned to [an imperial audience in] the Hall of Great Unity, after which an imperial decree granted him residence in the Hanlin Academy. Emperor Xuanzong leniently let things be in the empire, and a favorable wind led the way. Thereupon Wu submitted his *Xuangang lun* 玄綱論 [The Mysterious Mainstays; DZ 1052] in 3 sections, which was rewarded with an imperial decree praising and welcoming it. Determined to preserve his integrity and study immortality, Wu repeatedly memorialized the throne, begging to be allowed to retreat so he could be like the birds and fish and find contentment in marshes and ponds. (Quan, *Preface*; De Meyer 2006, 34; Kirkland 1986, 326)

Finally succeeding in this endeavor, Wu Yun left the court around the time of An Lushan's 安錄山 rebellion in 755, drifting southeast to a region relatively unaffected by the ensuing chaos (Kirkland 1986, 755; De Meyer 2006, 51). He stayed on Mount Mao 茅山 near modern Nanjing in Jiangsu at the religious center of the Highest Clarity school for some time, then moved on to Mount Lu 盧山 where he wrote eight poems, two rhapsodies, and one inscription, the latter containing a eulogy for the famous fifth-century Daoist Lu Xiujing 陸修靜 (406-477). [9] It was composed in 761 (*Quan Tangwen* 926; see Schafer 1981, 384; Kamitsuka 1979, 35; trl. De Meyer 2006, 385-403). He seems to have enjoyed his time there, as expressed in the following poem:

A long time I have been burdened by idle fame,
Causing me to leave the realm of retirement.
I always wished that my path should meet no obstructions,
What I secretly cherished, I have now indeed obtained.
My friends live among cloud-covered mountain peaks,
In their company I again shall find repose.
The wild goose has penetrated the blue depths of the sky,
Forester: put away your stringed darts.
(DZ 1051, 2.35a; De Meyer 2006, 56)

In the late 760s Wu Yun seems to have submitted once again to wanderlust and traveled widely to a number of sacred mountains in the southeast, including Mount Tianmen 天門山 on the banks of the Yangtze, Mount Beigu 北固山 near modern Zhenjiang 鎮江, and Mount Dadi 大滌山 (i.e., Mount Tianzhu 天柱山) in Yuhang 餘杭 near modern Hangzhou. No longer a refugee from the capital, but a well-respected Daoist priest and poet, Wu finally settled down and

---

[9] For these works, see *Zongxuan xiansheng wenji* 宗玄先生文集 (Collected Works of the Master of Ancestral Mystery, DZ 1051). For an outline, see Baldrian-Hussein in Schipper and Verellen 2004, 437-38. For translation of poems, see Schafer 1981; 1982. For a translation and discussion of most works, see De Meyer 2006.

organized a group of poets into a kind of "drink-and-sing" association under the protection of the local magistrate Yan Zhenqing 顏真卿 (Kamitsuka 1979, 36; De Meyer 2006, 63; 67). Li Bai 李白 (701-762) joined the group, and the two poets allegedly became good friends. For the next several years, he went on occasional travels to further mountains but for the most part seems to have engaged in advance Daoist practice, rituals, alchemy, and meditation. Wu Yun died in the first month of 778. He was honored with the posthumous title Zongxuan xiansheng 宗玄先生 (Master of Ancestral Mystery).

A prolific author, Wu Yun's wrote some 450 pieces, of which only a fraction remain: 130 poems, eight rhapsodies, three discourses, one memorial, two inscriptions, and the *Xuangang lun*. For this volume, his most important work is the essay *Xinmu lun* which is a fictional dialogue between the mind and the eyes on who has predominance and should carry more responsibility in the process of meditation. Also important are his *Shenxian kexue lun* 神仙可學論 (Immortality Can Be Learned, DZ 1051, 2.9b-16a; see De Meyer 2006, ch. 8) and his *Xingshen kegu lun* 形神可固論 (Body and Spirit Can Be Maintained, DZ 1051, 2.20a-26a; De Meyer 2006, ch. 9). While even these prose works are highly erudite and full of beautiful phrases, Wu's poetry is truly outstanding, revealing a first-hand experience of immortality and Daoist spiritual attainment, as Cycle 6 from his *Buxu ci* 步虛詞 (Songs on Pacing through Emptiness, DZ 1051, 2.31a; Schafer 1981; Kohn 2009, 229) shows:

> The jasper terrace, measurable in kalpas,
> Glitters alone beyond even Grand Network.
> Always there are the clouds of Three Simplicities,
> Crowding their brilliance, flying all around.
>
> Feathered luminants drift by in bright morning light,
> Rising and falling—how ever light and hazy.
> Phoenixes cry forth in elegant melodies,
> Perching and soaring above the rosy woods.
>
> All jade emptiness, there's neither day nor night,
> The wondrous luminants, blazing ever brightly.
> I take a look at the Highest Capital
> And know how small really all the heavens are.

Chapter Four

Main Texts

The four Tang masters, besides all their other accomplishments, have written, edited, or annotated the key texts on sitting in oblivion that have survived from the middle ages and provide essential information on the integrated practice. They center in the eighth century, with one dating from the early ninth and two possibly from the late seventh. They also all center around the *Zuowang lun* and stand in close relationship to it, just as their authors were connected within the Daoist network of the high Tang.

The Tang constellation of texts on sitting in oblivion shows that there was a rather strong school of meditation in the Daoism in this period. Centered around Sima Chengzhen and located in the Tiantai range, in close proximity to the Buddhist school named after this mountain, it combined ancient *zuowang* practices with inner observation and Buddhist mindfulness meditation. It also seems that some of the materials, and most probably the *Zuowang lun* itself, go back to a series of lectures on the practice that—not unlike the "Recorded Sayings" of contemporaneous Chan masters such as the Sixth Patriarch (see Yampolsky 1967)—were recorded by disciples and later compiled into a more formal document.

The likelihood is that the original lectures were given in the 720s and compiled into a first collection after the master's death. This then formed the basis for the inscription which was engraved on Mount Wangwu in 829, providing an early, authentic record of the work. Versions in the *Yunji qiqian*, in Tang literary collections, and in the Daoist canon followed, editors formalizing and standardizing the text. The *Daozang* edition, moreover contains an appendix, which turns out to be the text of the *Dingguan jing*, a work in verse that also survives separately with extensive commentary. This text, next, contains the outline of a series of "five phases" of achieving mental concentration and "seven stages" of attaining various levels of bodily sublimation and eventually immortality. These form the core of the *Cunshen lianqi ming*, a text otherwise dedicated to meditation practice and associated with Sun Simiao of the seventh century.

Beyond these four closely interrelated core texts, the *Tianyinzi* is commonly linked with Sima Chengzhen, contains a concise description of *zuowang*, and provides a comprehensive outline of eight sections of the Daoist path which nicely supplements the *Zuowang lun* itself. The *Neiguan jing*, dated to the seventh century and probably the oldest source in the group, claims to be revealed by Lord Lao—central Daoist deity at the time and widely venerated throughout the empire—and outlines the proper vision of the human body with its various energies and spirit entities. It adds a dimension of detail to the otherwise more general transformative vision, enhancing our understanding of how Daoists viewed the human body and mind at the time.

The *Wuchu jing*, both in its verses and commentary full of the same vocabulary and extremely subtle in its approach to human mind and perfection, serves to enhance the wider cosmic perspective of the practice. Linked with Yin Yin, it is placed right in the time of the original creation of the *Zuowang lun* and addresses much the same audience. Wu Yun's essay on "Mind and Eyes," the *Xinmu lun*, finally allows a glimpse of the more poetic and literary interpretation of the interior agents and dynamics of the human body, a vision of meditative attainment in powerful parables and metaphors.

While all these texts are thus close in authorship, time of origin, perspective, and content, they each have their own unique history and complex textuality. Existing in various editions, dated differently by scholars, and studied under multiple auspices, they deserve to be considered carefully one by one.

Zuowang lun

The *Zuowang lun* outlines a gradual progress to immortality in seven steps. Practitioners begin with "Respect and Faith," i.e., they have to have heard of the practice, believe that its promises are real, and trust that they have the capacity and energy to attain them. Next, they work on "Interception of Karma," which in essence means detaching themselves from society and, at least for a practice period, withdraw from ordinary life.

Third, they dedicate themselves to "Taming the Mind," which means the establishment of access concentration with the help of breath observation combined with an increased awareness of just how jumpy and fickle the ordinary mind is. Next, "Detachment from Affairs" sees the first conscious turning away from things, an initial level of forgetfulness, where one can let go of worldly achievements which are now merely "superfluous gratifications of passions and desires."

Step five is called "Perfect Observation." Integrating the basic tenets of insight meditation, it leads practitioners to a reorientation within self and world, gaining a deeper appreciation of the workings of karma, letting go of attachments to body and self, and increasingly overcoming dualistic evaluations and value judgments. It sees the completion of the first state of oblivion, closely followed by the second, a deep trance state called "Stability of Cosmic Peace." Here even the inner agent that gave rise to the various mental states is actively forgotten. Practitioners find themselves in deep, stable serenity, a restfulness within that needs no stimulation or outer action, but is at the same time accompanied by a radiant heavenly light, the pure energy of the Dao shining through, the power of penetrating wisdom and sign of enlightenment.

Finally, in the last step called "Attaining Dao," adepts realize oneness with Heaven and Earth, a life as long as the universe, and various spiritual powers. As perfected beings they can live among fellow men and spread the purity of the Dao by just being themselves; or they can ascend spiritually to the heavens where they take up residence among the immortals

The *Zuowang lun* survives in two main editions: one appears in the *Yunji qiqian* of the year 1019 (ch. 94) as well as in the *Quan Tang wen* 全唐文 by Dong Gao 董誥, dated to 1819 (ch. 924). The other is in the Daoist canon (DZ 1036) and can also be found in the *Daozang jiyao* 道藏輯要 (Collected Essentials of the Daoist Canon, Maoji 5.39a51a).[1] It has both a preface and an appendix not found in the other version.

The preface claims to be by a certain recluse or retired scholar called Zhenjing 真靜 and is dated to a *dingwei* year. There is the slight possibility that the characters for Zhenjing, which occur only once in the text, are an error for Jingzhen, which would mean that the author of this preface is one of Sima Chengzhen's foremost disciples, Jiao Jingzhen 焦靜真. If the edition was indeed put together by her, the year would refer to 767. However, not only is the probability of a mistake in the name of the editor very slight, but there are also indications that the relationship of the editor to the author was not of a very close personal nature. Sima Chengzhen is called by his posthumous name Master Zhenyi, and it is explicitly mentioned that he was of the Tang dynasty. Moreover the preface

---

[1] This compilation was first published during the Jiaqing reign (1796-1820), consisting of 173 texts, all from the Ming-dynasty canon, and probably compiled by Jiang Yupu 蔣予浦 (1755-1819), a central figure in a spirit-writing group based at the Altar of Awakening in Chengdu. It was republished several times, most recently in 1906, with more texts added, so that it contains today 287 works. For indexes, see Chen 1987; Komjathy 2002. For ongoing research on the collection, see Esposito 2009.

mentions that the *Zuowang lun* was then printed. Printing becoming common only in the following centuries (Goodrich 1925, 41), this makes such an early date unlikely.

The *Zuowang lun* by Sima Chengzhen is first mentioned in the bibliographical chapter of the *Tangshu* as consisting of one *juan*. Ouyang Fei 歐陽棐 in his *Jigu lumu* 集古錄目 (Catalogue of Collected Ancient Inscriptions; see Hervouet 1978, 199) of the year 1069 gives the text of a stele inscription merely mentioning the title *Zuowang lun* and naming a Baiyun xiansheng 白雲先生 (Master White Clouds) as the author (5.5a). As the stele was placed before Sima Chengzhen's temple, the rather common title Master White Clouds in this case probably refers to him.

Another mention of the *Zuowang lun* is found in Wu Zeng's 吳曾 *Nenggai zhaiman lu* 能改齋漫錄 (Revised Record of Zhaiman) of 1157 (Hervouet 1978, 290).[2] According to this, Sima Chengzhen received the teachings of Master Tianyinzi from Wu Yun and rephrased them to produce a text on mystical attainment, later called *Zuowang lun* (5.42ab). Wu Zeng cites several passages from this, but they do in fact come from the appendix, the *Dingguan jing*, rather than from the *Zuowang lun* proper. He also notes that these references go ultimately back to Hong Xingzu 洪興祖 (1019-1155) and that they are not from the *Zuowang lun*. In conclusion he remarks that, since his seniors exchanged a passage from the *Dingguan jing* with one from the *Zuowang lun*, the latter must have originally been based on it.

Zeng Zao's *Daoshu* of 1151 contains a lengthy section under heading "Sitting in Oblivion" (2.2b-4a). It cites the *Dingguan jing*, includes the *Tianyinzi*, and contains a summary of the *Zuowang lun* which turns out to be very close to the text of the inscription of 829. In other words, by the middle of the twelfth century, the three key texts on oblivion in the Tang were closely connected if not actually conflated in the minds of scholars and collections.

This inscription, while containing much of the same information, is by no means identical with the *Zuowang lun* in seven sections. It compounds the complexity of the textual transmission and questions of authorship since it mentions a text entitled *Zuowang lun* written by a certain Zhao Jian 趙堅 (Wu 1981, 47a). Serious questions as to who wrote the *Zuowang lun* were also posed by Lu You 陸游 in his *Weinan wenji* 渭南文集 (Collected Works of Master Weinan; Hervouet 1978, 418). In one of the fifty-eight postscripts contained in this collection, he mentions that he himself saw a *Zuowang lun* stele on Mount Lu. He

---

[2] Before Wu Zeng, there are two other mentions of the text, in Chao Buzhi's 晁補之 (11th c.) *Jile ji* 雞肋集 (Chicken Bone Collection) and in Ye Mengde's 葉夢得 (1077-1148) *Yujian zashu* 玉潤雜書 (Miscellaneous Writings from Jade Creek; Wu 1981, 46a).

describes its text as consisting of eight sections and notices that such a text was written by Zhao Jian who, being Sima's senior, must thus have been the true author of the text (28.14b-15a).

The *Zuowang lun* in seven sections plus an appendix is mentioned by Chen Zhensun 陳振孫 (1190-1249) in his *Zhizhai shulu jieti* 直齋書錄解題 (Explanatory Comments on Books and Records in the Studio of Uprightness; see Hervouet 1978 198; 9.23a). Around the same time, Chao Gongwu 晁公武 also refers to it in his *Junzhai dushu zhi* 郡齋讀書志 (Record of Readings in the Provincial Studio; Loon 1984, 109; 34a). Similarly Ma Duanlin 馬端臨 in his *Wenxian tongkao* 文獻通考 (Pervasive Examination of Literary Offerings; Hervouet 1978, 174; ch. 225) speaks of a *Zuowang lun* by Sima Chengzhen in seven sections. He mentions a postface to the text by Wenyuan gong 文元公, i.e., Chao Jiong 晁迥 of the early Song. This would imply that the text existed in the tenth century.

I have not been able to locate this particular postface. From the information gathered so far, however, it has become clear that there were possibly as many as three different texts with the title *Zuowang lun*: the text contained in the Daoist canon and the *Yunji qiqian*; its appendix, transmitted separately under the title *Dingguan jing*; and the inscription. All three date from the late Tang, share a basic concern for Daoist immortal transformation, and present a system divided into stages of gradual refinement, leading from ordinary consciousness to a mind unified with Dao.

Inscription on Oblivion

The inscription is the shortest of the three texts and the one most precisely dated (ed. Wu 1981; Chen et al. 1988, 176). It is well connected with other texts of the period. Like the *Zuowang lun*, it outlines the fundamental steps to oneness with Dao, i.e., the recognition of the delusions that make up everyday consciousness, the attainment of a concentrated mind, the arising of insight, and the finding of oneness with Dao. Like the *Dingguan jing*, it mentions the gradual refinement from body through *qi* and spirit to union with Dao. Like Wu Yun's *Shenxian kexue lun*, it relies on the *Yijing* and makes allusions to alchemical practice.

As noted in the *Jigu lumu* (5.5a), it was engraved in 829 by the Daoists Liu Ningran 柳凝然 and Zhao Jingyuan 趙景元 on Mount Wangwu, where Sima Chengzhen spent the later part of his life (Wu 1981, 46a; Robinet in Schipper and Verellen 2004, 307). The old Wangwu, says Ding Shaoji 丁紹基 in his *Qiushi zhai beiba* 求是齋碑跋 (Postface to Inscriptions of the Studio for Pursuing Rightness; 3.12b), is today in Jiyuan District in northwestern Henan. This is the place where Gu Xieguang 顧燮光 of the Ming also found the stele, located in front of the Ziwei gong 紫微宮 (Temple of Purple Tenuity). He describes it under the title "Stele of the Ancestral Temple of Master Zhenyi" in his *Heshuo xin beimu* 河朔新碑目 (Catalogue of New Inscriptions from Heshuo; 3.12a). The place is on the northwestern border of present-day Henan, almost directly north of Luoyang, still under the name of Jiyuan.

The text of the inscription was written by Zhang Hongming 張宏明, a Daoist of Wangwu. Its contents was brought there by a certain Mr. Xu 徐氏, otherwise unknown (Wu 1981, 47a). He received it on Mount Tongbo, where Sima Chengzhen's teaching seems to have been transmitted orally. According to the text of the inscription, Sima Chengzhen once met the Daoist Zhao Jian who had written a treatise on "sitting in oblivion" in seven sections. However, this treatise was so carefully phrased that people would forget their practice of oblivion and rather become absorbed in the beauty and sophistication of the text. Sima criticizes this treatise sharply.

It appears, furthermore, that there was a work on *zuowang* by Wu Yun, who supposedly gave Sima the teachings contained in the *Tianyinzi*. There is indeed a *Zuowang lun* by Wu Yun mentioned in a catalogue of books lost in the imperial libraries compiled in the Southern Song (Loon 1984, 109). Moreover, there is a fair amount of overlap between the *Zuowang lun* inscription and Wu's *Shenxian kexue lun*. Although not explicitly mentioned as a disciple of Sima Chengzhen, he certainly moved in the same circles and was very likely part of a living oral tradition of Sima Chengzhen's teachings in the Tiantai mountains.

To sum up, several treatises on "sitting in oblivion" seem to have circulated in the eighth century: by Zhao Jian, Wu Yun, and Sima Chengzhen. While Wu Yun's was lost early, the work of Zhao Jian was still known under the Song, but today only Sima's work survives.

Dingguan jing

Another candidate for an early *Zuowang lun* is the *Dingguan jing* which appears three times in the Daoist Canon: as appendix to the *Zuowang lun*, as a separate text (DZ 400), and sharing the same chapter with the *Neiguan jing* in the *Yunji qiqian* (1.6b-13a).[3] Called by its full title *Dongxuan lingbao dingguan jingzhu* or "Scripture on Stability and Observation of the Mystery Cavern of Numinous Treasure, With Commentary," it is a short but powerful document consisting

---

[3] For a general discussion and dating, see Schipper in Schipper and Verellen 2004, 332). He translated *dingguan*, in adaptation of Buddhist *samadhi* as "Intent Contemplation."

of forty-nine stanzas of two or more lines, each with four or occasionally six characters. It presents a survey of the mental transition from an ordinary perspective, characterized by impurity, cravings, vexations, emotions, and desires, to a state of mental stability, peace, and quietude. Once stability (*ding* 定) is reached, the mind will observe (*guan* 觀) all dispassionately and gain the necessary insight that will take one to immortality.

The development of the mind is outlined in five phases, the immortalization of the body in seven stages. This system repeats the pattern described by Sun Simiao in his *Cunshen lianqi ming*. In addition, the text is noteworthy for its practical details concerning the various mental states the adept undergoes when passing through the process of attainment. Throughout, purity and total abstention from intentional thinking and acting are emphasized.

While the editions in the Daoist canon and the *Yunji qiqian* show only minor variation in characters, the *Zuowang lun* appendix version adds two sections: a paragraph reviewing the fundamental concepts of the *Zuowang lun* inserted after about the first third of the text; and a list of the five phases of the mind before the seven stages of the body Neither section is phrased in the same verse-like pattern as the remainder of the text, nor does it have commentary, with only a few extra words supplemented to its citation in the *Daoshu* (2.2b-4a).

The *Dingguan jing* seems to have been a highly popular text. A concise synopsis, which substitutes "quietude" (*jing* 靜) for "stability" (*ding*), appears under the title *Guanmiao jing* (DZ 326), dividing into three parts: 1. an initial section containing a short synopsis of the basic practical instructions of the text which yet leaves out four lines dealing with the ordinary mind and the initial difficulties of mental concentration; 2. paragraph similar to the *Zuowang lun* in that the arising of the heavenly light is mentioned yet also like the *Cunshen lianqi ming* in that it emphasizes the non-active way of attainment plus a summary of the central section of the *Dingguan jing*; 3. a final section which includes the five phases of the mind and the seven stages of the body.

Another indication of the text's popularity is its frequent citations. The earliest appears in the commentary to two mystical poems collected under the title *Xuanzhu xinjing zhu* 玄珠心鏡註(Annotated Mysterious Pearly Mirror of the Mind, DZ 574; Reiter in Schipper and Verellen 2004, 300-01; Kohn 1989a), which were published with commentary on Mount Wangwu, the former residence of Sima Chengzhen, in 817. The poems go back to a revelation by Jiao Shaoxuan 焦少玄, the wife of Lu Chui 盧陲, located in Fujian. Originally an immortal from the heaven of Highest Clarity, she departed this world, leaving behind only an empty coffin. Her husband implored her to give him some instructions regarding Daoist attainment; in response she returned to earth and revealed the poems. The first poem speaks of the restraint needed to guard the One:

Attainment of the primordial power of the One
Is not a gift from Heaven.
Realization of great nonbeing
Is the state of highest immortality.
Light restrained, a hidden brilliance, the body one with nature:
There is true peace, won but not pursued.
Spirit kept forever at rest.

In serenity and beauty: this is true being!
Body and inner nature, hard and soft
All is but cinnabar vapor, azure barrens.
One of the highest sages—
Only after a hundred years
The tomb is discovered empty.

The second poem has:

The Dao is nonaction, yet nothing is left undone.
Purity of mind does not come from knowledge and wisdom.
What is knowledge? What is purity?
Knowledge is to give up all wisdom. Purity is to be empty in going along.

Going along, not following: this is pervasion of mind.
Pervade the One and all affairs are done!
The One is the root, affairs are the gate.
When affairs return to the One, the One is always there.

The commentary cites the *Dingguan jing* twice. First the exhortation to observe
with proper awareness and to never abandon the radiating mind in the first part
of the text is used to explain the line: "The Dao is nonaction," pointing out the
need to immediately eradicate whatever thought arises (DZ 574, 6b). Second,
commentary to the last line of the first poem refers to the *Dingguan jing* saying,
"Guard emptiness and nonbeing and naturally you will live forever," then lists
the five phases of the mind and seven stages of the body in explanation of the
process (9b-10b).

The text as cited in the *Xuanzhu xinjing zhu* is close to Sun Simiao's version of
the five phases and the seven stages, allowing the conclusion that the *Cunshen
lianqi ming* circulated among the same practitioners as the other texts. In the
added section, moreover, the independent will of the individual is emphasized
more strongly than is common in such texts. Similarly, this version notes that
later the body-self rather than the body-form is the basis for refinement to *qi*.

Another prominent reference to the *Dingguan jing* is found in Du Guangting's
Guangsheng yi, where he uses the text to elucidate the meaning of *Daode jing* 79,

especially to the line: "Therefore the sage keeps his left-hand portion [of a contract] and does not blame the other party." Du interprets "left-hand portion" to refer to the mind, while he sees the passage as a whole concerning the sages' transmission of the true doctrine. He describes the nature of the sage as having permanent control over the mind while trying to reform others. He then illustrates the quality and development of the sagely mind by citing the *Dingguan jing* (49.8b). He also substitutes "sage" for "perfected" in the description of the final realization, a variant that also appears in the *Dadao lun* (15b-16b).

Last but not least, the *Dingguan jing* is cited in the *Zhuzhen neidan jiyao* 諸真內丹 集要 (DZ 1258; see Reiter in Schipper and Verellen 2004, 1185), a Yuan-dynasty text on internal alchemy, to illustrate the process of introspective observation. The work uses the exhortation to practice diligently day and night and only get rid of the agitated mind in the beginning of the text with a variant commentary. In addition, the final realization of the adept, described as "Never being not alive, never being not changing" (5a), is explained by reference to the last three stages of the mind.

Cunshen lianqi ming

A forerunner of Sima Chengzhen's *Zuowang lun* and a key source for the five phases and seven stages appears in the *Cunshen lianqi ming* (DZ 834, YQ 33.12a-14b) of Sun Simiao, his senior and almost contemporary. The text, which may have been collated and attributed to Sun Simiao later (Lévi in Schipper and Verellen 2004, 375), closely relates to his *Zhenzhong ji* and is grouped together with it in the *Yunji qiqian*. In both outlook and contents it is very close to the other meditation works of the eighth century.

Beyond the more specialized focus of the *Zuowang lun*, Sun here not only gives a practical method for taming the mind, i.e., focusing one's entire attention on the Ocean of *Qi* in the lower elixir field, but also emphasizes the need for physical preparation by means of fasting before one can begin meditating. He says: "If you want to learn the technique of refinement of *qi* you first of all have to refrain from eating grains" (1ab). Then, by means of focusing one's attention on the abdomen one will attain control over the mind as well as a feeling of natural satiation. Sun Simiao explains these preliminaries as "the cultivation of one-pointedness" and divides them into a minor cycle of one hundred and a major cycle of two hundred days. By this process, he claims, the body will spontaneously fall into a harmonious rhythm with nature, and "when one must eat, one eats, when rest is required, one rests. Thus one lives forever in freedom and without obstruction."

Daoist meditation can therefore be seen as structured according to the three fundamental levels of body, i.e., preliminary purification, mind, i.e., the actual practice of sitting in oblivion, and Dao, i.e., the spontaneous stages of the body once the mind is fully controlled and has attained serenity. These three fundamental levels are in turn divided. Bodily purification, as Sun points out, has a minor and a major cycle. Taming the mind is divided into five phases, and the final realization of bodily union with Dao takes place in seven stages.

Tianyinzi

Another text that places *zuowang* into a larger context and is closely related to Sima Chengzhen is the *Tianyinzi*, the "Book of the Master of Heavenly Seclusion," an otherwise rather obscure master.[4] In content, it divides into eight sections, beginning with a general outline of the ideal of "spirit immortality," presenting the same theoretical framework as found in the *Zuowang lun*. Next, it emphasizes the basic attitude of "simplicity," again echoing the other meditation texts, then it prescribes the "gradual progress toward Dao," strongly warning against overeager expectations and "suddenness."

This progress, then, divides into five levels which constitute the remaining sections of the text. The first is "fasting and abstention," the physical foundation of meditation, echoing Sun's admonition to practice abstention from grains. Next comes "seclusion," which details the lay-out of the quite chamber and matches Sima's second section on leaving society and "intercepting karma." Third, "visualization and imagination" describes basic methods of concentration and inner observation, echoing the "taming of the mind" section of the *Zuowang lun* as much as the *Neiguan jing* and the *Xinmu lun*. "Sitting in oblivion" is the title of the fourth section. It cites the original *Zhuangzi* passage and stresses the need to make the mind unmoving. The process culminates, fifth, in "spirit liberation," marked by liberation into Dao and the attainment of magical powers.

The text is contained in DZ 1026, but has been edited many times both in Daoist and secular collections (Kohn 1987b, 4). Its edition was fully established in the Song and has remained standardized, with only two variants (in the *Daoshu* and in the *Congshu jicheng*, Kohn 1987b, 5) and an introductory section added later (Loon 1984, 84). As regards the authorship of the text, the common view was first that the Master of Heavenly Seclusion was a mysterious figure whose teachings Sima Chengzhen adopted and summarized. An alternative arose in 1162, when Hu Lian 胡璉 wrote a postface to the text (*Shuofu* 75), in which he first praises Sima's mystical attainments, then cites a poem by Su

---

[4] An extensive discussion and translation of the text appears in Kohn 1987b. It is also transated in Komjathy 2008, #9; examined by Robinet in Schipper and Verellen 2004, 303.

Dongpo 蘇東坡 which mentions a work in eight sections on "quietude, nonaction, oblivion, and radiance." As the number of sections matches those in the *Tianyinzi*, Hu concludes that Su is speaking of the *Tianyinzi* as written by Sima Chengzhen himself, reaching the hypothesis that he actually wrote the text and only attributed it to the legendary master (Kohn 1987b, 4). This vision of the text was duly adopted by other scholars, becoming a popular alternative to the earlier view.

Another postface to the text, which does not appear until Ming editions, claims to be by Sima himself. Upon receiving the text, it says, he first recited it for three years, then gradually practiced according to its instructions with good results: "I awakened to the peace of body and mind and realized the insignificance of fame and profit." After three more years, Tianyinzi himself appeared to him and gave him oral instructions on how to practice the meditation methods. A further practice round of three years, then, should allow the adept to "feel purity and harmony in the body," eventually reaching a point when "the Dao of immortality is no longer hard to attain" (Kohn 1987b, 5).

The *Tianyinzi*—besides being reprinted in numerous collections—with its eight-step outline has remained a major mainstay for practitioners of both meditation and qigong to the present day. It forms part of the modern compilation *Qigong yangsheng congshu* 氣功養生叢書(Collected Works on Qigong and Nourishing Life, Shanghai 1999), on par with a number of classical works on internal alchemy and some more recent treatises on meditation (see Komjathy 2002, 106).

Neiguanjing

The *Neiguan jing*, on the other hand, is placed in the mouth of Lord Lao. Extant in two editions that are very close to each other (DZ 641; YQ 17.1a-6b) It consists of thirteen paragraphs of differing length and deals with the spiritual and psychological makeup of humanity, encouraging inner observation of the body gods from a state of stability and quietude, emptiness and serenity. More focused on the human body, it explains it in terms of the five phases and inner organs, but also through the divinities and internal passageways described in early medieval texts on Daoist visualization. It defines psychological terms, then integrates the Daoist system with Buddhist conceptions of consciousness, ego, and the senses. Following this, the text outlines the way of internal purification and concludes with the statement that "there is no teaching to transmit or receive, thus there is nothing that is not ultimately transmitted or received" (YQ 17.6b).

The *Neiguan jing* can be dated to the late sixth century, since it is cited extensively in the *Chuanshou jingjie falu lueshuo* 傳授經戒法籙略說 (Short Exposition of the Transmission of Scriptures, Precepts, and Registers, DZ 1241), "a survey of Daoist initiations and ordinations that describes admonitions, texts, oaths, pledges, and various other aspects of the rite" (Benn in Pregadio 2008, 1237; see also Cedzich in Schipper and Verellen 2004, 458). The text, by Zhang Wanfu, a priest at the Taiqing guan 太清觀 (Monastery of Great Clarity) in Chang'an, is dated clearly to the year 713 and is best known for its appendix that describes the formal ordination of two Tang princesses to the priestly rank of Numinous Treasure (see Benn 1991; Schipper 1985, 129-31).

It cites the *Neiguan jing* in its second chapter in a section that deals generally with internal deities and their cultivation (2. 5b-7a; Schipper in Schipper and Verellen 2004, 500). Using the text in its *Yunji qiqian* version, it presents parts of the first two sections (2ab, 3b-4b) as well as excerpts from the last three paragraphs (5b-6a), thus creating a comprehensive summary of the meditation work. Another, later citation of the *Neiguan jing*, appears in the Song treatise *Dadao lun*, in the section on "Mind Practice" (17b), referring to the nature of the mind.

Wuchu jing

The full title of this text is *Laozi shuo Wuchu jing* 老子說五廚經 (Scripture of the Five Kitchens as Revealed by Lord Lao, DZ 763). Edited and commented by Yin Yin in the early eighth century (Mollier 2000, 62), and presented to the court in 736 (Verellen in Schipper and Verellen 2004, 351), it was also interpreted by the Celestial Master Zhao Xianfu 趙仙甫 in the late Tang and the focus of a miracle described by Du Guangting in his *Daojiao lingyan ji* 道教靈驗記 (Record of Daoist Miracles, DZ 590; Verellen 1992, 250-51). A variant version appears in YQ 61.5b-10b under the title *Wuchu jing qifa* 五廚經氣法 (Energetic Methods of the Scripture of the Five Kitchens). The methods of the text are advocated further in Sima Chengzhen's *Fuqi jingyi lun* (DZ 277, 9b-10a; YQ 57.10-11b); they have matching versions in esoteric Buddhist sutras of the same period (see Mollier 2000; 2008).

In content, the *Wuchu jing* is a highly abstract mystical poem in twenty verses which guides adepts toward a mental state of detachment, non-thinking, and equanimous perception by cultivating the energy of universal oneness (*yiqi* 一氣) and merging with cosmic peace and harmony (*taihe* 泰和). This will lead to complete physical satisfaction: "The five organs are abundant and full; the five spirits are tranquil and upright." This in turn, means that all sensory experiences are calmed and all cravings and desires eliminated—including those for food and drink.

The text is dedicated to the five organs. Cosmologically the five organs (*wuzang* 五臟) match the five phases (*wuxing* 無行) and determine the horizontal structure of the universe, while the three elixir fields (*san dantian* 三丹田) match the three forces (*sancai* 三才: Heaven, Earth, Humanity) and create the vertical pillar of the world. Within this scheme, the Five Kitchens (*wuchu* 五廚) refer to human *qi*-processing on a subtle-body level, signifying the yin or horizontal structure and complementing the Triple Heater (*sanjiao* 三焦), a set of three transformative or yang organs that rest vertically between chest and abdomen. In other words, the Five Kitchens signify the energetic, transformative power of the five organs, both on the physical and spiritual levels.

Despite this concern with the body, the work strongly emphasizes mental restructuring over bodily practices, in fact saying that "accumulating cultivation will not get you to detachment" and that methods of ingestion are ultimately useless. On the other hand, the recitation of the scripture is beneficial, especially if combined with intellectual, mental, and ethical practices, so that "you will easily get the true essentials of cultivating the body-self and protecting life." More specifically, chanting the text one hundred times and practicing the harmonization of the five *qi* allows adepts to abstain from grain and eliminate hunger (Mollier 2000, 62-63).

This feature of the text as a talismanic work to be chanted for protection makes it a popular scripture even today. It still appears as a recited work in various Daoist temples, where its text is being distributed on flyers—such as the one I picked up at the City God Temple in Shanghai—showing the more devotional dimension of meditation in a contemporary light

Xinmu lun

Wu Yun's essay on "Mind and Eyes" is a brief exposition that creates an imaginary dialogue between the eyes, the senses' foremost representative, and the mind, the seat of the spirit in the human body and ruler of all sensory functions. The text appears twice, in almost identical editions, in the Daoist canon, once among Tang-dynasty essays on Daoist mysticism (DZ 1038) and once in Wu Yun's collected works (DZ 1051, 2.16b-19b).

It can be divided into an introduction and five sections of dialogue that lead from the recognition of the basic problem to the mind's attainment of Dao. The introduction sets the scene and explains the inherent opposition of mind and eyes. The dialogue part begins with the mind accusing the eyes and their undisciplined activity of causing its confused and agitated states. The eyes counter this accusation by placing the responsibility for order within the body squarely on the mind, who after all is the ruler of the senses and thus causes whatever erratic actions they exhibit.

Next, the mind responds to this, showing itself deeply moved, and develops a new resolution by envisioning itself as a flying immortal and entering the celestial spheres in joint cooperation with the senses. The eyes, however, counter yet again. They agree that the basic intention of the mind is sound but also make it clear that more is needed than just a vision of immortality, however enchanting it may be. They cite the examples of various sages to bolster their argument, teaching the mind that it must actively work for emptiness and vacuity, search to attain forgetfulness and serenity.

In the last section of the text, the mind finally comes to change its fundamental attitude. It eases up on thoughts and does away with hesitations and insecurity, reaching a state of oblivion and thereby attaining clarity and liberation. The mind ends the dialogue with a delightful chant on the intensity of liberation and the joys of non-sensory existence.

Chapter Five

The Integrated System

These core texts document sitting in oblivion as a complex system of meditation, outlining a series of procedures leading to inner peace, cosmic perfection, and oneness with Dao. Addressed to a general audience and members of secular society, the system centers on Sima Chengzhen's *Zuowang lun* and the seven steps it describes, the other documents adding more details in terms of precise methods to follow and mental states to pursue or eliminate. In addition, some works, such as the *Dingguan jing* and *Cunshen lianqi ming* as well as Wu Yun's ecstatic poems and *Xingshen kegu lun*, illuminate advanced states while others, such as the *Tianyinzi* and related Tang works outline details of the foundational work necessary for successful practice.

All the documents make it clear that the advance is gradual, but the *Tianyinzi* spells it out most clearly. It patterns the main stages of practice on the hexagram Jian 漸, "Gradual Progress" of the *Yijing* (no. 53). Here the six lines are metaphors for the flight of the wild geese. After a preliminary first approach to the shore, the second line represents their initial sitting on the rocks, i.e., finding a secure position. Next, they fly off to the plains, but this is too far off civilization, so in the following step (line 4) they fly to a group of trees where they can take rest. Thereafter they reach a high mound, a peak, to finally soar off to the vastness of the skies above (Wilhelm 1950, 204; Kohn 1987b, 9).

Matching this outline, adepts ready themselves for their endeavor by developing the right attitude and undergoing various forms of physical preparation. Second, they "sit on the rocks," i.e., establish the organizational set-up and physical preparations that facilitate practice. Next they engage in various forms of meditation, beginning usually with concentration and moving on to observation, which may come in the form of visualization or as detached insight. They reach out and move into new and exciting states but often find themselves too far off. Eventually they find a way of practicing that allows them to get a firm foothold in Dao, like the geese resting on the trees. Their peak is reached when they find the state of sitting in oblivion, also called the stability of cosmic peace. From there they soar off into a state of spirit pervasion which signifies the ultimate attainment.

Fundamental Attitudes

The *Zuowang lun* begins its discussion with the necessity to develop "Respect and Faith" (sect. 1), which means that to set out for the ascent to Dao one must first of all have heard about such things as sitting in oblivion and believe that it is possible to reach a state of mind free from all distinctions which will lead to oneness with Dao. One must trust in Dao and have a deep respect for the teaching. Paraphrasing the classical *Zhuangzi* passage, one must accept that "sitting in oblivion means the annihilation of the myriad states of mental projections" and have faith in the process as taught by the masters.

Along the same lines, the *Tianyinzi* begins its presentation with a general overview of "spirit immortality," defined as "settling the spirit within and letting its radiance shine without." It emphasizes the need to turn away from the seven emotions (joy, anger, sadness, happiness, love, hate, and desires) while working to eliminate the eight excesses of *qi* (wind, damp, cold, heat, hunger, satiation, labor, and idleness) (sect. 1). It then insists that the path is essentially simple and gradual, requesting that adepts put their trust in teachings that are straightforward and practical and eschew any expectations to rise up into the clouds in one swift motion (sect. 2-3).

The initial request for faith and trust in these texts closely reflects the fundamental requirement Sun Simiao formulates in his *Zhenzhong ji*, i.e., a sense of "prudence" (*zishen* 自慎) rooted in an attitude of "awe and care" (*youwei*憂畏). In this he follows the *Shenxian shiqi jin'gui miaolu* 神仙食氣金櫃妙錄 (Wondrous Record from the Golden Casket on the Spirit Immortals' Practice of Eating *Qi*, DZ 836), ascribed to Master Jingli 京里 who supposedly lived in the fourth century. The text may be a Tang compilation but in contents predates the Sui (Loon 1984, 130; Lévi in Schipper and Verellen 2004, 355).

Both insist that progress begins with awe and care which encourages moral actions and virtuous thoughts. "Awe and care are the gateway of life and death, the key to rites and good teaching, the cause of existing and perishing, the root of good and bad fortune, as well as the prime source of all auspicious and inauspicious conditions." They assure that sons have filial devotion, parents have kindness, ministers have merit, and rulers preserve peace (Engelhardt 1989, 280). If lost, "the mind will be confused and not cultivated, the body will be restless and not at peace, the spirit will be scattered, the *qi* will go beyond all bounds, and will and intention will be deluded" (*Jin'gui lu* 14b; *Zhenzhong ji* 1b). In other words, respect and faith, awe and care are prime conditions allowing the mind to become calm and focused. They also set the person up for moral integrity, expressed in the *Zhenzhong ji* as a series of prohibitions and precepts like those typically associated with Daoist practice (Engelhardt 1989, 283-85).

Echoing this and clarifying exactly what kind of "faith" Sima may have had in mind, Wu Yun in his *Shenxian kexue lun* requires seven positive attitudes when working with Dao and outlines seven potential hindrances. The first wrong attitude is the obviously Buddhist idea that "life is an illusion" and that body and spirit are mere ephemeral phenomena; rather, they are the storehouse of inner nature and need to be seriously cultivated. Second is the erroneous idea that immortality literally means never to die; rather it means that one returns to one's origins in Dao and spiritually co-exists with Heaven and Earth, reaching a state where physical death has become negligible (De Meyer 2006, 296). Third, people are guided away from true attainment by "foreknowledge," the belief in reincarnation and specific visions of the afterlife, hoping for a better existence beyond the world when all efforts should be directed to the here and now.

A fourth hindrance to attainment is the lure of material wealth and physical pleasures, "to think of official carriages and ceremonial caps as sources of satisfaction, to consider achievement and fame imperishable, to find pleasure in sex and indulge in music, to wear fancy clothing and crave delicious food" (De Meyer 2006, 299). Fifth is the pursuit of long life with the only goal of continuing indulgence; sixth, the dabbling in operational alchemy and search for medicinal substances instead of doing the interior work; and seventh, the adoption of priestly rank and status for mundane motives and worldly goals (2006, 300).

As regards the seven positive attitudes, they are modes of behavior and states of mind that each serve as a preparatory stage for the real work, "elements that bring one closer to the path leading to immortality" (2006, 303). They include:

> —having few desires and taking pleasure in the mysterious void;
> —controlling emotions and cultivating purity;
> —fulfilling one's duties with moral integrity;
> —letting go of possessions and taking things easy;
> —committing to honesty and finding quietude;
> —releasing past errors and doing good;
> —behaving virtuously and with rectitude. (De Meyer 2006, 303-06)

To sum up, before one can even begin the first step of practice, one's attitude has to be correct, one has to have firm roots in moral integrity, and one needs to find an inner distance to the pleasures and pursuits of the world—thus setting one's intention firmly on Dao.

Establishing Distance

Having found the correct fundamental attitude, one next must establish physical distance to the common world to create a space in which inner peace can flourish without distraction. The *Zuowang lun* calls this "Interception of Karma" (sect. 2), saying that "free from affairs and in peaceful leisure, one can finally cultivate Dao." The inscription, not quite as explicit on this point, also emphasizes the need for "placidity and freedom from desires." The *Dingguan jing* in its appendix version outlines three initial "precepts" of leaving affairs: detachment from karmic conditions, freedom from desires, and stillness of mind.

Already the *Daode jing* makes this point: "Cut off all contact, shut the doors, and to the end of life there will be peace without toil" (ch. 52). Sima sees the meaning of these lines as referring to people's relation to society and business, adding a passage from the *Zhuangzi*: "Don't be an embodier of fame, don't be a storehouse of schemes, don't be an undertaker of projects, don't be a proprietor of wisdom" (ch. 7). Both, Guo Xiang and Cheng Xuanying agree that these lines mean that it is much better to leave affairs to take care of themselves than to meddle with them. Cheng sees the problem slightly more psychologically than Guo Xiang who never tires of emphasizing that it is most of all necessary to forget oneself and spontaneously go along with the nature (DZ 745, 9.20b)

Sima's reading of the *Daode jing* lines in terms of social activities is not common among commentators. Rather, they tend to see their meaning in terms of spiritual practice. Thus Heshang gong takes *dui* 兌, here given as "contacts," to mean the eyes, whereas *men* 門, "doors," refer to the mouth. He says: "Eyes and mouth should not see or speak anything false, then the body will not be labored" (DZ 683, 3.12a). Similarly Wang Bi interprets "contacts" as the origin of desires, whereas "doors" for him means the actions undertaken on the basis of desires and passions. The passage thus comes to refer to the state of freedom from desires as the foundation of salvation (DZ 707, 7.23b-24a).

Xuanzong of the Tang follows along these lines, too, but adds the aspect of seeing dui as *le* 樂, "pleasure," which arises through the six senses and their being deluded by the apparent beauty of outer things. The "doors" in his commentary are the gates of the spirit through which it leaves people due to the delusion caused by pleasure (7.23b). Du Guangting, in his *Guangsheng yi* does not deviate from this line but adds a reference to *Xisheng jing* 7: "Sight and hearing of eyes and ears keep people in a state of imbalance. All the joys of the senses must be given up" (2.11b).

On the whole, the requirement to establish distance from society is a practical consequence of the precept of freedom from desires, also noted in the introduction to the *Zuowang lun*, which cites *Daode jing* 1: "Let there always be no desires so that the wondrous may be observed." More than merely saying that the senses are corrupting spiritual purity and that this must be prevented, Sima Chengzhen tells his audience how to go about doing this. Creating some distance to social interaction is thus the first active measure on the path.

The *Tianyinzi* sees this requirement in even more concrete terms as going into "Seclusion" (sect. 5) by setting oneself up in a simple hut described in terms of the oratory or quiet chamber (*jingshi* 靜室) of early medieval Daoists. A single detached building anywhere from ten to twenty square meters in size, the classical oratory should be covered by a thatched roof, surrounded by running water, and protected by a wall (Yoshikawa 1987, 129). It was to be erected well away from human activity and had to be kept in strict simplicity without any ornamentation. As Lu Xiujing says in his *Daomen kelue* 道門科略 (Abbreviated Rules for Daoist Followers, DZ 1127; see Schipper in Schipper and Verellen 2004, 126-27):

> Its outside should be separate and cut off, not connected with other buildings. Its interior should be pure and empty, not cluttered with superfluous objects. Opening and closing the door, never recklessly bang it or rush through it. The chamber should be sprinkled, swept, purified, and revered. It should always be thought of as a dwelling of the spirits. (Bumbacher 2000, 482; see also Nickerson 1996)

The oratory was thus kept extremely simple. It should not have more than four pillars, three rafters, and two beams, and they should all be made from the same simple, local wood, not from a variety of fancy imported timbers (Yoshikawa 1987, 129). As the *Tianyinzi* also notes, the ideal room should have windows to allow a maximum control of wind and light and a screen-door entrance that could be easily moved. A wooden bench should be placed in the center, according to one measurement given, approximately 2.5 x 1.9 meters in floor size and 31 centimeters high. In addition, the oratory was to contain only four things: an incense burner, incense lamp, table for petitions, and writing knife (Yoshikawa 1987, 128-29; Bumbacher 2000, 481-82). Adepts should enter it with circumspection and only after extensive purification. All actions in the oratory should be accompanied by ritual formality and conscious awareness of the divine (Yoshikawa 1987, 140-44).

The purpose of having a separate chamber—still part of Daoist practice in the Ming dynasty and even today (see Liu 2009; Kohn 1993b)—is to allow the physical separation of the practice from ordinary life and to create a good balance of yin and yang. It is desirable but not essential in the effort of intercepting karma and moving toward more focused practice.

Physical Preparation

Another important prerequisite for the practice of sitting in oblivion is mentioned in the *Tianyinzi* even before seclusion. "Fasting and Abstention" (sect. 4) involves modifying one's diet toward more fresh and organic foods; establishing a routine of moderation and the avoidance of all exertion; as well as practicing breathing, self-massages, and healing exercises to open the *qi*-flow in the body and cure acute or latent diseases. In other words, it means to undertake various physical longevity techniques to ready oneself for meditation proper.[1]

The *Zhenzong ji* discusses this aspect both under the headings "Prohibitions" and "Healing Exercises." It first encourages closer alignment with Dao by observing moral precepts, temporal taboos, and dietary regulations.[2] Besides avoiding all lascivious and immoral acts, practitioners should be very careful on days including the cyclical signs *jia* and *yin* which mark the time when the demons fight each other and people are given to nervous tension. In terms of food, they should abstain from eating meat and the five pungent vegetables (garlic and all kinds of onions), reflecting the classic demands of Daoist eating (Kohn 2010, 79-87).

The text also advises practitioners to keep themselves and their surroundings scrupulously clean and always maintain emotional harmony. They should move frequently to prevent getting involved with ordinary people and to avoid deep relationships with the opposite sex. Female adepts should not get pregnant; male practitioners should not approach pregnant or menstruating women. Both should strive for greater self-reliance and venerate the gods and goddesses but not dream of engaging in sexual intercourse with them (Engelhardt 1989, 284).

All this leads to the third section on "Healing Exercises," which specifies concrete daily routines of physical movements and self-massages. It says:

> When you get up in the morning, balance the *qi*. To do so, sit up straight and interlace the fingers behind the neck. Face south and raise the head, resisting this movement with your interlaced hands. Do this three or four times. This will make your essence harmonious and open your blood arteries. By doing this you will prevent all sorts of diseases.

---

[1] Similar methods are also found in the *Zhonghuang jing* 中黃經 (Scripture of Central Yellow, YQ 13) and the *Benqi jing* 本起經 (Scripture on the Original Arising, YQ 10), both from the Tang period. See Eskildsen 2007.

[2] Dietary regulations included avoidances of meat products, the five strong vegetables, and various tabooed foods as well as of all processed, conserved, or fermented products. It also involved taking herbal supplements and concoctions and undertaking advanced breathing exercises. For details, see Arthur 2006; 2009; Eskildsen 1998; Kohn 2010a.

Next, [stand up and] bend the body forward, stretching all four extremities and extending the sides by rotating to the right and left. Shake the hundred joints. Repeat three times.

Again, when you first wake up, rub the neck, the four sections of the face, and the ears with the soft inside of your hand, then cover the entire area with a hot, moist towel. Next, comb your hair and massage the top of your head for a good long time, then move both hands over the face and the eyes, covering them for a good while. This will make your eyes naturally bright and clear and prevent all wayward *qi* from accosting you.

When you are done with all this, swallow the saliva thirty times, guiding it deep inside the body. To count the number of repetitions as you swallow, maybe press your ears to the right and left. This way you won't lose count and at the same time prevent deafness in the ears and stuffiness in the nose.

Always, during the time of rising, living *qi* swallow the saliva twenty-seven times while pressing on any area of the body that is sore or painful. To do so, sit down, close your eyes, and inwardly envision the five organs and six viscera. With prolonged practice you will naturally become clear, discerning, and adept. (YQ 33.8ab; Kohn 2008a, 141; Engelhardt 1989, 285)

This is a typical daoyin sequence, as first documented in medical and longevity sources and integrated into Daoism with the inception of Highest Clarity whose practitioners used routines such as these as preparations for advanced practice.[3] Their most detailed account in the Tang appears in Sima's *Fuqi jingyi lun* which outlines the different aspects of physical cultivation in nine steps. According to this, one should begin by establishing a clear medical diagnosis, evaluating one's physical condition and taking special care to spot latent diseases that may or may not erupt in the future. In a second step, one should treat these disease tendencies with various *qi*-balancing methods, then move on to energize the five inner organs, making sure they store ample *qi*, and take care to live in moderation, avoiding excessive strain or emotions.

Moving into more active practice, one should begin to replace ordinary food with herbal concoctions, allowing the body to cleanse and refine as it opens to subtler states. This, then, can be supplemented with "talisman water," i.e., the ashes of a burnt talisman mixed with water. Taking this, adepts align themselves with the higher energies of the cosmos. The last three steps involve heal-

---

[3] Sun also provides a similar outline in *Qianjin fang* 27, based on the *Daolin shesheng lun* 道林攝生論 (Discourse on Protecting Life by Master Daolin, DZ 1427) (Kohn 2008b, 137).

ing exercises, the absorption of *qi*, and the ingestion of the five sprouts, the pure *qi* of the five directions of the universe, which firmly places the adept into the larger cosmic context of Dao (see Engelhardt 1987; 1989, 273-77).

All these practices, while ostensibly physical in nature and geared primarily toward the healing of diseases and establishment of an energetic balance in the body, are also meditative in that they require an inward focus and increasing awareness of the presence, quality, and movements of *qi* within. They lead almost seamlessly into the practice of mental concentration, the starting point of meditation proper and the main focus of the *Zuowang lun* and its related texts.

Concentration

The first step in meditation is the establishment of something called access concentration, which creates the mental focus and sensory calm necessary for further practice. It stands in contrast to attainment concentration, the complete one-pointedness of attention and the utter absorption in a single object which signifies a state of inner bliss and the overcoming of ego—the "Stability of Cosmic Peace" of *Zuowang lun*, sect. 6.

Access concentration commonly begins by focusing the mind on the respiration, anchoring it with the help of kinesthetic, visual, or auditory awareness, i.e., feeling it at a certain point in the body, focusing the gaze on an object or image while breathing, and using either a count or set phrase while breathing in and out.[4] It can also involve the guiding of *qi* and controlled forms of breathing: deepening, holding, or reversing.

The point of the practice is to take control of the mind, make it behave in an orderly fashion and be calm when required, in other words "tame" it like one would a wild animal—a metaphor common in Buddhist sources and also used in the *Zuowang lun*. Called "cessation" in Tiantai, it leads to "the termination of all sorts of perversions and attachments obstructing the mind from seeing the true nature of dharmas" (Ng 1993, 135). Although the texts agree that the mind is generally indestructible, boundless, shapeless, and unpredictable, it has two basic natures. It is either agitated and impure (*dongzhuo* 動濁), hasty and competitive, creating all sorts of stress and causing people to get ever more involved with the world; or it is still and clear (*jingqing* 靜清), all-pervasive like spirit itself, bringing people closer to the gates of Heaven and giving them joy

---

[4] For breath observation to establish access concentration in Buddhism, see Fryba 1989, 114-23, 208-25; Humphries 1968, 30-56; Kamalashila 1992, 16; Rosenberg 1998; Solé-Leris 1986, 44-47, 78-81; Thera 1962, 108-13.

and peace. The goal of this level of practice, then, is sit in stillness (or practice quiet sitting, *jingzuo* 靜坐) and calm or give peace to the mind (*anxin* 安心).

Sun Simiao describes the impure mind in his *Cunshen lianqi ming.* "The mind experiences much agitation and little stillness. One's thinking is conditioned by a myriad different projections, it is full of grasping and rejecting and without any constancy. Dreads and worries, plans and calculations keep racing on like mad horses. This is the normal mind" (1b-2a). From here, by anchoring the mind to the breath as felt in the rising and falling of the belly, one gradually moves through several stages of increased calmness: mostly agitated, half and half, mostly still, and being "turned entirely to clarity and stillness."

The *Zuowang lun*, in its section on "Taming the Mind" (sect. 3) emphasizes the need to sit quietly and get rid of all thoughts, i.e., mentally abide in non-existence and take no foothold anywhere. If one has to deal with affairs, take care of them with a clear mind, stopping all thoughts as soon as the business is completed and eliminating all fantasies and foolish ideas. This will lead to an empty mind detached from all outside affairs, to a peaceful mind turned away from ordinary things. Then, whatever one may hear or see, it will feel as if one had seen or heard nothing.

This state of "no-mind" (*wuxin* 無心) is a completely new experience for the mind which was used to relate to outer things and affairs all along. The freshness of this mental independence may bring about a certain confusion for the practitioner, but this must be checked at once. The mind should be fully immovable, it should be blindly concentrated. Once blind concentration is established, the mind will finally be tamed, just as oxen and horses, merlins and goshawks gradually get used to being handled.

The dangers of this process are manifold. When one does not control the mind enough, defilements overgrow it, one will float around in dissolution and be in no way different from ordinary people. By abiding in emptiness as in a concrete place, one will produce new mental projections and illusions about the nature of reality. By trying to hasten the development of concentration, one will only injure it and create another load of karma. Any kind of forceful action will agitate the mind. Diseases are the consequence, as are intense emotions, the "thorns and brambles" or overgrowth of the mind made up from love, sight, thoughts, and ideas. Another danger is that one only talks about it, missing the effect of the method in practice and moving further away from Dao. Ultimately Dao is realized by living with an empty mind in the midst of society, at the center of affairs. However to get to the point of having an empty mind that is also stable one must get away from society for a period—like a crane soaring majestically into the sky after nourishing on regurgitated food.

The same vision, much abbreviated, also appears in the inscription which emphasizes the necessity to establish concentration in order to experience the ultimate mental state as opposed to the mere theoretical understanding of the fact that "glorious positions are worthless and vain, that life and death are one whole." It is found in most detail in the *Dingguan jing*, which begins with the requirement to "give up all affairs," then sit quietly and at peace, systematically eliminating all mental disturbances that might arise due to the "six impurities," i.e., data absorbed through the senses, and "projected reality," i.e., the—fundamentally illusory—understanding of the world in one's own terms and due to personal likes and dislikes. "Mind and reality both forgotten, there are neither afflictions nor irritations" (7b). This, a "stabilized mind in a state of non-arising" (9a), is experienced for a short moment at first, then more frequently, and eventually becomes the solid foundation of all further practice.

Mind and Eyes

More details on the transition from agitated to stable mind are given in Wu Yun's *Xinmu lun*, which begins with the mind expressing its desire "to forget all emotions in withdrawal and retirement . . . and leave the realm of life and death" (1b) while accusing the eyes of distracting and disturbing it. The eyes, here representative for all the senses—"the body doting on beautiful ornaments, the mouth desiring rich tastes, the ears being fond of harmonious sounds, and the nose delighting in fragrant smells" (1b-2a)—counter by insisting that "disorder is never the fault of those below," holding the mind responsible as the central governing agency of the self and accusing it of living according to its own version of projected reality, "discriminating between beings and self, illuminating right and wrong" (2a).

In other words, adepts working to tame the mind need to begin with a strong determination to pursue inner stillness and let go of sensory attractions, but they cannot blame the senses for presenting them with outside information as long as they still evaluate it in terms of good and bad, right and wrong. Instead, they need to move away from their conceived understanding of reality and set their vision on immortality and ecstatic freedom, following the call to Dao. In Wu Yun's essay, the mind proposes such a vision and the eyes appreciate it but they warn against yet another level of likes and dislikes: "You would desire stillness yet follow things in haste, push out defilements yet stir up more dregs" (3a), expressed in Twofold Mystery as the perception of partial emptiness.

Following the model of the *Zhuangzi*, Wu Yun in his discourse uses various water metaphors to describe the activity of the mind. In the early part of his essay, he emphasizes the distraught and unhappy state of the mind with words like "confused" (*luan* 亂) and "muddled" (*lun* 淪). In the following sections, he applies images like to "ride on pure chaos" (*cheng hundun* 乘混沌), a watery state of primal merging, and become "one with the vast expanse" (*hanman* 汗漫), an ocean of vast openness, to express the mind's longing for clarity and freedom. Abstract purity and defilement, too, are expressed in water-terms: *qing* 清, open clarity, is an image of standing water that is lucid to the bottom; *zi* 滓, the sediments and dregs, are a metaphor for the deep defilements that lurk in the depth of the mind: stirred up, they cause great agitation and harm.

The ideal state found through spiritual practice, too, is seen through the metaphor of water. The mind becomes "shoreless" (*wuya* 無涯) and "limpid" (*bo* 泊). It is the ocean of Dao within, and just as "rivers rise, and dragons come to coil in them," so "spirit rests in an empty hollow." Roaming in "vast, deserted wilderness," the mind wanders freely around "the boundless source." Free from all, it overcomes the various turbid and whirling motions of its impure state and remains unmoved by the flow of activities around it, however violent they may be. Neither "whirling storms" nor "heaving oceans" or even "sky-high floods" can shake it any longer.

Detachment from Affairs

Only when the mind "adopts a relaxed attitude" and "finds placidity," it is purified of thoughts and stops pursuing things, reaching an intermediate stage the *Zuowang lun* calls "Detachment from Affairs" (sect. 4). This signifies an inner separation from the world and new understanding of oneself and one's needs. Most importantly it involves the realization that life goes on by itself, that things are neither good nor bad but just what they are. At this point worldly achievements become "mere gratifications of passions and desires" and one can live in purity, giving up "whatever is not essentially necessary to sustain life," dedicating oneself solely to Dao.

Of central importance here are the notions of essential inner nature and original destiny, the parameters one is born with that prescribe what is right for one's particular situation. As Sima says: "Knowing that life has allotments, one should not be concerned with what one is not allotted;" and, citing the *Zhuangzi*, "He who has mastered the perfect nature of destiny does not labor over what destiny cannot do" (ch. 19).

The classic explication of these concepts, on which Sima draws here, is found in Guo Xiang's commentary to the *Zhuangzi* (DZ 745), the first to connect the concept of share or allotment (*fen* 分) with inner nature (*xing* 性) and the concept of principle or cosmic order (*li* 理), with destiny (*ming* 命) (see Robinet

1983a; Knaul 1985b).[5] According to him, all beings have their share in the organic process of life, which in concrete terms means that everyone has certain inherent limitations and life conditions. Essential inner nature accordingly means the intrapersonal aspect of people's share in the cosmos, indicating the way they are created by nature, their genetically determined abilities, character, and natural way of being. Independent of people's subjective wishes of what they would like to be or do, it works in complete disregard of all aspirations, hopes, conceptions, and feelings.

Governing people's lives from within, essential inner nature is the individual's Dao, "what people rely on spontaneously without ever being conscious of " (2.35b). This can be a positive and comforting concept in the sense that one has a built-in direction and perfect abilities in this world. It becomes problematic and threatening when one tries to change it or go against it. Then it becomes the root of much suffering.

Sima Chengzhen understands inner nature as inborn qualities that remain in people's unconscious. There is no way to really know one's inner nature as an object. It is only by learning to accept oneself as one is within the framework of one's natural allotments and limitations that one can avoid being "concerned with what is not allotted." This unconcern will provide freedom from strife and tension, bringing inner peace and happiness.

The other main concept of Guo Xiang is original destiny, which he sees in relation to principle or cosmic order, a term indicating that all living beings are bound by cosmic rules. He says: "Each single being has its inherent order, as much as each individual affair has what is appropriate for it" (3.14b). Cosmic order is the outer framework in which human life is set; it cannot be escaped because in every single instance it defines the particular circumstances of one's existence. It is also the function which connects individual beings with the whole of the cosmos, defined as the flow of existence.

Like cosmic order, destiny in Guo Xiang is an ordering factor that structures human life from the outside. It means the life that one is "ordered" or "commanded" to live by Heaven. "That which one is given is destiny," Guo Xiang maintains, "one cannot shape it at will" (4.10b; 19.43b). Within cosmogony the pair order/destiny is placed prior to allotment/inner nature. That is to say, according to Guo Xiang, when the cosmos first came into being, things received their structure and their outer framework before they were defined in their inner characteristics and specific ways of participation in the universe. Like with

---

[5] These works are based to a large extent on Japanese research. See Aoki 1979a; 1979b; Fukunaga 1954; 1964; Hachiya 1967; Horiike 1972; Nakajima 1970; Nakano 1990; Seki 1965; 1974; Togawa 1966. The work by Brook Ziporyn (2003) studies Guo Xiang purely as a Confucian thinker and makes no reference to these works nor does it examine his Daoist vision.

inner nature, the goal is to recognize destiny and accept whatever it may be as something which they cannot do anything about (6.3b; 8.38a).

As existence is naturally flowing along, so life should just be part of the rhythm of Dao. The only reasonable and proper way to deal with allotted inner nature and the *a-priori* structure of one's destined life is to "base one's actions on the changing situation, to adapt to circumstances without imposing fixed rules" (Graham 1969, 143). In describing this ideal attitude, Guo Xiang uses a great variety of terms ranging from "accord with" and "correspond to," to "let go," "follow along," and even "being content with" or "resigning oneself to." This kind of attitude toward a life which is governed by forces beyond individual will and intention enables the person to "live in the midst of action full of serenity, to remain among beings without attachments," as the *Zuowang lun* has it. The knowledge that one's inner nature is only a share in the cosmos and that one's destiny is merely the individual manifestation of cosmic order makes such an attitude possible. The calm and concentrated mind is thus given a new way of looking at the world, readying it for the more advanced stages of oblivion.

Seeing the Self

Just as this stage in the *Zuowang lun* is at the half-way point from ordinary to perfected perception, so essential inner nature and original destiny are at the mid-level of the vision of body and mind in the greater system of Daoist cosmology. This vision rests on Dao and inherent potency (virtue) as the fundamental powers of creation, the root of all existence and phenomena. Through the medium of *qi*, the vital energy that makes all things come to life in visible, tangible, and audible form, they manifest in the two fundamental constituents of the human being: spirit and body-form (*xing*).

Spirit is the intangible power of Dao, which comes to inhabit the body as pure form—which, unlike the body-self (*shen*), is free from personal preferences and identities and essentially just a microcosmic replica of the greater universe. The body is thus the "habitation of the spirit" (*Zuowang lun*), "the carriage of the spirit, the habitation of the spirit, the host of the spirit" (*Xisheng jing* 7.5; Kohn 2007, 145). Li Rong comments, "The body can carry the spirit, the spirit can ride within the person, thus the image of the carriage is applied. The body can give a home to the spirit, the spirit can use the body as a habitation, thus the term habitation is used. The spirit comes from outside and takes up temporal residence within the body, thus it is said that the body is the host of the spirit" (DZ 726; 4.4a). The body is accordingly also called the "root of the spirit," where the latter resides as a ruler in his country (*Huangting neijing jing* 27.6). Similarly it is the "vessel of Dao," and one need only look inside to find Dao

(*Xisheng jing* 12; *Huainanzi* 11,7b; YQ 58.1b). Spirit is thus the resident of the body-form; combined they make individuated physical reality come to life.

Within the individual, they further appear as two forces often described as "souls" which define the fundamental attitudes and urges of the person. Thus, the spirit or cloud soul (*hun* 魂) connects people to Heaven, is yang in nature, and governs the person's overall attitude to the outside world and supports intellectual, artistic, and spiritual endeavors. [6] At death it returns to Heaven, transforming into the ancestral spirit that is worshiped on the family altar. The material or white soul (*po* 魄) connects the person to Earth, is yin in quality, and controls basic survival instincts, such as the need for food, sleep, and sex, and in general manages the physical aspect of the individual (Jarrett 2006, 30). At death it returns to Earth by staying with the corpse; it is nurtured in proper burial sites and procedures as well as through sacrifices at the tomb.

How these two function specifically is defined by essential inner nature and original destiny, the inborn/genetic and outer/social conditions of life, two agents that represent an even more individuated connection to Dao. They shape the concrete fulfillment the souls will strive for—be it artistic, musical, intellectual or spiritual for the *hun*, finding most satisfaction in food, sex, wealth, status, or comfort for the *po*. They also determine the direction the next two psychological forces take: the will (*zhi* 志; yin) and intention (*yi* 意; yang), which function in close relation to the kidneys and spleen. They represent the general power of thinking and planning in the intention and the more focused determination directed toward a specific objective in the will.

So far, the human being can function perfectly within Dao without having to resort to conscious evaluations or emotions in any form. Inner nature and destiny defining one's inner gifts and urges as well as outer situation and circumstances, one can live one's life in perfect harmony with body, family, society, state, and cosmos—provided everyone does the same and they all follow their perfection as given by Dao. This, then, is Guo Xiang's ultimate vision, what Isabelle Robinet calls "le monde comme absolu" (1983); it is also the ideal of Great Peace, the political and social utopia of ancient and not-so-ancient China.

It gets problematic when people—as they are wont to do—deviate from their cosmically ordained life path. The main culprit, according to the texts, are the senses, the six robbers, the six defilements which cause disruption in the all-

---

[6] It is also the agent that is called back in the ritual known as "Summoning the Soul" (*chaohun* 招魂). A shaman or priest climbs to the roof of the house and calls out in all directions to the departed soul to return, depicting each region as dreary and dangerous. The rite, as much as the three-day delay of the burial, makes sure that the soul is not just on temporary leave or the person in a state of suspended animation. For original chants, see Hawkes 1959. For Han beliefs, see Yü 1987. For modern Hong Kong, see Chan and Chow 2006.

encompassing sphere of cosmic harmony and universal oneness. The senses stimulate people into having reactions of right and wrong, good and bad, likes and dislikes, and other forms of craving and aversion. The result are intellectual classifications and artificial categories—what the texts describe as mental projections or partial views—and reactive feelings or emotions which in turn produce a sense of insufficiency, frustration, yearning, and general dissatisfaction—what Buddhists describe as thirst (*tan* 貪), suffering (*ku* 苦), afflictions (*fan* 煩), and irritations (*nao* 惱) and Daoists talk of in terms of vexations (*huan* 患) and confusion (*luan* 亂). From here the ordinary mind and the body-self arise, both factors that determine so much of actual life and that yet could not be further removed from who we really are in Dao.

The system of sitting in oblivion serves to reverse this process. Detachment from affairs, building on taming the mind through concentration exercises and karmic de-conditioning by putting some distance between self and society, is the point where adepts for the first time have a clearer vision of who they are now and who they ultimately should be. It sets the stage for the more advanced practices that lead eventually to attainment of Dao and the ecstatic freedom of immortality.

Chapter Six

Advanced Stages

The more advanced practices consist of various further forms of meditation, including traditional visualization, Buddhist-inspired insight or mindfulness, deep levels of absorption, as well as shamanic flights into the otherworld and intimate contact with gods and immortals. The individual is transformed from an ordinary person into an immortal, a metamorphosis that completely reorganizes feeling and thinking and acting in alignment with Dao. The aim is to develop one's body identity from an individual entity to being part of the larger framework of nature, to complete oneness with the cosmos at large. No longer a means toward sensual gratification, the body becomes a vehicle of perfection and emotions become powerless. The aspiring immortal is systematically trained to see and feel a distance between the underlying truth of perfection and the surface waves of emotions or "passions and desires," as the texts have it. Worldly tasks and pursuits are found shallow and even considered hindrances to the goal.

The conscious mind, too, undergoes a similar change through rigorous reprogramming. The arising of mental projections and "foolish imaginings" is first observed, then controlled, and eventually stopped altogether. The understanding of oneself as an individual with a set, socially and emotionally defined personality is lost in favor of a wider sense of oneness with the universe, the Dao. In the final stages, adepts acquire powers that otherwise are considered "supernatural," but really only one's birthright in Dao. They pass through a series of stages that each deliver them to a new and higher level of subtlety until they finally find their right place in the heavenly spheres and live in ecstatic, untrammeled freedom—whether on this planet or in the galaxies beyond.

Inner Observation

The first practice described in the texts, and the next stage in Sima Chengzhen's work, is observation. The Chinese term for "observation" is *guan* 觀, explained in the Han dictionary *Shuowen jiezi* 說文解字 (Elucidating Phrases and Explaining Words) as "to scrutinize." The term denotes "looking at something in an examining fashion," thus the usage of *guan* as "observatory" or Daoist monastery (Schafer 1980, 18). In Tang meditation texts, it indicates two major types of practice: the "inner observation" (*neiguan* 內觀) of the different parts and aspects of the body, including the visualization of its energetic patterns and residing divinities; and the "perfect observation" (*zhenguan* 真觀) of reality which involves the establishment of a witness consciousness that allows the detached inspection of one's life and self in order to attain a purified view of the world. In the latter sense, *guan* adopts the Buddhist practice of *vipaśyanā* or insight meditation, also translated with the term *guan*, in combination with *śamatha*, cessation or full concentration (*zhi* 止).[1]

Inner observation is a form of visualization, defined as the active, intentional use of imagery to alter or transform mind and emotions. Objects of visualization can be colors or colored energies imagined to pervade parts of the body; they can involve static objects, such as a vase, a diagram, a landscape, or the statue of a deity; and they can be focused on an entire sequence of activities and events, almost in movie fashion, either for detached viewing or active engagement. Since the brain does not distinguish outside stimuli from imagined ones, visualization is a powerful mode of accessing the subconscious mind to retrain brain mechanisms and transform emotional reactions.[2]

In Daoism, the earliest form of visualization is the infusion of colors into the inner organs, hinted at in the Heshang gong commentary to the *Daode jing* and documented in more detail in the *Taiping jing shengjun bizhi* 太平經聖君秘旨 (Secret Instructions of the Holy Lord on the Scripture of Great Peace, DZ 1102), a Tang-dynasty redaction of meditation methods according to the Han-dynasty *Taiping jing* (see Kaltenmark 1979b; Schipper in Schipper and Verellen 2004, 277-80; trl. Hendrischke 2006). Like later methods that involve ingesting cosmic energies into the organs, such as the "Five Sprouts" (*wuya* 五芽), the key technique here is to see the body energized by *qi* of different colors as as-

---

[1] *Guan* in the Buddhist context is also translated as "view" or "contemplation." See Ng 1993, 136.

[2] See Begley 2007, 9, 151-52. In visualization the brain uses the same regions as in physical actions; it recreates the experience as if done physically (Ratey 2002, 147). For more on visualization in general and as used in healing, see Epstein 1989; Korn and Johnson 1983; Samuels and Samuels 1975.

sociated with the five phases.[3] By the third century first visualization manuals appeared that described deities who resided in the starry constellations above but who were also present in the human body—now seen as a veritable storehouse of divine agencies, palaces, and figures. The most important works here are the *Huangting jing* and the *Laozi zhongjing* 老子中經 (Central Scripture of Laozi, DZ 1168, YQ 18-19),[4] but related methods also appear in Ge Hong's 葛洪 *Baopuzi* 抱朴子 (Book of the Master Who Embraces Simplicity, DZ 1185; trl. Ware 1966) of the mid-fourth century and become the central mode of Daoist meditation in the school of Highest Clarity (see Robinet 1993).

According to these sources, the head is the cosmic paradise of Mount Kunlun or the administrative center of the Yellow Court; it contains nine palaces, each the residence of a divine being and thus matching starry mansions. Most important among these nine palaces were the Hall of Light, located in the center of the eyebrows about one inch into the head; the Grotto Chamber, one inch further in; and the Niwan Palace in the very center, also known as the upper elixir field. There are three elixir fields in the body: the upper one just mentioned; the middle one in the solar plexus or heart area, also known as the Numinous Terrace, the Scarlet Palace, and the Square Inch; and the lower one in the abdomen, an area also called Mount Kunlun, the Gate of Life, the Primordial Pass, and the Ocean of *Qi*. In all three, celestial rulers reside, the so-called Three Ones, whose presence ensured the practitioner's successful ascension.

Inner observation guides practitioners to transform personal identity as formed by subjective perception of the body into a sense of cosmic oneness and alignment with the stars and divinities above. This practice of visualization, moreover, could lead to a deep trance state, during which adepts left their ordinary environment to go on ecstatic journeys into the supernatural realm, both on the earth, exploring its far-off corners, and in the heavens, visiting the gods. Their goal was to become so familiar with the otherworld that their main reality was over there, to experience—by seeing and feeling the gods and their palaces—a cosmicization of self and world.

The *Tianyinzi* places "visualization and imagination" (*cunxiang*) third after physical preparation and seclusion. It defines this in terms of concentration as "returning to stillness" and in terms of inner observation as turning the eyes inward and to "visualize the spirit and imagine the body-self."

---

[3] On these methods, see Kohn 1989a. For more on the Five Sprouts, see Jackowicz 2006; Kohn 2008b, 155-57; Robinet 1989, 165-66; 1993, 176-78.

[4] On the *Huangting jing*, see Baldrian-Hussein 2004; Homann 1971; Kohn 1993a, 181-88; Kroll 1996; Mugitani 1982; Robinet 1993, 55-96; Schipper in Schipper and Verellen 2004, 347-48. On the *Laozi zhongjing*, see Lagerwey 2004; Schipper 1979; in Schipper and Verellen 2004, 92-94.

The most explicit Tang text on this form of practice is the *Neiguan jing* which describes the different aspects of body in cosmic terms: the five phases, the three spirit souls, the seven material souls, the eight phosphor stars, and the various chambers and palaces of the gods. The key deities it tells adepts to maintain are those residing in the three elixir fields: the Great One in the head, the Ruler of Destiny in the heart, and Baiyuan and Taohai in the abdomen. "Radiating through the hundred joints, they give life to the hundred spirits"(2a).[5]

The text encourages practitioners to give up all delusions and fantasies, limit sensory input and attachments to things, get rid of emotions and entanglements, and "observe that the body-self has arisen from emptiness and nonbeing" and in essence is nothing but a randomly individualized manifestation of Heaven and Earth (3a). The body deities are forms of cosmic spirit while the mind as apparent in day-to-day consciousness is a deviation that keeps people separate from Dao. By becoming aware of one's connection to the greater universe and overall dependence on Dao one can make the mind empty and stable, attain clarity and stillness, and allow spirit to shine forth in stillness.

The *Neiguan jing* compares the presence of spirit in the body-form to the oil in a lamp, which in turn needs the wick to create fire. It explains: "Brightness karmically depends on spirit radiance; spirit relies on the mind being fully present; the mind exists only within the body-form; and body-form is only complete through Dao" (5b). It makes use of the concept of spirit as internal brightness or light (*shenming* 神明), which goes back far in ancient China.

Originally related to the ancestral cult, spirit light is first mentioned in the ancient expression for ancestral spirits meaning "blossom of radiance." Philosophers, next, defined inherent potency as the "light of inner vision" that direct outer behavior toward goodness. Thus spirit as the agent active in human potency is the force of light, which in turn is the visible pure *qi* of yang. The personal light of inner vision, moreover, is the same as the light of the cosmos. As both participate in one another, they become the stronger the more harmoniously they shine forth. This is the power that renders ritual objects potent (Vandermeersch 1985). The Daoist concept of light is a direct continuation of these ancient notions. Many Daoist practices thus aim at strengthening the inner light of the adept (Robinet 1979, 94), inner observation being foremost among them in the Tang.

---

[5] This is a variant version of the meditation on the Three Ones. See Andersen 1980; Kohn 1993a, 204-14; Robinet 1993, ch. 4.

Perfect Observation

The other major form of observation is perfect observation. As outlined in section 5 of the *Zuowang lun*, it also focuses on strengthening spirit by seeing the universal connection of self and reality. It adapts Buddhist insight or mindfulness practice, which teaches the practitioner "to engage the object actively, contemplating it in terms of Buddhist doctrine until he has brought about a change in the way the object occurs to him" (Bielefeldt 1986, 137). To do so, the method establishes a detached, objective observer or witness consciousness in the mind. This is a mental position of distanced seeing, a faculty of taking a step back from involvement with experiences and emotions. The detached observer is something all people have at times, such as the ability to laugh at themselves when in a strange situation or the faculty to take a step back and examine circumstances from a distance.[6]

Through insight meditation, practitioners strengthen this observing faculty and make it accessible at all times. Learning to both feel an experience immediately and see it from a distance, they begin to identify, observe, and cleanse negative emotions while cultivating positive states, such as compassion and kindness, calmness and equanimity, peace and joy. They also come to see the world increasingly in new terms, understanding that neither mind nor self are immutable, firm entities; that life is constantly changing and essentially unsatisfactory; and that true contentment can only be found in the present moment. As a result, mindfulness meditators engage with reality in a detached yet intensely present way.

The *Zuowang lun*, matching concepts and phrases used in the Tiantai school, encourages adepts to understand the interconnectedness of all phenomena and realize the full power of karma and retribution. The text, moreover, takes the practice into daily life. How, for example, should one relate to such worldly necessities as food and clothing? One should recognize them as a vehicle, a means of transportation, necessary but to be abandoned in due course. Like a boat that is used to cross an ocean, it cannot be given up before one has completed the trip, yet should not be carried around afterwards.

Then again, how does one eliminate all feelings of enmity and hatred? One must come to regard them truly, to realize that "to see another do evil and give

---

[6] For a detailed analyis of the objective observer, see Deikman 1982. The central text on the practice in ancient Buddhism is the *Satipatthāna sūtra*, which divides it into four types: mindfulness of body, sensations, mental states, and mental contents. On the text, see Brazier 1995, 70; Bucknell and Kang 1997, 19-25; 50-54; Fryba 1989, 245-73; Silananda 1990; Solé-Leris 1986, 74-78; Soni 1980; N. Thera 1962; S. Thera 1998.

rise to enmity and hatred in one's own mind is just like seeing someone kill himself and promptly sticking one's own neck out to accept the other's blade and get killed oneself." What if I am deeply distressed by the state of extreme poverty that I am in? Echoing the *Zhuangzi*, Sima Chengzhen says one should try to find out who made you poor. Heaven and Earth?—Why should they? Your parents?—Certainly they wanted you to be happy! Spirits and other men?—They are far too busy with their own troubles to make you poor. The conclusion must be reached that all one experiences is due to the karma produced by oneself and the destiny one has been given by Heaven. One has to accept whatever cannot be avoided, one cannot run away from oneself.

As the text notes, the situation of the adept at this point of his development is comparable to that of a knight fighting with a band of brigands. He can either fight the various vexations and illusions with the strong sword of observation and insight and thereby establish the lifelong merit of happiness for himself. Or he can flee the battlefield and abandon his weapons, thus succumbing to the enemy and ending up in disgrace and defeat. Another comparison is found in the *Zhuangzi* metaphor of the "sobered man who now can see the drunkard's evil deeds the wrong of which he was totally unaware as long as he was drunk himself."

Body and Self

What the drunkard did not realize but what meditators come to see at this point is that there is no continuity in one's body, whether as cosmic form or personalized self. Merely the "shape one has taken in this particular life," the body-form (*xing*) is basically part of the continuous flow of existence, a temporary, fleeting phenomenon that has arisen from the eternal process of universal transformations yet contains the spirit and one's connection to Dao. On the other hand, the body-self (*shen*) becomes a dwelling place for vexations, pain, and suffering.

In whichever dimension body is so unstable, as the *Neiguan jing* (3b) and the *Sishen jue* 思神訣 (Secret Instructions for Meditation on the Spirits, YQ 55, 1a) agree, because it is assembled from *qi*. Already the *Zhuangzi* has, "Human life is a coming-together of *qi*. If it comes together there is life. If it scatters there is death" (ch. 22; Watson 1968, 235). The body is thus only a form that takes part in the continuous natural transformations of *qi*; it is merely "borrowed from Heaven and Earth" (*Liezi* 1; Graham 1960, 29) and duly is bound to "return to dust and ashes" (*Xisheng jing* 7). As a consequence of this vacillating nature of the body, it is also unstable within. As mentioned above, the *Zhuangzi* emphasizes the notion that "there is no true master" of body and mind (ch. 2). It also assures us that we do not have any real possession of the body and that we can not control its development in any way (ch. 22).

Yet far from being able to just let it go on changing as it pleases, people personalize the body due to the senses and their reactions to them. From a body-form determined by the changes of Heaven and Earth it becomes a body-self, turning into "the reason why I have terrible vexations. If I didn't have a body-self, what vexations would I have?" This famous citation from *Daode jing* 13 is quoted in the *Zuowang lun*, in the inscription, in the *Xisheng jing*, and many in other meditation works. Li Rong explains: "Having a body means having vexations and adversities. Frustrated by sight and hearing, tortured by taste and smell, one is subject to pain, irritation, heat, and cold" (DZ 726, 2.9b); and: "As soon as there is a body-self, the hundred worries compete to arise, and the five desires [of the senses] hurry to make their claims" (4.5b).To escape from all this, ideally "the sage desires to return to the beginning, to the state before he was born" (XSJ 7.17; Kohn 1991, 261). This is also the key feature in the Heavenly Worthy's "Explanation of the True Father and Mother," i.e., Dao:

> This body-form is nothing that I have. It only comes to life as it follows empty nonbeing and cosmic spontaneity. In accordance with karma I was entrusted to the womb, underwent several transformations, and took birth. The parents who conceived me are not my real origin. They are just taking the part of the parents in this world. My true parents are not here, they are noble and honorable, most venerable and lofty. The parents who conceived me in this world were merely predestined to graciously give me nourishment and education. I bow to them in accordance with propriety and honor them as my parents.
>
> But ultimately whatever I received as "my" body-form is not really mine. I only use it as a temporary residence, a shelter like a thatched hut. Looking down on it, I recognize it as a body-form; analyzing it, I find it does not really exist. So the "I" who has attained Dao is said to have no more body-form, no more body-self, no more spirit! Once the body-self merges with universal oneness, the perfect body-self makes its appearance. Then I can return to the cosmic parents who originally gave me life and fully attain Dao. (YQ 31.9b-10a)

The value of the body in the Daoist path is thus twofold: it can be used to make people realize the impermanent nature of all apparently solid phenomena; it also serves as the basis for the cultivation of spirit or Dao, of essential inner nature or potency. It is important not to confuse the two. The inscription says,

> If one did not have a body-self and thus returned to nothing, shouldn't that be called the loss of the basis of eternal life? No, I answer, what you would call not having a body-self does not actually refer to not having

this body-form. Rather, the expression means that the bodily structure is unified with the Great Dao, that one is never influenced by glorious positions, nor ever seeks after speedy advancement. Instead, it indicates that placidly and without desires one forgets the experience of this body-self which is so dependent on all kinds of things.

Daoists at this stage increasingly identify with Dao as it governs and inhabits the body, thus loosening attachments to their limited physical and personal selves. They begin to develop a new and wider identity as part of the universe at large, coming to see themselves as beings of spirit that are merely housed in this fragile physical framework which will be subject to all the transformations the spirit transcends.

Oblivion

Finding rest within the body and letting the changes of the universe go along as they please, practitioners enter a state of deep absorption or complete oblivion. This is a trancelike or enstatic state of complete immersion in Dao to the exclusion of all else, characterized by unconsciousness and immobility. The *Tianyinzi* describes it as both the culmination and oblivion of the previous level, as a stage where there is no more seeing or hearing, no more conscious acting or sense of self. At this point, as both the *Zhuangzi* and the *Zuowang lun* say, "the body-form is like dried wood, the mind is like dead ashes; there are no more impulses, no more searches."

The *Tianyinzi* goes on to describe an almost Zen-like dialogue where a disciple asks about mind and Dao, and "the Master of Heavenly Seclusion remains silent and does not answer." Another question elicits a similar response: "The Master closes his eyes and does not look." Like in a koan, the Daoist master here takes the disciple out of his intellectual mode and into the core of the practice by demonstrating the form the practice should take (see Hori 2000). When he finally talks, it is only to note that in a state of "self and other both forgotten, nothing is left to radiate forth."

Generally, descriptions of this state speak of "preserving," "embracing," "harmonizing," and "recovering." Rather than in terms of flux and going along, it is a state of fullness and stability, an intense tranquility and restfulness which pervade the adept. The imagery used is one of union, oneness, and merging; it is full of darkness and the shading of light, showing a mind full of innocence and simplicity, purity and resting in Dao. People in this state are like an uncut block of wood; their time has stopped and there is no more progress, no more decay. They have fully joined the One at the source of creation, the deep underlying root on whose basis change takes place, the center from which all universal development springs. This source of the universe is what is truly permanent, it is "being" in its truest form. Unless this is recovered and preserved, unless one has is completely one with this, immortality cannot be had. The underlying ground is static—and so in this phase of realization is the immortal state.

The *Zuowang lun* calls this level *taiding* 泰定, which at first glance means "great stability." The term goes back to the *Zhuangzi*, which says *yu taiding fa hu tianguang* 宇泰定發乎天光 (ch. 23). Burton Watson translates: "He whose inner being rests in Great Serenity will spread a heavenly radiance" (1968, 254). James Legge speaks of the "mind being grandly fixed" (no. 7), A. C. Graham reads the initial *yu* as a noun and understands *tianguang* as the source rather than the effect of radiance, thus rendering the sentence: "What is ultimately fixed in the cosmos-as-spatial goes on issuing from the light of Heaven" (1981, 103). Victor Mair mixes these readings and says: "when space is serenely stabilized" (1994, 231); Brook Ziporyn follows him to say, "empty space is vast and un-shifting" (2009, 98). In my earlier translation of the *Zuowang lun*, I had "intense concentration" for *taiding*, reflecting the continuity to section 3 on "Taming the Mind," which focuses on concentration, and emphasizing the increased intensity of this absorbed state.

However, a different dimension to the term becomes obvious in the *Zhuangzi* commentaries. Both Guo Xiang and Cheng Xuanying explain *tai* and *ding* as equal yet separate characteristics of the meditative state. Guo Xiang says: "If virtue rests in *tai* and *ding*, a heavenly light is brought forth" (25.10b). Cheng Xuanying, too, supports this by giving *antai* 安泰 (peace) for *tai* and *jingding* 靜定 (quiet) for *ding*. The Tang text that uses this distinction most explicitly is the *Wuchu jing*, which makes it very clear that *tai* is a separate word and not a modifier. Focusing largely on the absorption level of the oblivion process, its key concept is *taihe* 泰和, which is parallel to *taiding* but, instead of indicating "great harmony," means *tai* and harmony. The text has:

> "Attaining universal oneness" means: on the inside, dwell in the *qi* of universal oneness to nourish essence and spirit; on the outside, make physical form and life whole to abide in *tai*. (1a)

What, then, is *tai*? One major meaning of the word is "peace," but this peace is significantly different from *an* 安, which is personal and internal and means resting in deep inner and mental calm, and also from *ping* 平, which is social and political and means the balance and harmonious interaction of agents and forces, as in *taiping*, Great Peace. Thus I now render the word as "cosmic peace," indicating that at this level of practice, which is also the full attainment of the state of oblivion, adepts find a level of mental immersion that allows them to participate in cosmic harmony while resting in deep mental stability.

Stability

Ding, the term used for "stability," too, comes with an extensive set of connotations. In Buddhism it is used to translate *samādhi* (*zhengding* 正定), a state of deep absorption that allows Buddha-nature to shine forth and is the beginning of enlightenment. It also renders *dhyāna* in the compound *chanding* 禪定 and thus indicates a concentration so deep that one is pervaded by feelings of happiness and bliss. Buddhist *dhyāna* is "a mode of meditative concentration, not a content" (King 1980, 41). It can be described as:

> a state in which attention is locked in on one specific datum to the total exclusion of all others; for practical purposes and with respect to ordinary awareness, the subject is in full trance and operatively unconscious; the lucidity is actually a description of the immediately ensuing moments, when the mind reawakes to the world around it, but sees that world in the mood of the just ended higher state of consciousness. The calm, undistracted post-dhyanic mind now sees clearly. (King 1980, 48)

In classical Buddhist literature, *dhyāna* is explained as the state reached when the five hindrances (tiredness, agitation, craving, aversion, and doubt) are completely overcome and only a sense of deep joy and harmony remains. It consists of eight progressive levels of absorption which, like Daoist oblivion, are characterized by a significant slowing of respiration, the absence of thought, an expansion of mental openness, a feeling of the disappearance of the bodily self, the closing off of sight and sound, and an overall deep and blissful serenity (Austin 1998, 475).

As they advance in the practice, meditators reach in the first *dhyāna* where they still experience thought—not the fleeting, wandering puppy mind of the beginning, but sustained clear and conscious thought—while those in the second *dhyāna* are free from thought and only feel a deep inner confidence and singleness of mind. The third *dhyāna* eliminates the factor of happiness as joyful excitement, leaving the meditator in a state of unified bliss. The fourth, next, sees the emerging of a complete unity that is so deep that it is not even blissful any longer, but pure equanimity and steadiness of mind. Following these, there are four further stages, known as formless *dhyānas*, extremely subtle states of consciousness that leave behind all component elements of existence. They allow the meditator to dwell in boundless space, boundless consciousness, nothingness, and in a state of neither perception nor non-perception. [7]

---

[7] For descriptions of the Buddhist *dhyānas*, see Brazier 1995, 59-60; Humphries 1968, 187-93; King 1980, 41-54; Solé-Leris 1986, 56-73; Kamalashila 1992, 66-87.

The Daoist system matches this in that with the attainment of the "stability of cosmic peace," the adept has left all worldly involvements and deliberations behind and, as the *Zuowang lun* says, has reached "the first foothold of Dao." The state of mind he finds himself in is characterized by a twofold structure, perfect serenity on the inside and a "heavenly light" radiating on the outside. This pair is also described as tranquility and wisdom in accordance with *Zhuangzi* terminology or as concentration and insight following Buddhist usage.

Formulated in more concrete terms, at this stage one has to "make sure to always note the disadvantages whenever one recognizes an advantage, and to calm the mind whenever one feels anxiety about misfortune." On the other hand, one should continue to "diminish, forsake, purify, and cleanse the mind." This will lead to a perfect stability of mind, one will be unperturbed even by "sudden clashes of thunder." As a result, "unmoving in the stillness, one will imperceptibly enter enlightenment." In addition to this outline of what one has to do, some explanations on the nature of the human mind are given. The mind is inscrutable, never to be grasped or understood, it is extremely powerful in its manifestations such as anger or goodwill, hatred or benevolence. It reaches through the eight directions, can be anywhere and nowhere, and it is never far-off the Ninefold Darkness below or the Threefold Clarities above.

The inscription quotes the same *Zhuangzi* passage, then proceeds to interpret "great stability" as resting in "emptiness and oblivion, merging one's mind with the realm of solitude and stillness." It makes it very clear that this is the state of "sitting in oblivion."

The most detailed presentation of Daoist absorption appears in the *Wuchu jing*. It speaks of the *qi* of universal oneness (*yiqi* 一氣) as the origin of the cosmos and foundation of human life. One is to merge back with this *qi* and forego all sorts of mental and physical interaction:

> When people are first endowed with the *qi* of universal oneness, they are [innately] merged with the harmony of cosmic peace. By [later] dwelling in harmony and attaining universal oneness, they can merge with cosmic order and find overarching peace. As utmost harmony flourishes freely, not only is there no more [sense of] oneness, but there is also no [conscious awareness of] harmony any longer. (2a)

The main work of the meditator at this level is the continued maintenance of deep concentration and inner calm. Spirit should be focused to a "state of profound luminosity," using the word *zhan* 湛 which means "softly brilliant" or "translucent" like standing water, "making it vague and vacuous, and letting it merge with the state before thoughts arise." At this point all mental activity is obliterated and "all knowledge is forgotten" (2b). It is important to realize that this is state of unknowing and non-thinking is a spontaneous inner unfolding and not an intentional or controllable process: "If you knowingly pursue non-thinking, you are already mired in delusory perception and are thus in a state no different from thinking, intending, and the like"(2b).

Echoing the *Zhuangzi*, the *Wuchu jing* further describes the mind at this stage as being "like a deep abyss: unadulterated, it regards the myriad phenomena equally", i.e., makes all things equal. Reminiscent of both *Zhuangzi* and Chan metaphors, it emphasizes that it should be bright and clear, "a mirror of [universal] light, where the [world's] dust and grime have no place to stick" (3b). Subtle nuances of intensified oblivion follow: the mind dwells in the elimination of all; it is free even of itself as perceiving agent and reaches a point of non-dwelling (4a).

Full oblivion, the state in which one "casts off form and does away with knowledge," is found when the world is completely "eliminated on the outside" and consciousness no longer has an active agent on the inside" (4b). Instead, "things just arise and pass away one after the other," one is fully merged with the natural processes and completely free from all reactions, feelings, classifications, and evaluations. Then "there is just personal karmic functioning and no more self-based knowing" (5a).

Wisdom in Dao

Self-based knowing at this point is radically replaced by wisdom or insight, expressed with the two terms *zhi* 智 and *hui* 慧. While Buddhists use them interchangeably to refer to wisdom in the sense of *prajñā*—the understanding of world and self in terms of suffering, impermanence, and no-self—Daoists tend to be very much aware that *zhi* is originally derived from *zhi* 知, knowledge. Thus they make a distinction between wisdom as based on human knowledge and insight developed through the practice of meditation, attaching highest value to the concept of non-knowledge or unknowing (*wuzhi* 無知).

Unknowing in medieval Buddhist texts is also a way of understanding *prajñā*. Thus Sengzhao 僧肇 in his *Panruo wuzhi lun* 般若無知論 (*Prajñā* Is Non-Knowledge) says:

> The empty mind is a mysterious mirror. It is a state when knowledge is closed in and perception obstructed. Only then can one be aware of the darkest mystery. Therefore, when the deep dark mirror develops from knowledge, it is non-knowledge. When spirit applies itself fully to encountering and corresponding, it is utterly free from thoughts. Only spirit free from thoughts can be aloft, beyond the world. Only knowl-

edge which is non-knowledge can mysteriously reflect what is beyond things. (T. 45, 153b).

The true knowledge of non-knowledge is thus "the way a pure sagely mind relates to the world." It represents insight and not wisdom, pure going along and not acting, the pervading power of Dao and not strenuous human effort.

Already the *Zhuangzi* notes that sensory input and knowledge can harm people and that it is much better if "the eye does not see, the ear does not hear, and the mind does not know" (ch. 11; Watson 1968, 119). Li Rong in his commentary to the *Xisheng jing* similarly describes the mystical process as a loss of conscious knowledge. "All knowledge of the principles, all wisdom of the classics is utterly submerged in darkness. Pursuing the lightless, one becomes darker and more obscure" (2.5a). Consequently the final state is one of submersion and complete unknowing: "Being ignorant and unknowing is following life, thereby one does not deviate from Dao or err from the root" (2.2b).

The resulting personality is entirely unbound by physical limitations, by emotional engagements, intellectual divisions, and arguments of reason. Any conscious ego identity that was there before is lost, and it is hard to determine at what point exactly the individual ends and the Dao begins. All is in continuous flux, moving along smoothly with the changes of the greater universe.

Coming out of enstatic immersion and the complete cessation of all physical, sensory, and mental functions, adepts at this stage fully attain Dao and transcend all in open pervasion. They undergo an increase in movement, openness, joy, light, even ecstasy, until they rise up to heaven and take up their rightful place among the immortals.

The imagery of this level is ecstatic and shamanistic: flight into higher realms, experiences of altered states of consciousness, freedom from worldly imitations. Attaining Dao means getting lighter and brighter; the higher one ascends, the purer the spirit becomes, the more light one will radiate. The worldview that underlies this model is one of "becoming:" the universe is in a constant flux, and nothing stands ever still or stops for a moment. Time is conceived as cyclical, eternity can only take place in an eternal return. By reaching this, the Daoist has become one with Dao in both its key aspects, as the quiescent, underlying power of all and as the creative power of the world, continuously moving and forever transforming

Dao is the most basic of all forces of the universe, "undifferentiated and yet complete, it existed before Heaven and Earth. Soundless and formless, it depends on nothing and does not change; it operates everywhere and is free from danger" (*Daode jing* 25). Not having a better name for this invisible, inaudible, and subtle force, it is called Dao (14). It is the basis of all creation. "Dao is free from life and death, but all embodied beings must live and die. . . . They only come to life when they attain Dao; they die once they lose it," as the *Neiguan jing* maintains (4b).

As the key force that makes *qi* assemble and causes everything to exist, Dao occupies a position in Daoist mystical thought very similar to that of the spirit. As Li Rong says: "Spirit functions in giving life to embodied beings. Without this, there would be no life. . . . It is only upon borrowing spirit that embodied beings can come to life. Spirit uses them as a habitation in order to attain completion. Without the joining of the spirit and embodied beings, there would be no life nor completion" (4.14b). "Spirit," the *Tianyinzi* says, is "that which "arrives without moving and is swift without hurrying, what transforms along with yin and yang and is as old as Heaven and Earth" (sect. 8). The *Neiguan jing* provides more details:

> Spirit is neither black nor white, neither red nor yellow, neither big nor small, neither short nor long, neither crooked nor straight, neither soft nor hard, neither thick nor thin, neither round nor square. It goes on changing and transforming without measure, merges with yin and yang, greatly encompasses Heaven and Earth, subtly enters the tiniest blade of grass. Controlled it is straightforward, let loose it goes mad. Clarity and purity make it live, turbidity and defilements cause it to perish. Fully bright, it radiates to the eight ends of the universe. Darkened, it confuses even a single direction. Keep it empty and serene, and life and Dao will spontaneously be present. (2b)

Oneness with spirit means its liberation (*shenjie* 神解) and the attainment of spirit pervasion (*shentong* 神通), which means the emitting of a bright radiance and attainment of supernatural powers. Perceiving fully with spirit instead of the senses, Daoist immortals as much as enlightened Buddhists are omniscient and can penetrate all phenomena with equal ease.[8]

The *Zuowang lun*, too, describes Dao in terms of spirit as a most "spiritual and wonderful thing," always there, yet never to be grasped or fathomed. As Dao fills the body-mind of the adept, he becomes a spirit person, someone whose "body is pervaded by Dao and unified with spirit," thus reaching a life co-eternal with Heaven and Earth. The *Xisheng jing* agrees: "I don't see, don't hear, don't know—the spirit does not leave the body-self and I live as long as Dao" (16.4). Li Rong comments: "Not seeing means that one is not blinded by colors.

---

[8] For Buddhist desriptions, see *Yuanjue jing* 圓覺經 (Perfect Enlightenment Sutra, T. 17.913a); *Weimo jing* 唯摩經 (*Vimalakirti nirdesa sūtra*, T. 14.539a). The former is a work on Buddhist meditation central to Tang practitioners that has been explicated variously, including by such important figures as Zongmi 宗密 (780-841) who uses Tiantai materials that have also influenced the *Zuowang lun*. See Bielefeldt 1986, 133.

Not hearing means that one is not deafened by sounds. Not knowing means that one is not obstructed by thinking. Abandon sights and sounds and be pure. Get rid of all patterns and distinctions and be non-acting. Then spirit will not leave." Only in an utterly empty mind Dao comes to stay—but it does so naturally and quite independently of the wishes of the practitioner.

Alchemy and Ecstasy

Both the *Dingguan jing* and the *Cunshen lianqi ming* outline seven stages that adepts undergo as they attain Dao, the *Dingguan jing* beginning with mental stability, a stage not found in the other text. Here the first stage is the strengthening of vigorous health, with "the body-self growing light and the mind translucent," in a state full of joy and peace and completely free from emotions. From here, adepts attain long life and recover youth, moving away from the general pattern of aging and pervading the numinous. Next, they become "immortals," ageless and light, "flying or walking, spontaneously present everywhere" as well as guarded by a host of divinities.

Stage four (five in the *Dingguan jing*) signals new levels of refinement: leaving the body-self to become pure *qi*, adepts attain the level of "perfected" which comes with the ability to appear and disappear at will and move through the grottoes and heavens of the divine. Next, they refine *qi* to spirit and become "spirit people," powerful enough to move Heaven and Earth. From here, they purify "spirit to unify with the world of form" and are called "utmost beings." Their appearance and body-form no longer definite, they "change according to occasion and go along with things to appear in different forms." The final stage (only described in the *Cunshen lianqi ming*) signals ultimate transcendence: "whirl out of all relations and reside next to the Jade Emperor of the Great Dao."

Unlike these texts, which describe the final transformation in purely meditative terms, the inscription, like in Wu Yun's *Xingshen kegu lun* (De Meyer 2006, 374-77), in addition recommends the use of "gold and cinnabar" in order to extend one's attainments as far as the body. Thereby the "transformation of wings" (*yuhua* 羽化) will be reached, i.e., one will become truly immortal and "enter the gateway of the boundless." [9]

Ultimately the successful adept will ascend into heaven. Sima himself is said to have anticipated his transformation, then sat quietly in meditation until he rose into the clouds, accompanied by white cranes, purple clouds, and celestial mu-

---

[9] Later practitioners of internal alchemy formalized both stages and ascension methods, making the spirit exit the body through a hole in the head and engaging in formal visualizations and encounters with gods. For more, see Eskildsen, 2004; 2007; 2009a; 2009b.

sic. His contemporary, Huang Lingwei 黃靈微, the Flower Maiden similarly ascended bodily to the immortals. As her biography in Du Guangting's *Yong-cheng jixian lu* 墉城集仙錄 (Record of the Assembled Immortals in the Heavenly Walled City, DZ 783), has it, after her passing in 721,

> In the ninth year of the Opened Prime reign period [721], when the Maiden was about to ascend and transform, she told her disciples: "Because my transcendent journey has become urgent, I cannot stay here any longer. After my body is transformed, do not nail my coffin shut. Just cover the coffin with crimson silk gauze."
>
> The next day she came to her end without even being sick. Her flesh and skin were fragrant and pure, her physical form and breath warm and genial. A strange fragrance filled the courtyards and halls. Her disciples followed her orders and did not nail her coffin shut, simply covering it with crimson silk gauze.
>
> Suddenly they all heard lightning and thunder strike. On the top of the silk gauze was a hole about as big as a hen's egg, and in the coffin were only her shroud and some wooden [text] slips. In the ceiling of the room a spot had been penetrated [leaving a gap] big enough for a person to pass through. At the base of the coffin, where offerings had been placed, a gourd sprouted creepers several days later and then set two fruits like peaches. (Cahill 1990, 33-34; 2006, 125; see also Despeux and Kohn 2003, 124-25; Kirkland 1991)

Another way of ascension is by just vanishing completely. Again, the successful adept is ready to transform and has been in contact with the divinities, then announces his or her supernatural state and gets ready for departure, but the setting is less formal. Instead of a visible transformation and a non-decaying or vanishing corpse, here the person just vanishes into thin air. This form of ascension, not as celebrated and rather less well prepared, often leaves friends and family in a state of confusion. An example from the late eighth century is the story of Qu Boting 瞿柏庭 of the Taohua guan 桃花觀 (Peach Blossom Monastery) in Langzhou, found in the *Huang xianshi Qutong ji* 黃仙師瞿童記 (Record of Immortal Master Huang and Lad Qu) which says:

> In the summer of the eighth year of Great Succession [773] in the evening of a dragon day of the fifth month [27th], Lad Qu put on formal dress, paid obeisance to the gods, and stepped outside into the courtyard. He said that a numinous appointment was waiting for him, and that he could not linger much longer. . . . He proclaimed: "The chronograms come to meet me, even the year star is descending now."
>
> On the side of the courtyard was a huge chestnut tree, not more than a couple of yards from where everyone was standing. Lad Qu turned his back to the crowd and very slowly walked over to stand next to the tree. From there he gradually dissolved and vanished into thin air. (Sunayama 1987; Kohn 1993a, 329-30)

His fellow Daoists were stunned and did not believe their eyes. For several days, they combed the area but they could not find a trace of him or his body. In either case, the subjective experience is something like Wu Yun's description in Cycle 4 of his *Buxuci* (Schafer 1981; Kohn 2009, 227-28):

> My inner being changes into congealed pure *qi*;
> My body quite refined, I become perfected, an immortal.
> My heart oblivious, I match the primal ancestor of all—
> Reverting to my roots, I'm one with spontaneity.
>
> The Emperor Great One settles in my heart;
> As streaming light pours from my elixir field.
> The gods, like Wuying and Taohai,
> Chant brightly from the chapters of long life.
>
> My six viscera glow with luminous morning light;
> My hundred joints are like a net of purple mist.
> My whirlwind carriage traverses endless spaces:
> Slow and steady I rise on light itself.
>
> Unaware how far the road of clouds,
> In an instant, I wander through ten thousand heavens.

Chapter Seven

The Buddhist Dimension

The system of sitting in oblivion in its Tang heyday owes much to Buddhism both in underlying worldview and concrete practice instructions. At the same time, oblivion as an ideal state and form of meditation has also made a serious impact on Chinese Buddhism.

Buddhist features, especially the ideal of the renunciant, basic precepts, karma and retribution, as well as key features of the pantheon, scriptural structure, and community organization, were first adopted into the Numinous Treasure school in the fifth century and since then came to shape Daoism as a whole. In this respect, the Buddhist dimension of the *zuowang* system merely reflects the status quo at the time, and it would not have occurred to Sima Chengzhen or any of his contemporaries to think, for example, of *ye*, lit. "action," as anything but karma.

As regards concrete practice instructions, certain aspects of the *zuowang* system, especially those on "perfect observation," work strongly with methods adopted from Buddhist insight meditation. At the time, the practice formed a key aspect of the Tiantai school, founded in the sixth century as part of the overall drive for unification and the integration of teachings. Its founder Zhiyi 智顗 (538-597) wrote several important works on "cessation and insight"—or "Stop! Look!" as Michael Saso renders it (2000, 1)—which provide instructions on basic practice as well as descriptions of stages, hindrances, and resulting states. Sima Chengzhen, as much as Wu Yun, a resident of Mt. Tiantai and well informed of the various methods of the day, adopted the practice into his system, matching yet also transforming the Buddhist way.

The impact of *zuowang* on Buddhism, on the other hand, is most obvious in the focus on the abdomen, which is quite different from Indian practice, where the breath is observed at the nostrils and the belly plays only a secondary role. As Michael Saso points out:

> Daoist breathing techniques, are always based on focusing attention on the lower elixir field [in the abdomen], which vastly facilitates the contemplative process itself, making an hour seem like ten minutes, rather than ten minutes seem like an hour. This point cannot be overemphasized, and is a basic component in all the masters' teachings.
>
> When Buddhism came into contact with Daoism, such as at Mount Tiantai, the focus on the belly also became part of Chan practice, now known as "just sitting" (*shikantaza* 止觀打坐), as well as of the practice of elementary cessation and insight, outlined in the *Xiao zhiguan* 小止觀 text of Zhiyi, which attests to this influence.
>
> Thus, even today, when learning *xiao zhiguan* on Mount Hiei [near Kyoto], the belly is kept as focus, as it is also in martial arts, calligraphy, and in Mikkyo meditation: the *vajra* or thunder world, which purifies, burns away, and empties all images before achieving meditative union, is placed in the belly of the meditator, while the lotus mandala is in the heart and the dharma in the mind. (Personal communication, April 2010)

Both in medieval China and today, Buddhist Chan (Jap.: Zen) practice instructions and explanations show many similarities with *zuowang*. It has long been recognized that the *Zhuangzi*, the root source of oblivion, has influenced it Buddhism, and scholars have pointed to various medieval intermediaries, such as Daoan or Sengzhao, who brought Daoist terms and concepts into a Buddhist context. Oblivion as both the ultimate state and practice procedure, however, is the clearest and most pervasive example on how Chan was shaped by Chinese culture. Similarities and connections abound—yet there is no denying the uniqueness of the Buddhist approach and the potent transformation they have wrought on the Chinese and Daoist patterns.

The Buddhist World

Buddhism first arrived in China in the first century c.e. but did not emerge as a strong religious force until the early fifth century, when the Central Asian scholar-monk Kumārajīva (d. 413) from Kucha came to head a translation institute in the northern capital of Chang'an.[1] Due to his efforts, and after several centuries of variegated transmissions and unregulated organization, Chinese Buddhists finally had texts that represented accurate presentations of doctrine

---

[1] For details on the early history of Buddhism in China, see Ch'en 1973; Tsukamoto and Hurvitz 1985; Zürcher 1959.

and worldview, rules and rituals. Both metaphysical speculation and monastic discipline improved vastly, leading to an upsurge in Buddhist activity in the country and inspiring Daoists to imitate the foreign religion.

The leaders in this effort were Daoists of the Numinous Treasure (Lingbao 靈寶) school, initiated by Ge Chaofu 葛巢甫 in the 390s on the basis of the Highest Clarity teachings, from which he adopted the ideas of multiple layers of heaven, celestial administration, and an extensive host of divine beings. In addition, he also returned to Han-dynasty cosmology of the five phases, the ideas and practices of Han recluses and masters of magic, and Celestial Masters ritual.

Once the newly translated Buddhist materials became available, Ge's disciples integrated them into their form of Daoism, using aspects of Buddhist cosmology, worldview, scriptures, and practices, and compiling a vast new collection of Daoist texts in close imitation of Buddhist sutras. Most specifically, they adopted the notion of multiple layers of heaven and consecutive world ages or kalpas, the doctrine of karma and retribution, visions of various hells and torture chambers for the dead, sets of systematic precepts and community rules, savior figures that would come and take people to the otherworld, as well as all sorts of new rituals and purification practices (see Zürcher 1980). Through their efforts, Daoism in fifth-century south China transformed into a complex and sophisticated organized religion that has had a strong impact on Chinese culture ever since and set the standard under which Sima Chengzhen and the other Tang masters operated.

The most important aspects of the rather extensive Buddhist imports into Daoism for sitting in oblivion include the organizational setting of meditation practice in monastic institutions, the formalized ethical requirement in the taking of precepts and refuge in the Three Treasures, the doctrines of karma and retribution, the five paths of rebirth, and the various layers of hell, as well as the vision of the body-mind in terms of multiple aspects, defilements, hindrances, and purification.

The first Daoist monasteries evolved under direct Buddhist influence and were actually called si 寺, using the term reserved for "administration of foreigners" under the Toba-Wei (r. 386-535). Even when the first guan was established at Louguan in the late fifth century, its organizational structure—from architectural features through daily schedule and administration to rules and regulations—closely followed the Buddhist model (see Kohn 2003). Thus, halls were set up on a north-south axis, with more public ones first and holier sanctuaries later, plus administrative, kitchen, and dormitory facilities on the sides. In their daily schedule, too, Daoists matched Buddhist convention and divided the day into six periods of worship—midnight, cockcrow, dawn, noon, dusk, and early evening (Pas 1986; Kohn 2003, 175).

All the various monastic rules and regulations, moreover, as much as the basic precepts, were inspired by Buddhist models, in some cases imitating them directly—as in the case of the five precepts (*pañcaśīla*) or the 250 rules for monks (*Pratimokṣa*)—in others tailoring the rules to specific Daoist needs (see Kohn 2004a). An example of the latter is found in guidelines for vestments which, unlike in Buddhism where monks' robes were made from rags, were highly ornate and inhabited by personal deities and divine protectors (Kohn 2003).

As regards meditation practice, not only was the monastic institution its central location but—again in adaption of Buddhism—it opened its gates to the laity for one-day retreats or for longer periods of abstention and purification (zhai). As still true today (see Goullart 1961), lay followers would join the monastics in their daily routine, take additional precepts, and undergo training in elementary forms of practice. Based on this one may assume that Sima's original lectures on sitting in oblivion were delivered at his monastic center on Mount Wangwu to aristocratic lay followers eager to find peace in their busy lives.

Not only the physical setting, the worldview underlying oblivion practice also shares basic Buddhist features. Most important is the doctrine of karma, which states that all actions have inevitable consequences and, after a period of maturation, revert to their perpetrator. As the individual's consciousness is the carrier of this load, it must continue to be embodied in a physical form to receive the rewards and punishments necessitated by its former actions. Thus the notion of rebirth revolving in the five realms—of gods, humans, animals, hungry ghosts, and hell dwellers—became a close correlate to the idea of personally created and suffered-through karma (Mahony 1987, 262).

In the Daoist system, the lowest levels are described as the "three bad rebirths," the "five realms of suffering," the "eight difficult conditions," and the "ten situations of intense suffering." As described in the fifth-century *Jieye benxing shangpin miaojing* 戒業本行上品妙經 (Highest Wondrous Scripture of Controlling Karma and Rooting [Good] Conduct, DZ 345), the three bad rebirths are in the hells, as hungry ghosts, or among animals, while the five realms of suffering include all areas of rebirth. The eight difficult conditions are life on the borders or among the barbarians, as a slave, orphan, indigent, or handicapped person as well as in an environment devoid of Dao. The ten situations of intense suffering, moreover, are specific punishments in the hells, envisioned as supernatural courts of inquisition and torture, such as the mountain of knives, the tree of swords, and the cauldron of boiling water (see Lagerwey in Schipper and Verellen 2004, 242-43).

The entire complex of understanding the mind and its workings, finally, presents an intricate mixture of ancient Daoist and Buddhist concepts. The mind, both traditions agree, is the personalized functioning of cosmic root consciousness (spirit; Buddha-nature), determined in its content by concrete mani-festations of reality (*fa* 法, dharmas; *xiang* 相, phenomena; Soothill and Hudous 1937, 267, 259). These reach it through the six senses, also known as the "six robbers," the creators of the six emotions (*qing* 情) or sensory impurities (*liuchen* 六塵, *guṇas*; 1937, 406). Classifying and evaluating sensory data, the mind sways between craving and aversion (*aiwu* 愛惡; *rāgadveṣa*), never resting, always agi-tated (*dong* 動), unsteady, and impermanent (*wuchang* 無常). This agitation is more specifically described in terms of defilements and impurities (*ran* 染,) as well as, irritations and afflictions (*fannao* 煩惱, *kleśa*; 1937, 304, 406).

In terms of thinking, a very similar structure holds true. On the basis of sensory input, the conscious mind, the thinking, reflecting, critical, and divisive factor of perception (*shi* 識, *vijñāna*; 1937, 473) creates mental projections which it then regards as objective reality (*jing* 境, *viṣaya*; 1937, 421). In fact, it is subject to the so-called six taints (*liuran* 六染; 1937, 135), aspects of the wrong percep-tion of apparent reality (*jia* 假), which is ultimately empty (*kong* 空). The include being attached to apparent reality and failing to eliminate it, giving rise to dis-criminating consciousness and accepting sensory data as real as well as mentally seeing apparent reality and continuing a. primal karmic relationship to it. Each thought (*nian* 念, *smṛti*, 1937, 258) is yet another manifestation of this funda-mentally deluded (*wang* 妄) way of being in the world, perpetuating mental ten-sion and agitation and thus karmic involvement. The practice of sitting in obliv-ion, as much as Buddhist insight meditation and *zuochan*, begins accordingly by anchoring the mind in stillness, then moves on to releasing built-up intellectual and emotional fallacies.

Insight Meditation

The central Buddhist method of meditation, as first recorded in the sermons of the Buddha, is insight or mindfulness (*vipaśyanā*), while its way to stillness is concentration or cessation (*śamatha*) (Faure 1986, 103). The latter is usually es-tablished by focusing the mind on the breath with "mindfulness of breathing" (*ānapānasati*). Allowing the breath to flow naturally and remaining aware of its movement, meditators begin to observe their mind and find that it is like a wild monkey, run-away horse, or excited puppy that never stops for an instant. Over a period of days or weeks, the mind calms down and is ready for insight prac-tice, the detached observation of body sensations and sensory impressions. Practitioners scan their bodies systematically time and time again, noticing dif-ferent feelings and becoming aware of changes while understanding that they are impersonal and beyond their control. They also learn to take this detached awareness into other aspects of life, practicing walking meditation, mindful eating, and generally maintaining calm observation (see Rosenberg 1999).

Remaining still and nonreactive, meditators allow subconscious patterns to emerge, become conscious, and evaporate. Gradually painful and unpleasant sensations and various accompanying emotions—also observed with detachment—give way to subtler and more pleasant feelings. Actively piercing through the apparent solidity of the body, they become aware of an underlying pulsation, an ubiquitous flow of vibration, a sense of subtle energetic oscillation. Realizing that this is the true nature of their selves, they see how little stability and solidity there is and start taking themselves less seriously, seeing their identity in a larger and more flowing context as taught by the tradition (Austin 1998, 129-37; Brown and Engler 1984). In Buddhism, this means rethinking the world specifically in terms of suffering, impermanence, and no-self. Eventually mental outflows stop completely and enlightenment begins to unfold.

In Tang China, this system was mainly represented by the Tiantai school named after its main mountain center. Its practices were widely known in the religious environment and even used by lay people as a means of healing or for pain relief (see Sakade 1989, 30; Ando 1970; Yamano 1984). Daoists learned the methods both from their wide use in Tang society and also directly from the center on Mount Tiantai, where many masters spent some time, including Sima Chengzhen and Wu Yun.

Founded by Zhiyi in the sixth century, the main Tiantai characteristic was its hierarchical integration of the various teachings and traditions within Buddhism, based on the theory that the Buddha taught his ideas in many different ways so as to adapt it to the individual preferences and specific abilities of his listeners. The system allowed Buddhists to integrate texts from widely variant and even contradictory schools into one organized whole, claiming that, whatever the form of a given teaching, it always went back to one original truth. This fundamental truth, moreover, encompassed all its concrete manifestations which at the same time also contained one another (see Hurvitz 1962; Swanson 1989; Ng 1993; Groner 1984; Ziporyn 2004a).

In other words, while it is essential to find liberation from the defilements of the mind and unwholesome karmic patterns of life, it does not matter which practice one begins with or which bodhisattva one invokes. Nevertheless, Tiantai followers placed the *Lotus sutra* at the top of all scriptures and Guanyin 觀音 (Avalokitesvara) at the center of their veneration. They strongly recommended the practice of cessation and insight as the most efficient vehicle to enlightenment. Zhiyi himself is the source of three important treatises on the practice that each share something with the *Zuowang lun*.

Most extensive among them is the *Mohe zhiguan* 摩訶止觀 (Great [Outline of] Cessation and Insight, T. 1911; trl. Donner and Stevenson 1993), which outlines the practice in a rather scholastic fashion. He describes cessation in three parts: putting an end to something, dwelling in something, and as an arbitrary name for reality, then emphasizes that it should lead to observation of all reality as empty (see Donner 1987). The closest match in Daoist materials appears in the *Daojiao yishu*, which details three forms of observation: of apparent existence, of emptiness, and of the middle (Kamata 1963, 211). Zhiyi next divides insight into ten different modes that all lead to the understanding that "all possible determinacies are . . . identical to each moment of experience, just as a thing is identical to its own characteristics and properties, or to its own process of becoming and perishing" (Ziporyn 2004b, 549). The main thing that this text has in common with the *Zuowang lun* is that it was transcribed by a disciple on the basis of the master's lectures. In this case, they were delivered during the summer retreat of the year 594 and edited by Guanding 灌頂 (561-632).

Second is the scholastic *Jueyi sanmei xingfa* 覺意三昧行法 (How to Cultivate Samādhi with Aware Intention, T. 1922), which details four major kinds of absorption along Mādhyamika lines. The ultimate transcendence of all functional perception is achieved after undergoing six kinds of preparation which bear a certain similarity to methods used in the *Zuowang lun*. They include establishing firm determination (through the bodhisattva vow), taming the mind (or controlling negative qualities with the help of the Six Perfections), eliciting mental phases (by seeing the mental factors or *skandhas*), general discernment of the mind (i.e., observation of perceived reality in terms of the two truths and four Mādhyamika propositions), and specific discernment amidst all activities (i.e., while walking, staying, sitting, and lying down) (see Stevenson 1986, 82-83). As a result, the meditator comes to fully realize that the mind "is pure in its essential self-nature and free of any change or transformation" and reaches illumination or universal awareness (1986, 84).

The closest connection with the Daoist system is found in Zhiyi's more elementary *Tongmeng zhiguan* 童蒙止觀 (Cessation and Insight for Beginners, T. 42).[2] This probably served as the ground model for the *Zuowang lun* for the simple reason that it "represents the first practical manual of meditation available to the Chinese" (Bielefeldt 1986, 133). Although not quite the same in basic outlook—it was addressed to initial monastic practitioners and not to lay followers and accordingly includes a lot more technical details—the text yet shows clear overlap in its emphasis on general modes of practice and the healing of diseases. For example, it works with physical practices such as simple

---

[2] English translations appear in Bucknell and Kang 1997, 55-63; Lu 1964; Saso 2000. The most extensive studies are in Japanese: Sekiguchi 1957; 1974; 1975.

stretches, breath control, and the six healing breaths (Saso 2000, 88-91)—all derived from Daoist exercises (see Despeux 2006; Kohn 2008a)—which in Daoist meditation literature appear in related texts, such as Sun's *Zhenzhong ji* and Sima's *Fuqi jingyi lun*. The section on "Harmonization," furthermore, "on the control of body, breath, and mind could [also] serve as a handy, nonsectarian guide to the basics of Buddhist mental discipline" (Bielefeldt 1986, 133).

In terms of overall organization, Zhiyi divides his treatise into ten stages which, as Yoshiko Kamitsuka (1982) has shown, bear some resemblance to those of the *Zuowang lun*.

Zuowang lun	*Tongmeng zhiguan*
1. Respect and Faith 敬信	1. Fulfilling Karma 具緣
2. Interception of Karma 斷緣	2. Rebuking Desires 訶欲
4. Detachment from Affairs 間事	3. Removing of Screens 棄蓋
3. Taming the Mind 收心	4. Harmonization 調和
	5. Expedient Means 方便
5. Perfect Observation 真觀	6. Proper Cultivation 正修
6. Cosmic Peace and Stability 泰定	7. Goodness Manifest 善發
	8. Recognizing Mara 覺摩
	9. Healing Diseases 治病
7. Attaining Dao 得道	10. Realizing the Fruit 證果

Chan

Moving in the opposite direction, there is also a school of Buddhism quite indebted to the Daoist tradition in theory and practice. This is the Chan 禪 (Zen) school, which traces itself back to the Indian monk Bodhidharma who supposedly arrived in China around the year 520. As first described in Song histories, the school claims to have emerged as a movement against the set ways and rigid patterns of established Buddhism. Hoping to return to the original pursuit of personal enlightenment rather than serving the aristocracy with devotional rituals and enjoying the luxuries of sponsored living, select monks dedicated to contemplative practice took to the mountains where they practiced deep meditative absorption, called *chan* after the Sanskrit word *dhyāna*. They eschewed the use of scriptures, rituals, devotion, and formalized training, increasingly inspired young seekers, and soon saw their followings grow into substantial groups which first received official recognition in the seventh century (see Dumoulin 1965; McRae 1983; Yampolsky 1967).

Contrary to this traditional vision, recent studies have shown that the claim to being iconoclastic and unconventional was part of the rather romanticized Song vision of an ideal Chan which supposedly flourished in the Tang and consisted of a few dominant lineages. Rather, it emerges, Chan began—and for several centuries continued—as a multifaceted localized development with enormous regional diversity and a strong "plurality of doctrinal standpoints and soteriological approaches" (Pocesci 2007). It was not until the late Tang that it developed into specific lineages and adopted the features that shaped it in the centuries to come (see McRae 2003; Faure 1997; Adamek 2007; Poceski 2009a).

More strongly connected to the Chinese tradition than other Buddhist schools, Chan made ample use of Daoist terms and concepts, especially those derived from the *Zhuangzi*. The two traditions accordingly share numerous basic ideas (see Brazier 1995, 191; Kasulis 1981, 29-38; Watts 1957, 3-28). For example, both emphasize the experience of immersed oneness, described as "making the body like dried wood and the mind like dead ashes" both in *Zhuangzi* and Chan sources, which also speak of "dropping off body and mind." Similarly both favor a state of oblivion or no-mind where the person as person has "lost himself":

> Zuikan was a Zen master who always used to address himself. "Zuikan?" he would call. And then he would call "Yes!" "Zuikan!" "Yes!" Of course he was living all alone in his small zendō, and of course he knew who he was, but sometimes he lost himself. (Suzuki 1970, 81)

Both also favor the transformation of conscious and sensory experience toward a subtler, deeper, and no-self level. Sitting firmly in a full or half lotus posture without moving and calming the breath to a very slow rhythm is the foundation of Chan practice as well as of Daoist oblivion. Keeping the body stable, the mind comes to rest, but thoughts continue to arise and pass away and the main task is to break the addiction to conscious evaluations and critical judgments. Thus the modern master Shunryu Suzuki says: "When the fish swims, water and fish are the fish. There is nothing but fish. . . You cannot find Buddha-nature in vivisection." Similarly the Japanese master Bassui (1326-1387) echoes *Zhuangzi* in asking: "Look! Look! Who is the master that is seeing and hearing right now?" (Suzuki 1970, 134; Braverman 1989; Austin 2006, 3).

Both Chan practitioners and Daoists, moreover, tend to undergo five phases of increased mental focus. Just as Sun Simiao outlines in his *Cunshen lianqi ming*, so traditional Buddhist texts describe five levels of concentration on breathing, after the initial stage of counting: staying, returning, accompanying, observing, and purifying (Link and Lee 1966, 192). The same is also borne out in modern meditation research, which finds that Zen practitioners undergo five stages of mental awareness in their basic training:

1. Focus on breathing. Reactive effect, alteration in occurrence and response to breathing.
2. Attention wanders. Habituation to the task of breathing.
3. Focus returns to breathing. Eventually "effortless breathing": relaxed attentive awareness, without reactive effect, without habituation.
4. New thoughts occur and are watched with relaxed awareness and continued focus on breathing. Global desensitization. Thought stopping.
5. Absence of internal chatter; categories suspended; receptivity to internal/external stimuli. "Mind as mirror." (Shapiro and Zifferblatt 1984)

Beyond that, however Chan practice is quite different in aims and methods. Fujiyoshi Jikai (1974) delineates the differences as follows:

	zuochan	*zuowang*
aim	liberation from all	union with Dao
method	increased awareness, awakening	darkening, obscuring, oblivion
oblivion	seen as delusion	true state of Dao
ideal	remain individual, but free	dissolution in cosmos
worldview	no fixed position	assumption of underlying One

Despite these differences, both in Daoism and Chan, the human mind is the key factor which, in its original clarity, connects to the universal network without effort. Its universal and originally pure nature, in Daoism called "spirit" and in Chan called Buddha-nature, is the cosmic mind of creation—described in most detail by the Yogacara school, which speaks of storehouse consciousness (*zangshi* 藏識, *alayavijñana*) or mind-only (Chatterjee 1962; Keenan 1993). According to this, mind-only is at the root of all existence, and a human mind in vibrant connection with it conducts all activities of life to perfection, knowing spontaneously and immediately what is what and what needs to be done—without reflection, interference, or conscious thoughts.

Chan practice, like sitting in oblivion, reduces conscious activity and sensory mediation to zero in order to break through to this underlying connectedness, to the pure existence of mind-only. On the way to this breakthrough, practitioners work hard and sit intensely, undergoing a variety of distracting experiences: from heat and cold through trembling and shaking to hallucinations of light, visitations by specters, and visions of divine beings (Dumoulin 1981, 142)—just as outlined in the *Dingguan jing*. The eventual breakthrough, then, is often experienced as a sudden opening of consciousness and not as the gradual emergence of a new state. Thus Chan masters speak of "sudden" enlightenment—unlike Daoists who emphasize the slow, one-by-one overcoming of inherent patterns in gradual progress.

Another aspect of Chan is koan practice, where adepts immerse themselves in paradoxes, using them in a deep state of absorption to break open the conscious mind and let universal mind come to the fore. [3] While Daoists never developed the paradox to quite this level or formality, the *Zhuangzi* contains numerous examples. For example, there frequently are questions like: "What is really me?" "Where is there a true lord in the body?" "What is real?" "Am I Zhuang Zhou dreaming that he is a butterfly, or a butterfly dreaming that he is Zhuang Zhou?" (ch. 2; Watson 1968, 38, 41, 49; Graham 1981, 58, 59, 61; see also Hansen 2010). Similarly Zhuangzi tells Yan Hui to consider what it would mean to "fly by being wingless, know by being ignorant" (ch. 4; Watson 1968, 58; Roth 2010, 198). The text constantly questions the relation of self, others, and language: "Without an other, there is no self; without a self, there is no choosing one thing over another" (Graham 1981, 51). And: "The one and what I said about it make two, and two and the original one make three. If we go on in this way, then even the cleverest mathematician can't tell where we will end, much less an ordinary person . . . Better not to move, but to let things be!" (Watson 1968, 43; Graham 1981, 56; Roth 2010, 207).

Later Daoist texts, like the *Xisheng jing*, use the same words on different levels and with different nuances, such as when Laozi insists that he does not know what good and evil are, then immediately states that "accumulating goodness" is the key to perfection (37.6-7). In addition, Daoists have a long tradition of eccentric and unpredictable sages and immortals, and on occasion report absurd dialogues, such as the one in the *Tianyinzi*, where the master either remains silent when confronted with a question or responds entirely out of context.

One Chan text that shows the closest similarities to Daoist notions is the *Linji lu* 臨濟錄 (Recorded Sayings of Linji), a collection of lectures by and stories about the Chan master Linji Yixuan 臨濟義玄 (d. 866), one of the best known iconoclasts in the tradition.[4] He was ruthless when it came to eliminate sensory and evaluative reactions:

> Followers of the Way, if you want to get the kind of understanding that accords with the dharma, never be misled by others. Whether you are facing inward or facing outward, whatever you meet up with, just kill it! If you meet a buddha, kill the buddha. If you meet a patriarch, kill the patriarch. If you meet an arhat, kill the arhat. If you meet your parents,

---

[3] For koans and their practice, see Miura and Sasaki 1965; Austin 1998, 110-19; Dumoulin 1979, 65-76; Heine 2002; Loori 2006; S. Suzuki 1970, 80-83; Watts 1957. About 1,700 koans were collected over the centuries, most in books like the *Hekiganroku* (Blue Cliff Record; trl. Cleary 1977) and *Mumonkan* (The Gateless Gate; trl. Cleary 1993).

[4] The text was probably edited and possibly even expanded by Song redactors, yet it does reflect realities of Chan practice. See Welter 2008; Poceski 2009b.

kill your parents. If you meet your kinfolk, kill your kinfolk. Then for the first time you will gain emancipation, will not be entangled with things, will pass freely anywhere you wish to go. (Watson 1999, 52)

This closely reflects the vision of the ideal state in the *Zhuangzi* as the ability to move about everywhere in ecstatic freedom. Another common point is the perfected and Linji's "true man without rank," both living in ordinary society yet being free from it. Without pretensions, he does whatever is necessary, menial or noble, important or petty: "When hungry, I eat; when thirsty, I drink" (Schloegl 1976, 37, 52). In addition, the true man has the power to traverse wide ranges and create harmony in the world around him:

Followers of the Way, he who at this moment, before my eyes is shining alone and clearly listening to my discourse—this man tarries nowhere: he traverses the ten directions and is freely himself in the Three Worlds. . . In traveling everywhere through every land, in bringing enlightenment to sentient beings, he is never separate from his present mind. Everywhere is pure, light illumines the ten directions, and the ten thousand things are one. (Sasaki 1975; Yixuan 1976)

Related Concepts

While Chan and Daoist masters both inherited and developed the ancient classics, and the *Zhuangzi* in particular, Chan as part of the Mahāyāna tradition also drew on a rich foundation of philosophical speculation and analysis which yet in many ways matches Daoist concepts.

For example, in addition to working with the two truths and four propositions of the Madhyamaka—as Daoists do in the school of Twofold Mystery, where oblivion is first formally featured—Chan adopts the vision of *Avatamsaka sūtra* (*Huayan jing* 華嚴經, Flower Garland Sutra; trl. Cleary 1984) and sees the world as one integrated whole. Unlike ancient Buddhist worldview where *nirvāna* is the "other shore," the universe here is a complex network where every single part is interconnected with every other and where all is mirrored endlessly in all else (see Cook 1977; Gimello and Gregory 1983).

This closely matches the Daoist understanding of reality as consisting of interlocking fields that each pulsate at their own rate. Chinese cosmology speaks of them in terms of vibration and sound, all things having their own form or shape which inevitably vibrates at a certain frequency, creating a certain wave pattern and a specific sound. As a result, the entire universe is humming along in the joining of many different *qi*-sounds. The *Zhuangzi* accordingly talks about the "piping of Humanity," the energy waves people produce; the "piping of Earth," the vibrations of nature in different places; and the "piping of Heaven" the creation of the universe in its diversity through Dao. The description of the "piping of earth" is most vivid and also applies to the other forms. The text says:

> They roar like waves, whistle like arrows, screech, gasp, cry, wail, moan, howl. Those in the lead cry out *yeee*; those behind cry out *yuuu*. In a gentle breeze, they answer faintly; but in a full gale, the chorus is gigantic. And when the fierce wind has passed on, then all the hollows are empty again. Have you never seen the tossing and trembling that goes on? (ch. 2)

These various fields can come into harmony with each other and mutually support and increase their amplitude. But they can also interfere with each other and create disturbances. Since all fields interlock, even a small disturbance in any one of them carries into all the others.[5] This means that bodily transformations are of unlimited possibilities and the mind is ultimately nonlocal: it can be anywhere and exchange information with anything else instantaneously. It also means that any effort on the part of the meditator to reach a state of spontaneity or immediacy in absorption or oblivion makes a clear contribution to the harmony and purity of the cosmos.

Another result of this vision of the world as fundamentally and intricately interconnected is that each individual takes part in the entirety of the universe at all times and is, qua being human, fundamentally enlightened. The world as it is in all its apparent instability (*samsāra*) is already and essentially the same as its ultimate state (*nirvāna*). There is nothing to do, nothing to attain, nowhere to go. All aspects of existence are mirrored in all other aspects, without permanence, stability, or individual nature.

This is what Chan Buddhists, following the lead of the *Prajñāpāramitā sūtra* (*Panruo jing* 般若經, Perfection of Wisdom; trl. Conze 1978; 1990), mean by "emptiness," the recognition of the interconnectedness of existence and the ultimate identity of *samsāra* and *nirvāna*. A short, comprehensive summary of these doctrines, compiled in China in the sixth century but claimed to be of Indian origin (see Nattier 1992), is the *Xinjing* 心經 (Heart Sutra). Placed in the mouth of the bodhisattva Guanyin and consisting of only a few hundred characters, it emphasizes the fundamentally empty nature of all perceived existence, going one by one through the different *skandhas* or constituents of the mind. The text spread widely in the Tang and is still the most recited sutra in East Asia, together with the *Jin'gang jing* 金剛經 (Diamond Sutra; trl. Price and Wong 1969) playing a key role in modern Zen (Glassman 2000, 29-35).

---

[5] This vision of interlocking fields is not only common among medieval Chinese Daoists and Huayan Buddhists but also closely matches the understanding of the universe in quantum physics. For details, see Bohm 1951; Capra 1975; Nadeau and Kefatos 1999.

The Daoist match of the *Xinjing* is the *Huming jing* 護命經 (Scripture on Protecting Life, DZ 19; trl. Assandri 2009, 216-18), revealed by the Heavenly Worthy of Primordial Beginning (Yuanshi tianzun 元世天尊). Its next incarnation is the *Qingjing xinjing* 清靜心經 (Heart Scripture of Clarity and Stillness, DZ 1169), which consists of about 600 characters and probably goes back to the eighth century (see Kamata 1966; Fukui 1987; Schmidt in Schipper and Verellen 2004, 316). [6] Placed in the mouth of Lord Lao, it begins with a general description of Daoist cosmology in terms of yin and yang, pure and turbid, stillness and agitation. It then focuses on the mind and its power of either creating purity or disturbance and the need to eliminate desires. Next, it distinguishes three kinds of observation, resulting in the full perception of all reality as empty while yet realizing that nothing is really empty:

> Inwardly observe the mind and see that there is no mind.
> Outwardly observe the body and see that there is no body.
> Far off observe all beings and see that there are no beings.
> These three not seen any longer, one sees only emptiness.
> Observe emptiness and see that it is indeed empty—
> Yet there is nothing that is empty. (1a)

Outlining the process toward "attaining Dao," from the elimination of desires through stillness of mind to clarity of spirit, it reiterates once more that "there is nothing to attain." In the next section, it moves in the opposite direction and describes how one falls deeper and deeper into the rebirth cycle when one begins to perceive anything as "real," eventually undergoing the suffering of hell and being forever separate from Dao. It concludes with a set of verses praising the pure mind—again using imagery that is also found in Chan: "Your clear mind like a clear mirror: there are no more obstacles. No obstacles, no mind: the mind just rests in itself."

To sum up, Daoist oblivion as described in Tang-dynasty sources is closely connected to Buddhist theory and practice, yet it also maintains its own uniqueness. Continuing to be true to the *Zhuangzi* and pursuing their own specific goals, Daoists reconceptualize Buddhist features as much as they adapt them into their own repertoire. The close similarity, moreover, between oblivion and Chan—both arising in the seventh-to-eighth centuries on similar foundations—allows us to classify them as one single type of meditation. This "im-

---

[6] Its more popular and still much recited version is the *Qingjing jing* 清靜經(Scripture of Clarity and Stillness, DZ 620; see Schmidt in Schipper and Verellen 2004, 332-33 and 728-29, various commentaries); also translated in Kohn 1993a, 24-29; Komjathy 2008, #3; Wong 1992.

mediacy," as I have called it (2008a, 97), is clearly distinct as a type from all the others: neither oblivion nor Chan can be reduced to insight meditation, body energetics, visualization, or mere concentration. They may make use of the different techniques, as Sima clearly does in his *Zuowang lun*, but their core is the "dropping off of body and mind," the liberation from all personal identity, the freedom of oneness with Buddha-nature or Dao.

Tang writers, moreover, show that people at the time did not make too much of a distinction between the schools. Thus the poet Bai Juyi 白居易 describes taking refuge in meditation practice when suffering from profound grief after his mother's death in 814:

> My breath disturbed, I return to absorption and stability.
> Visualizing spirit, I enter a state of sitting in oblivion.
> Cutting off doubts, I pursue the sword of wisdom,
> Being saved from suffering, I reach the lifeboat of compassion.
> (Ch'en 1973: 197)

This shows the intricate mix of practices as understood at the time. Bo Juyi begins with calming his breath and reaching a state of mental calm, described in both Buddhist and Daoist terms, then reaches through visualization to oblivion as outlined in the *Zuowang lun* and *Tianyinzi*. From here, he comes to hold the "sword of wisdom," both a Buddhist term and a key idea in the *Zuowang lun*, to end on a clearly Buddhist note: traversing the sea of suffering in the "lifeboat of compassion."

Chapter Eight

Western Appreciation

Sitting in oblivion as outlined in the Tang sources comprises a series of techniques leading to the transformation and transcendence of personal self-identity in favor of oneness with Dao. These techniques include breath control and mental calming as much as restructuring of the body, detached observation, and introvert, enstatic absorption. Many of them have been adapted into a modern Western context. However, given the predilection of modernity with mundane success, they have in many cases been reoriented to serve more practical goals, such as self-improvement, healing, stress-reduction, pain-management, and increased productivity. Thus present-day psychology postulates the aims of meditation as being control over the mind, increase in psychological well-being, and development of advanced states of consciousness (Walsh 1984, 24). Also, given the modern preoccupation with science and technology, the techniques have been tested, evaluated, and reinterpreted in terms of physiology and neuroscience, made measurable in brain waves, blood pressure, neurotransmitters, endocrine activity, and the like.

This holds particularly true for the more elementary—and thus more easily accessible—practices of breath control and concentration as well as for basic methods of insight or mindfulness. Although it is regrettable that healing as a goal and scientific justification may in some cases reduce the power of the practices and somatize their understanding, the explanations of scientific studies help explain just why traditional texts demand specific methods and report certain effects.

Deep absorptive states and the complete "dropping off of body and mind" have so far escaped both the popular health quest and scientific pigeon-holing. Less prominent in modern societies, they are still the domain of long-term dedicated practitioners who seek transcendence and complete loss of identity rather than healing, efficiency, or stress release. Their efforts take place both beyond and within organized traditions, and some techniques—notably those of Buddhist heritage—are more widely known than others. A well-documented example of a non-traditional, very modern path that yet closely matches the transformation and vision of oblivion appears in the works of David Hawkins. Seeing this in comparison with the Tang masters' works reveals just how universal these practices and their goals are and how relevant sitting in oblivion can be in present-day society.

Deep Breathing

Modern societies are becoming increasingly conscious about the importance of breathing deeply, calmly, and with awareness in order to maintain and enhance health, well-being, and optimal functioning. Science has shown a clear connection between shallow breathing and stress, tension, and anxiety as well as between short, truncated breaths and heart disease and cardio-pulmonary ailments in a phenomenon known as the hyperventilatory response. Extremely widespread in modern societies, where deep abdominal breathing often ceases already in childhood, these various psychological ailments benefit tremendously from beginning meditation exercises which focus attention on the respiration, deepening and lengthening the breath.

More specifically, breathing serves to bring oxygen into the bloodstream and the circulatory system of the body while at the same time releasing carbon dioxide back into the atmosphere. As the diaphragm, the muscle that divides the lungs from the intestinal cavity, contracts, air is sucked into the lungs and ideally spreads into their far reaches, widening the space between the ribs and oxygenating the body. The lungs extract oxygen from the air and channel it into the bloodstream from where it goes into the heart and the brain and then throughout the body to nourish all of its cells. Blood that has been depleted of oxygen and instead carries carbon dioxide is then transported back to the heart through the veins, from where the lungs take over and expel the carbon dioxide in exhalation.

The process of breathing is intimately connected to the autonomic nervous system, which "oversees the body's vital functions through subconscious signals that originate in the anterior cyngulate gyrus and are relayed to the hypothalamus and spinal cord" (Ratey 2002, 171). It has two branches: the sympathetic and the parasympathetic. The sympathetic nervous system is the energizing part. It puts people into a state of readiness to meet challenges or danger, causing nerve endings to emit neurotransmitters that stimulate the adrenal glands to secrete powerful hormones which increase the heartbeat and the rate of breathing. They also influence the digestion, speeding up the metabolic function through increased acid secretion in the stomach. The parasympathetic nervous system, on the other hand, activates neurotransmitters like acetylcholine that lower the pulse and respiratory rate. Its responses are comfort, relaxation, and sleep. Any method of relaxation stimulates the parasympathetic nervous system and slows down the breath (2002, 172-74).

People are either in one or the other mode. If the sympathetic nervous system is "on," the parasympathetic is "off," and vice versa. Both, moreover, connect closely to the endocrine system which manages the hormones that control growth, activity levels, and sexuality. Endocrine glands secrete hormones known as endorphins and enkephalins that modulate reactions to stress and pain, affect moods and appetite, and support abilities of learning and memory. The more one is in the parasympathetic mode, as stimulated by quiet sitting and deep breathing, the better the endocrine system can do its work and the stronger one's immune system becomes. This, in a nutshell, explains why so many people today suffer from stress related ailments while practitioners of yoga, qigong, and meditation enjoy health and vitality and why all meditation systems begin with calming the breath.[1]

Calming the Mind

The breath, moreover, is often the main vehicle for calming the mind to a state of concentration, which meditation traditions use in two major forms: access and attainment. Access concentration is the foundation of all further practice, the basic level of mental focus and sensory calm necessary to engage in advanced methods. Attainment concentration is the complete one-pointedness of attention, the utter absorption in a single object, a state of inner bliss and oblivion, the overcoming of ego and identity. What Westerners commonly mean when they speak of the "meditative state" and what many scientific studies focus on is access concentration, a rather elementary achievement from the perspective of the old traditions.

To achieve basic concentration, then, practitioners focus their attention on the breath by anchoring it in one of three main modes of human perception. Kinesthetically they feel it either as it enters and leaves the nostrils or as it expands and flattens the abdomen (Rosenberg 1998, 24-25). Visually they link it with a simple and steady image, such as a vase, geometric diagram, image, or statue (Bucknell and King 1997, 41-52). Auditorily they associate it with certain words

---

[1] On the physiology of breathing and the autonomic nervous system, see Altose and Kawakami 1999; Borysenko 1987, 55-68; Fried 1993; 1999; Loehr and Migdow 1986; Von Euler and Lagercrantz 1987.

matching the inhalation and/or exhalation (such as "in-out"), by counting each breath up to a certain number, or by linking it with a prayer or chant (Easwaran 1990, 15).

Undertaken in a quiet setting and in a comfortable position with eyes closed or lowered and pursued for at least twenty minutes at a stretch, the basic practice is to remain focused. Usually the mind wanders away, chasing after thoughts, memories, and ideas. Rather than being exasperated and impatient, the point of the exercise is to become fully aware of the present moment, notice the mind's shenanigans, and bring it back to the breath—thousands of times if necessary. Eventually it calms down and is able to remain focused for a minute or more at a time. To use Larry Rosenberg's metaphor, from a mind unfocused like a sniffing dog, practitioners should strive to attain a mind like a sitting lion, majestically focused on the source (1998, 22).

Sitting quietly, breathing deeply, and calming the mind create a fundamental state of relaxation which, when combined with increased focus and heightened awareness, has a direct effect on brain chemistry and wave patterns. While the conscious mind works largely in beta waves, when quieted it changes to alpha, a state found in beginning practitioners. More advanced disciples or people in more absorbed concentration may also enter states dominated by theta waves that indicate a profoundly calm, yet conscious state (Shapiro and Walsh 1984, 363-534). Deep relaxation signaled by these patterns activates the parasympathetic response, increases subjective well-being, and has various beneficial effects.

However, its attainment is not the sole domain of meditation, and studies have shown that "resemblances undoubtedly exist between the meditative experience and that induced in various relaxation therapies, such as self-hypnosis, progressive relaxation, autogenic therapy, and perhaps biofeedback training" (Davidson 1984, 377). Since it is not usually possible to relate a particular effect on a person's subjective well-being to a specific method of relaxation employed, there is no one effect of concentrative meditation significantly different from that of comparable practices (Bono 1984, 209). Rather, "all that is clearly established . . . is the hardly surprising conclusion that meditators are in a state of relaxation" (Davidson 1984, 381). In other words, meditation methods—at least as used in modern societies under laboratory conditions—"are no better or any more effective than other kinds of relaxation and stress-reduction techniques" (Ospina et al. 2007, 4).

That said, modern physicians and psychologists make use of several practices simplified from traditional meditation systems to help patients release stress, reduce pain, and enhance well-being. Best known among them is the Relaxation Response, developed by Herbert Benson of Harvard University on the basis of Transcendental Meditation, a chanting-based concentration practice popular in the 1960s and 70s. Its practice involves sitting or lying comfortably, closing the eyes, and breathing through the nose while repeating a word or phrase of choice—often inspired by religious beliefs—either vocally or mentally. The practice should be continued for twenty minutes while maintaining a receptive, passive attitude and permitting relaxation to occur at its own pace. The Relaxation Response has been found most effective in relieving pain and anxiety. Patients working with the repeated utterance of a word, chant, or prayer relax deeply. This state encourages natural healing or allows a gradual drifting into death (Benson 1976; 1996; Benson and Proctor 1985; Fried 1993, 240-42).

Another method that uses concentration for healing works with visual methods adopted from hypnosis and is somewhat closer to Daoist practice. The Quieting Response by C. E. Stroebel consists of a series of ten exercises to be practiced daily over six months. The first exercise is to lie down and be comfortable with eyes closed. Next comes deep, easy breathing, followed by a series of gentle arm movements and face massages. This leads to visualization: patients are to imagine a spot of warm sunlight above their head and to feel their body as a hollow vessel. They then imagine the warm sunlight slowly seeping into the vessel, moving freely through chest and abdomen, arms and legs. Another visualization, while still paying attention to breathing, is to focus on a spot before their nose where they imagine a ball of blue, cooling energy. Allowing their mind to be filled with this energy, they float in a space of suspended thinking, deeply relaxed. From this state, they then conduct a review of their day, seeing their activities in reverse order as if on a movie screen while remaining calm and detached (Fried 1993, 242-43; Stroebel 1982).[2]

To sum up, deep breathing and basic concentration practice, at the foundation of sitting in oblivion and other forms of meditation, have a profound impact on human physiology and neurology, activating the parasympathetic nervous system and creating an inner state of receptivity and calm. This state is essentially a form of relaxation, which can also be achieved by other methods. While people today may be content with its healing and stress-reducing benefits, traditional Daoists use it as a stepping stone toward advanced transformations of the body and subtler explorations of the mind.

---

[2] For other stress-reduction methods and the possible use of Daoist methods in this context, see Santee 2008.

Adjusting the Body

Another important basic step in the Daoist system is the alignment and healing of the body, which means matching the patterns of yin and yang, avoiding polluted situations and substances, and strengthening the overall energetic network. Matching this in the West, the science of behavioral kinesiology—with recent support in the newly developing fields of energy medicine and energy psychology[3]—has developed a system that supports everything Daoists (and Chinese medical practitioners) say about the nature of body, self, and society. It also recommends a series of measures— social, physical, and psychological—to enhance bodily well-being which are very much in agreement with those described by Sun Simiao and Sima Chengzhen.

Kinesiology is the science of movement: how to move the body and use its joints, tendons, and muscles to create maximum efficiency and best performance. It is best known from sports culture and studied widely in departments of physical education at Western universities (see Luttgens and Wells 1989). Behavioral kinesiology adds the dimension of personal perfection into the mix: the attainment of health, the extension of life expectancy, and the realization of virtues and inherent goodness in self and society. In other words, it is the study of how we can realize ideal health and harmony by living and moving our bodies most efficiently.

The key factor in behavioral kinesiology, as described by John Diamond (1978), is the thymus gland. Located in the solar plexus, it was already seen by the ancient Greeks as the central seat of vitality. "Thymus is the stuff of life, vaporous breath, active, energetic feeling and thinking, a material very much related to blood" (Spencer 1993, 47). The gland, although known to exist, was ignored in Western medicine for the longest time as not having a specific function, since it—like essence in Chinese medicine and Daoism—grows during puberty, is reduced in adulthood, shrinks to a miniscule size during sickness, and shrivels up completely after death (Diamond 1978, 10). More recent studies have shown that the thymus gland, like the central elixir field and power house of qi, is the center of immunological surveying and works to produce lymphocytes,

---

[3] Energy medicine is developing a more scientific vocabulary for qi-related phenomena, such as bio-electricity, the living matrix, cytoskeleton, tensegrity, and so on, seeing the body increasingly as an integrated, coordinated, successful system. See Oschman 2000. Energy psychology works with the aura as much as with the meridians of the Chinese and the chakras of the Indian systems; it is developing energetic methods such as tapping to release psychological tensions and bring out positive change. See Feinstein et al. 2005, 201 Gach and Henning 2004; Gallo 2004. For a more detailed discussion of kinesiology and Daoism, see my paper on "Daoist Body Cultivatin and Behavioral Kinesilogy" (http://www.daoist-studies.org/dao/node/11739).

i.e., the white blood cells responsible for the immunological reaction in the body. Connected energetically to all the different organs and extremities of the body, it prevents disease and cancer if kept strong (1978, 28-29).

The lower elixir field, the center of transformation in Daoist practice, moreover, in Western physiology matches the abdominal brain, the seat of spontaneous intelligence, in the vernacular described as gut feelings or intuition. A popular medical idea in the late nineteenth century (see Bedell 1885), it has re-emerged in recent research as the seat of an active enteric nervous system that governs the well-being of the person (McMillin et al. 1999). Its activation is best known from Zen practice, which requires a tightly held upright posture as well as conscious breathing and control over the diaphragm (Sekida 1975, 84).

Another Daoist practice that finds a match in science is placing the tongue at the roof of the mouth—used to establish an energy circuit of the channels in front and back of the torso. Modern kinesiologists call this the "centering button," a place that opens the body's central power lines and releases stress (Diamond 1978, 31). In addition, matching traditional healing exercises and modern qigong, kinesiologists have found that when there is too much synchronous activity on either side of the body, it will suffer a cerebral-hemisphere imbalance and weakened muscles, a state they describe as "switching" (1978, 40). In other words, the subtle energy lines of the body need to be activated by using the opposite arm and leg as much as possible, creating a sense of good body coordination. The lines are also impacted by any kind of metal that may be placed in the body's center and prevent proper energetic integration (1978, 43). Positive energy is further enhanced by wide, open gestures, such as the spreading of arms in a blessing or the welcoming of loved ones at a reunion (1978, 49)—movements often seen in Chinese exercises where *qi* is gathered or spread by opening the arms wide.

Practices to stimulate the thymus gland and increase vitality as outlined in behavioral kinesiology closely match the repertoire of traditional Daoists:

> —deep abdominal breathing and control of the diaphragm;
> —self-massages of the chest and front line (Conception Vessel) of the torso;
> —tapping of major energy centers, especially the center of the chest;
> —upright posture that allows an equal flow of energy in all parts of the body;
> —conscious movement that alternates the body's two sides;
> —emotional refinement toward feelings of love and caring;
> —careful selection of food, avoiding processed, or chemically altered items;
> —wearing loose and pure clothes, using natural fibers;
> —environmental care, providing good air, light, housing, and natural settings;
> —support for peace in the world and the creation of a harmonious society (Diamond 1978).

Within this overall framework, John Diamond has a few specific recommendations. Most generally, he suggests that one should find a "homing" thought, a mental vision of oneself in a pleasant and stress-free situation, such as in nature, on a beach, or with loved ones, and practice smiling both inwardly and to others, to create an internal harmony and relax the facial muscles (1978, 47, 49). He also emphasizes the energetic benefits of beauty, as found in poetry, music, painting, art, and natural landscapes and suggests that one should regularly take so-called energy breaks by reciting poetry, looking at nature, viewing a painting, or walk about with the arms swinging (1978, 39). All these are practices Daoists have embraced for centuries, living in beautiful natural settings, pursuing arts and music, and practicing calming meditations, where the facial muscles are relaxed and the internal organs viewed with sympathy and kindness and energized through the presence of body gods.

In addition to widely recognized pollutants, such as denatured food, neon lights, smoking, and various irritating chemicals, Diamond also advises against contact with ugly sights and shrill or intensely pulsing sounds since they lead to "therapeutic weakening" (1978, 62). This matches traditional Daoist rules against energetic pollution through encounters with dirt, death, or violence (see Kohn 2004a). Diamond especially singles out the weakening agents of aggressive art work and advertising as well as noise pollution through traffic, television, and rock music (1978, 65-66). In terms of practical objects, he suggests avoiding the use of sunglasses, wrist watches, nylon hats, wigs, and high heels as well as of metal chairs and seat cushions, mattresses, sheets, and clothing made from synthetic fabrics (1978, 74-77)—a list that echoes the requirements for strict simplicity in the furnishing of the oratory as much as the lifestyle of *zuowang* followers.

Detached Observation

To transform the mind, moreover, Daoists develop "perfect observation," which in modern societies is best documented in the form of insight meditation, the empowering of the witness consciousness or observing faculty of the mind that guides practitioners to a state where they can simultaneously feel an experience and see it from a distance. Used today both in religious or medical settings, it trains practitioners to strengthen their faculty of detached observation and learn to develop a fundamental attitude of non-judgment, patience, acceptance, and trust, with a particular emphasis on non-striving, letting be, and allowing things to happen. They understand that they cannot change reality but have to accept it as it is and instead of passing judgment should cultivate a beginner's mind, the ability to see every moment afresh and with new eyes.

Doing so increases the activities of the right brain hemisphere, which—unlike the planning and controlling done by the left—is given toward the artistic and works in a more receptive mode of being. It also activates the parasympathetic nervous system and stimulates alpha and theta waves. The observing self as established in insight practice is a way of allowing both sides to integrate harmoniously. It is not part of the subjective oneness of the right hemisphere, nor can it be controlled and objectified as an outside entity. It is deeply part of the person and represents a totally subjective answer to the question of "who am I," yet it also has the detachment and distance needed for critical awareness and decision-making (see Deikman 1982).

Another scientifically shown effect of insight meditation is the transformation of emotional patterns. Emotions "provide a quick, general assessment of the person's situation that draws on powerful internal and external value" (Ratey 2002, 171). They relay essential information to the amygdala, the principal pleasure center in the brain which provides a preconscious bias of intensity to every stimulus and classifies all reactions to sensory data in terms of aggressive or defensive (2002, 174). Emotions divide into two major types: bad and good, pleasant and unpleasant. Usually the bad, unpleasant emotions are afflictive, negative, and destructive; they tend to cause people to withdraw or move away from the object or circumstance that caused them. Good, pleasant emotions are beneficial, positive, and engaging; they make people approach and seek out the object or circumstance that caused them (Goleman 1997, 34).

In terms of brain chemistry, withdrawal reactions are located in the right frontal cortex, while approach reactions are activated in the left frontal cortex. People are born with a tendency toward one or the other dominant activation, but this inherent pattern can also be changed through learning and systematic training. Overall, people who have more right frontal cortex activity are more emotionally volatile. They get sick easier, have a harder time recovering, suffer from numerous ailments, have difficulty in their community because of their actions, and die earlier. People with dominantly left frontal cortex activity are more positive, don't submit to stress, will not catch colds even if exposed to germs, and live longer and happier lives (Goleman 1997, 68-69; see also Begley 2007, 226-33; Ratey 2002, 232-42). Mindfulness practice has been found particularly effective in enhancing the activity of the left frontal cortex and thus the creation of positive, community-connecting emotions (Goleman 1997, 69-71; see also Goleman 2003).[4]

---

[4] This effect of the practice is used increasingly in a medical setting, following a model pioneered by Jon Kabat-Zinn of the Stress Reduction Clinic at the University of Massachusetts Medical Center in Worcester. For detail of his program and work, see Kabat-Zinn 1990; 2005. An East Asian variant is the Japanese therapy of Naikan (adopting the Daoist

In other words, the practice of detached observation along the lines of traditional mindfulness meditation in modern Western settings is associated with
the reduction of negative emotions and the strengthening of positive attitudes
toward self and society. This effect has been linked convincingly with the right
frontal cortex and connected to the concept of neuroplasticity, the understanding that the brain can be shaped even after many years of ingrained use.

Integrated Personality

Another effect of mindfulness meditation is the integration of the personality
on a different level, one that is reached by seeing the world increasingly as flow.
Doing so, practitioners come to understand that neither mind nor self are immutable or firm entities, that life is constantly changing and essentially unsatisfactory, and that contentment can only be found in the present moment—all
features clearly formulated in section 5 of the *Zuowang lun*.

To study this effect Daniel Brown and Jack Engler presented insight practitioners in the Burmese lineage of the Venerable Mahasi Sayadaw with the Rorschach test, a method that reveals a person's perception of reality and inner
conflict structure in the way he associates patterns on the basis of inkblots.

The subjects of the study were ranked according to five levels: beginners, concentration practitioners, insight meditators, advanced insight meditators, and
enlightened masters. While beginners were no different from ordinary people,
those on levels two and three exhibited signs of relaxation and greater levels of
concentration. A major change was found among subjects of the fourth group,
who had pursued the practice intensely for many years, making it the main focus of their lives. They tended to "perceive the inkblots as an interaction of
form and energy or form and space. That is, each of the subjects, in several
responses, perceived the inkblot primarily as energy-in-motion or as empty
space" (Brown and Engler 1984, 245). Moreover, the energies were often seen
as energies within the human body: "The number of references to bodily parts
and internal organs and the psychic energy centers within the body is very high.
One possible interpretation of this contiguity between body and energy responses is that insight into bodily (and mental) processes becomes a vehicle
through which to observe the fundamental energy transformations of body/
mind/universe" (1984, 248).

This description of the newly developed worldview of advanced insight practitioners matches the observation section of the *Zuowang lun* closely. Here, too,

---

term *neiguan*), developed in the 1950s by Ishin Yoshimoto. It involves an intensive
introspection and release of emotions in a retreat-like setting (Reynolds 1983; Krech 2002).

adepts reorganize their perception in terms of flowing energy, seeing everything as impersonal changing transformations. The body becomes the habitation of the spirit, the vessel of Dao, and is no longer seen as having any solid reality of its own. Where concentration was used to empty the mind, observation is applied to fill it again with new modes of perception.

The final state of unified consciousness, an utter oneness with Dao, is characterized by a complete loss of ego-identity. "Unify your mind with Heaven," the *Zuowang lun* admonishes its readers, "and you will have no more knowledge. Unify your body with Dao and you will be free from all bodily structure." Full enlightenment, too, as formulated in Western psychological terms, means that the individual's "intrapsychic structure has undergone a radical enduring reorganization" (Brown and Engler 1984, 260). The result is a mature and true being, "a whole unified person whose internal psychic differentiation and organization would simply represent his diversified interests and abilities" (1984, 260).

This maturity of a unified consciousness is obvious in the Rorschach data in two unusual features. First, the enlightened master "sees the inkblot itself as a projection of the mind. . . . the testing situation is a projection of the mind in a certain sense" (1984, 249). Second, the full set of ten cards is integrated into "a systematic discourse on the Buddhist teachings pertaining to the alleviation of human suffering." Such an integration without any "significant departure from reality" is extremely rare, it has also been found in the testing results of an Apache shaman who—like the Buddhist master—"used the ten cards as an occasion to teach the examiner about his lived worldview" (1984, 260).

What Daoists mean when they speak of having attained "union with Dao in mind and body" can therefore be expressed in modern psychological terms as having reached a state of perceptual unity after many years of dedicated practice. Any individual personal life is fully dissolved into Dao or any other greater source of being, adepts no longer conceive of themselves as persons with a certain knowledge, history, or identity, but rather as part of a greater entity which works through them to the best benefit of all. Whether this is ultimately appealing to Westerners with their strong sense of self and visions of pleasurable fulfillment remains to be seen.

The Presence

One Westerner who has achieved complete union is David R. Hawkins (b. 1927), a psychiatrist who first studied at Marquette University, then earned an M.D. from the Medical College in Wisconsin (1953). Working as a psychiatrist in New York, he became deathly ill and underwent a spiritual rebirth which led to an expansion of his practice. In 1968, he met John Diamond, learned about behavioral kinesiology, and got involved in the field. As part of a large-scale experiment, Hawkins did extensive testing on thousands of subjects in many different cultures and eventually established a universal scale for the moral and spiritual potential of the world at large.

This scale places people's responses in a range from 20 to 1000, with a watershed—the realm of courage—at 200. Anything below means people work entirely toward survival and generate wide ranges of negative emotions, such as fear, worry, anger, hatred, greed, and pride—feelings that pull the person away from Dao and in traditional China are associated with the material soul. Above 200, more intellectual and spiritual values dominate, including trust, goodwill, forgiveness, love, and reverence to the point of sagely qualities such as serenity and bliss—attitudes that support the spirit soul and unfolding of higher values. On the basis of this work Hawkins earned a Ph. D. from Columbia Pacific University in 1995 (see Hawkins 2002a). He then spent the next decades authoring a series of books that combine his personal quest with kinesiological testing. Currently retired, he resides in Sedona and does occasional interviews with alternative and spiritual groups, such as Beyond the Ordinary (www.beyondtheordinary.net).

As regards his spiritual journey, the first experience of an altered state he recalls was at age 12 he was a paperboy in rural Wisconsin and found himself in a 10-below blizzard.[5] While nestled in a snow bank for safety, he had a miraculous transformative experience. "I became oblivious of my physical body and surroundings as my awareness fused with this all-present illuminated state. My mind grew silent; all thought stopped. An infinite Presence was all that was or could be, beyond time or description" (2002a, 293). The Presence helped him during World War II, but he did not acknowledge it as something spiritual or divine, the overall stupidity and suffering of humanity causing him to become an agnostic.

In 1965, when he was 38 year old, he succumbed to a fatal disease which did not respond to any available treatment. In his final moments, as he felt himself

---

[5] The following biography follows Hawkins's own account in Hawkins 2002a. It is summarized comprehensively on www.consciousnessproject.org.

dying, he called out: "If there is a God, I ask him to help me now." The reaction was immediate. He was submerged in a profoundly altered state:

> The person I had been no longer existed. There was no personal self or ego, only an Infinite Presence of such unlimited power that it was all that was. This Presence had replaced what had been 'me,' and my body and its actions were controlled solely by the Infinite Will of the Presence. The world was illuminated by the clarity of an Infinite Oneness which expressed itself as all things revealed in their infinite beauty and perfection. (2002a, 294)

This state of clarity and stillness persisted for a total of nine months. It involved complete oblivion of self and others:

> That which is the Self is total and complete. It is equally present everywhere. There are no needs, no desires, or lack. . . . A glance a the body reveals it to be the same as everything else—unowned, unpossessed by an individual, equal to the furniture or other objects and merely part of all that is. There is nothing personal about the body and no identification with it. It moves about spontaneously, correctly executes its bodily functions, and effortlessly walks and breathes. It is self-propelled and its actions are determined and activated by the Presence. (2002a, 4)

Like Liezi's Master Hua who forgot everything, Hawkins seemed unable to function effectively in the world and, although friends and colleagues urged him to return to his practice, he found little motivation to do so. Living withdrawn and being taken care of by others, he gradually returned to his field, developing a new way of looking at human psychology and suffering. He understood that the origin of emotional sickness lay in people's belief that they *were* their personalities and was the consequence of the illusion of the ego, what medieval Chinese call illusory mental projections. "It was clear that all pain and suffering arises from the ego and not from God," he says (2002b, 340).

Eventually he resumed his clinical practice. Examining patients, he would see to their core with a sense of universal love and sympathy, and they would get better. Effecting almost miraculous cures, his fame spread, and people came from all over the United States. Over the following few years, he built the largest psychiatric practice in New York, with fifty therapists and other employees, treating thousands of patients each year.

In 1983, he had another mystical experience:

> The Presence suddenly intensified until every thing and person, which had appeared separate in ordinary perception, melted into a timeless universality and oneness. In the motionless Silence, I saw that there are no "events or "things" and that nothing actually "happens," because past,

present, and future are merely an artifact of perception, as is the illusion of a separate "I" subject to birth and death.

As the limited, false self dissolved into the universal Self of its true origin, there was an ineffable sense of having returned home, a state of absolute peace and relief from all suffering. For it is only the illusion of individuality that is the origin of all suffering; when one realizes that one is the universe, complete and at one with all that is, forever without end, then no further suffering is possible. (2002a, 297)

Following this, he closed his practice and went into writing and research, founding the Institute for Advanced Spiritual Research and giving lectures around the world.

His outline of the path to advanced spiritual states in many ways resembles the *zuowang* literature of the Tang, just as applied kinesiology matches the key Daoist energy lines and centers in the body and recommends a similar mix of physical, breathing, and meditative practices. Hawkins's outline begins with "one-pointedness of mind, the capacity for concentration and an unwavering fixity of focus," which "requires intense motivation and devotion," a total commitment to the task (2003, 27). It serves to quiet the mind, a "non-stop talking machine with a constant barrage of endless thoughts, ideas, concepts, leanings, memories, plans, apprehensions, doubts, repetitions, and nonsense verses" (2002a, 95-96). Once the mind is calmed, observation can set in, "remaining consistently aware of the totality of one's surroundings, with no focus, interest or selection" (2003, 28). Then again, a deeper level of concentration or one-pointed focus is attained. He compares it to target practice, and notes that it lets all thought stop: "Although the focus may shift from one object to another as required by the activity involved, the quality of absolute attention and focus remains the same" (2003, 29). Either way, the Presence becomes real and the world recedes as one find the ultimate state and lives in spontaneity:

Stilled by the Silence of the Presence, the mind is silent and wordless. No images, concepts, or thoughts occur. There is no one to think them. With no person present, there is neither thinker nor doer. All is happening of itself, as an aspect of the Presence. (2002a, 5)

To sum up, while many of the practices associated with oblivion as an integrated system are still present today—as much as *zuowang* itself is still practiced in Daoist communities—the focus for the most part has shifted toward the more immediate gratification of modern desires: stress release, pain control, healing, and enhanced success and well-being. In addition, there are certain branches of modern science, such as kinesiology and energy medicine, that allow the integration of traditional Daoist views of body and mind into a contemporary scientific framework and are shaping current new developments. Most impressive of all, there are practitioners today—both within and beyond traditional organizations—who are experiencing states that are very much like oblivion and recommend highly similar methods toward their attainment. Daoist sitting in oblivion and other forms of practice, it becomes clear, still have to make valuable contributions to people's lives today.

Translation

Text One

Sitting in Oblivion[1]

Sima Chengzhen

Preface by the Recluse Zhenjing

[DZ 1a] When Heaven and Earth first separated and the three powers took their positions, humanity's place was in the center between Heaven and Earth with the five *qi* coming together to form people's body-self. Therefore they could live long. Later, however, people obscured their inner nature, subdued their spirit, constricted their *qi*, and wasted their essence. For this reason their lives were no longer in harmony with Heaven and Earth; on the contrary, they accepted their crippled shortness [of life] and were sweet in their hearts about it [*Zuozhuan* 左傳 (Mr. Zuo's Commentary), Zhuang 9; *Shijing* 詩經 (Book of Odes), Ode 62]. I always feel intense pain about this state.

---

[1] The following translation is based on the edition in DZ 1036, but occasional recourse has been taken to its variant in *Yunji qiqian* [abbr. YQ] 94. The latter version is also found in *Quan Tangwen* 924. In case of discrepancies, I have preferred the YQ version and indicated it in a note.

Generally, the DZ numeration of the seven steps does not appear in the YQ. The YQ regularly substitutes the final particle *er* 耳 for *er* 爾 and often has the demonstrative *ci* 此 instead of *si* 斯. It also always inserts *gu* 故 before a quotation, and says *Zhuangzi yue* 莊子曰 rather than *Zhuang yue* 莊曰.

References to texts cited are placed in brackets in the text. Abbreviations include "DDJ" for *Daode jing*, "XSJ" for *Xisheng jing*, and "ZZ" for *Zhuangzi*. References to the letter follow *A Concordance to Chuang-tzu*, Harvard-Yenching Institute Sinological Index Series, Supplement no. 20 (Cambridge, Mass.: Harvard University Press, 1956).

The *Yijing* says: "By penetrating universal order and realizing one's inner nature one can fulfill one's original destiny" [*Shuogua* 1]. The *Daode jing* has: "The sage keeps his mind empty and his belly full" [3]. And "Let there always be no desires so that the wondrous can be observed" [1]. The *Lunyu* states: "There were four things that the master wholly eschewed: he took nothing for granted, he was never over-positive, never obstinate, and never egoistic" [9.4]. The *Mengzi* says: "People's inner nature is good" [3A.1]. And "I am good at nourishing my flood-like *qi*" [2A.2]. All these quotations illustrate how important inner nature and original destiny are.

Now, after having reviewed the books of the repository, I obtained the *Zuowang lun* in seven sections and one appendix by Master Zhenyi of the Tang. As the author's understanding and viewpoint are extraordinary indeed, he clarifies Dao very well. **[1b]** First he leads the reader to feel "respect and faith" so that his mind may be no longer in mad confusion. The he makes him "break off his karmic conditions" and factors, "tame his mind," and "detach himself from affairs" so that he can be serene in his physical structure and illuminated within. By the next step of "perfect observation" of center and periphery, being and nonbeing, he can then step into the "stability of cosmic peace," where the *qi* is peaceful and the spirit stable. Thus it is called "attaining Dao."

The items listed here are the steps of sitting in oblivion, gradually lead practitioners to complete oblivion. Yet generally speaking this is none other than a state of no-things, no "I," a state when not even a single thought arises. As clearly stated under "Respect and Faith": "On the inside unaware of one's body-self, on the outside not knowing there is a universe. Merged in oneness with Dao, the myriad plans and worries are all gone."

Carefully selecting and arranging the words of the scriptures, the author avoids discrepancies and carelessness. Rather, he meticulously sets forth the subtleties of sitting in oblivion. Spirit and *qi* spontaneously guard one another, they keep the hundred arteries moist and glossy and the three passes open and free.[2] Thus the perfect *qi* of heavenly yang comes to stay in the body-self. This is the untransmitted Dao of "long life and eternal vision" [DDJ 59]. Highly venerated spirit immortals of antiquity and modern times, being distressed that worldly people do not attain this, have always felt compelled to speak up. Students should thus calmly ponder and thoroughly consider their words, practicing ever so diligently. **[2a]** Never should they regard them as "the mere chaff and dregs of men of old" [ZZ 36/13/70] and thereby only gain the ridicule of having wasted their efforts.

---

[2] Arteries and passes are essential for the flow of *qi* through the body. See *Huangting neijing jing* 18:1, comm.

In the year *dingwei* [767], on the 9th day of the 9th month, when this text was carved in wood, the Recluse Zhenjing respectfully wrote this preface.[3]

Author's Preface[4]

[YQ 1a] What people esteem is life, and what life esteems is Dao. "People are in Dao like fish are in water" [ZZ 18/26/7]. Fish in a dried-up rut still long for a pitcher of water just as people having "lost their perfect home" [ZZ 6/2/79, 18/6/72] unconsciously strive for Dao. They hate the sufferings of life and death [*samsāra*] yet love its activity. They esteem words of Dao and inherent potency yet disregard their practice. Delighted by colors and flavors, they think they attain their will; demeaning stillness and plainness, they think of them as extreme disgrace. Exhausting themselves for "hard-to-get goods " [DDJ 3], they trade in the good fortune of their future life. Giving free rein to easily defiling passions, they destroy the Dao of their body-self. They call themselves wise and skillful, but in fact they live in nothing but a dream, a delusion. [1b] They come with life and go with death, revolving through the [rebirth] cycle for a myriad kalpas. One can only call them "upside-down" [ZZ 42/16/21]. Is there anything more preposterous?

Thus the *Miaozhen jing* 妙真經 [Scripture of Wondrous Perfection] says: "Human beings always lose Dao; Dao never loses them. Human beings constantly reject life, life never rejects them. Nourishing life therefore means being careful not to lose Dao. Practicing Dao means being careful not to lose life. This way one causes life and Dao to guard and preserve each other, making sure the two never get separated. Thus one can live long" [DZ 25, not found]. When it speaks of "live long," it means attaining the material base of Dao.

The *Scripture* has: "Life is the great potency of Heaven, the great happiness of Earth, the great good fortune of humanity" [unclear]. If a person of Dao

---

[3] Zhenjing could refer to the female Daoist Jiao Jingzhen 焦靜真 who, like the 13th patriarch Li Hanguang 李含光 (683-769), was a key disciple of Sima Chengzhen. According to her biography in YQ 16.5a, she once had a vision of a deity who directed her to meet her destined teacher. The story is also found in Sima's biography (DZ 296, 25.9ab).

[4] This preface also appears in the DZ, but in an abridged version, including the first paragraph and last two sentences, plus one additional sentence: "Upon properly investigating something, one's thoughts go usually straight, but when deluded they run around in circles. As time in its shortness always seems to be as eternal as a jade disk, my feelings of shame and regret now grow constantly deeper."

achieves it, this is not merely due to an allotment of destiny. As the *Xisheng jing* states: "My life is my own. It does not depend on Heaven" [ch. 26].[5]

Seen from this angle, the length of life depends on oneself: it is neither attained as a gift from Heaven nor lost through theft by people. Examining my heart, I regret that it is already late and that time cannot be detained. I deplore the short "years of the morning mushroom" [ZZ 1/1/10] and that I have already passed beyond fifty. I still have not yet mastered the central points of returning to Dao. [2a] As time is passing fast like a burning candle, I have made an effort to search the scriptures for passages with simple matter and straightforward meaning, easy to carry out practically and appropriate for spiritual sicknesses. Thus I wrote a concise treatise on the method of calming the mind and sitting in oblivion. I arranged it in seven sections, giving successive steps of cultivating Dao, together with an appendix on the central methods of its realization.

1. Respect and Faith

[DZ 1b] Faith is the root of Dao, respect is the stem of inherent potency. When the root is deep, Dao can grow tall, when its stem is strong, potency can flourish. However, though his gem gleamed with a brilliance worth a succession of cities, Bian He was brought to the point of punishment by loss of a limb. And though his words disclosed a plan for preserving the state of Wu, Wu Zixu went on to be executed.[6] In these cases, only the outer form was clear, while the mental inner structure was blurred. The plans of Bian He and Wu Zixu were straightforward, but the passions and thoughts of the kings were confused.

Utmost Dao goes so far beyond sensual perception, perfect inner nature is so far apart from anything one might desire, that it is impossible to "hear the inaudible, perceive the subtle" and believe one's senses, to "listen to the formless, recognize the symbolic," and not be perplexed.[7] If someone thus has heard words [YQ: methods] of sitting in oblivion, has faith in the central points of Daoist cultivation, respects and reveres them, and is determined and without doubt, moreover pursues his practice with utmost diligence, then he will certainly attain Dao.

---

[5] This statement first appears in *Baopuzi* 16 and is also found in Wu Yun's *Xingshen kegu lun* (DZ 1051, 2.23a) as from the *Guijia jing* 龜甲經 (Turtleshell Scripture).

[6] Bian He 卞和 presented an uncut gem to two rulers of Chu who both punished him with foot amputation before they recognized his sincerity and the value of the jewel. Later there was an offer to exchange fifty cities for it (*Hanfeizi* 12). Wu Zixu 伍子胥 offered the King of Wu advice which would have saved it from being absorbed by Yue. Instead, the king ordered Wu to commit suicide (*Shiji* 66).

[7] The two citations refer to DDJ 3, 12, 14 and ZZ 49/19/43.

The *Zhuangzi* says: "I smash up my limbs and physical structure, drive out perception and intellect, cast off body-form, do away with knowledge, and become one with Great Pervasion. This is what I mean by sitting in oblivion" [19/6/92]. [Guo Xiang adds:] "Practicing this oblivion, what would there remain unforgotten? On the inside unaware of one's body-self, on the outside never knowing there is a universe" [DZ 745, 8.39b]. Merged in oneness with Dao, the myriad plans and worries are all gone. [2a]

When Zhuang Zhou therefore speaks of becoming identical with Great Pervasion, these words may seem shallow, but their meaning is very profound. A deluded person will hear them but not believe them. How can he ever practice? Thus the *Daode jing* says: "It is only when one does not have enough faith in others that others will have no faith in oneself" [17, 23]. In our context this means that when faith in Dao is insufficient there will be the misfortune of distrust. On such a basis how could one ever aspire to Dao?

2. Interception of Karma

Interception of karma means eliminating the karmic conditions of action and worldly affairs. By abandoning affairs, the body-form is no longer labored; by resting in nonaction the mind finds peace of itself. Thus stillness and leisure will increase daily, while defilements and entanglements will diminish every day. The further one's traces are away from the ordinary world, the closer the mind approaches Dao. How could "utmost saintliness" [ZZ 24/10/90] and utmost spirit not begin with this? Thus the *Daode jing* says: "Cut off contacts, shut the doors, and to the end of life there will be peace without toil" [52, 56].

Now, there are people who show off their inherent potency and exhibit their skills, seeking to become others' protégés. Some call on people to congratulate or condole in order to foster social relations. Others feign [YQ: cultivate] a retired life while secretly yearning for promotion and advancement. **[2b]** Yet others freely distribute wines and foods in the expectation of future rewards. All these are accumulations of craftiness, "mechanical minds" [ZZ 31/12/56], only concerned with temporary profits. This is not at all in accordance with Dao, but rather obstructs right action [*samyakkarmānta*]. All behavior like this has to be given up completely. As the *Daode jing* puts it: "Go ahead, open up contacts and meddle with affairs—to the end of life there will be no salvation" [52].

"If I don't sing, then others won't fall in with me" [DDJ 22, 66]. And even if others are singing, then I just don't join them. This way old karmic conditioning will gradually dissolve and no new conditions will build up. Intoxicated partying and formal assemblies naturally will be less interesting day by day. Free from affairs and in peaceful leisure one can finally cultivate Dao. The *Zhuangzi* says: "Go after nothing, welcome nothing" [21/7/32]. [YQ: This means that] one should not get emotionally entangled in social relations. It also has: "Do not be an embodier of fame, do not be a storehouse of schemes, do not be an undertaker of projects, do not be a proprietor of wisdom" [21/7/31].

On the other hand, if there are affairs one has to take care of, do not deal with them egoistically but make sure you don't, because of them, give rise to love and mental entanglements, thus producing further karma.

3. Taming the Mind

The mind is the master of the body-self, the master of the hundred spirits.[8] When still it gives rise to insight, when agitated to confusion. [3a] Delightedly straying in delusions and projected reality, it speaks of obligation and greatly enjoys to be in the midst of action. Who would awaken to see this as empty and wrong?

Yet, as one realizes one's derangement of mind and consciousness being largely due to one's place of residence, one chooses a new neighborhood and goes to live there. This is already a great improvement. By a careful choice of friends one will profit even more. How much more should this process apply when the body-self leaves the realm of birth and death and the mind comes to reside in the center of perfect Dao? Without giving up the former, how could one ever attain the latter?

Therefore, when one first begins to study Dao one must sit calmly and tame the mind, let go of projected reality and abide in nonexistence [*avidyamāna*]. As one abides in nonexistence, without being attached to even one being, one naturally enters emptiness and nonbeing. Thus one joins Dao. The *Scripture* says: "The center of utmost Dao is serenity and nonexistence, where spirit is without bent and so are mind and physical structure. By going to the deepest source of mind and physical structure, one finds their root is Dao."[9]

On the other hand, when one lets one's mind and spirit become defiled, if the obscuring overgrowth becomes thicker and wilder day by day, then one is moving away from Dao. Rather, [YQ: having the ability of] scrubbing away the defilements of the mind, opening up consciousness of [YQ: insight into] the root

---

[8] See *Shijing*, Odes 252, 273; *Liji*, "Lijun." As body gods, they appear in the *Huangting jing* and *Laozi zhongjing*.

[9] Citation unclear. The YQ reads: "Thus the scripture speaks of 'perfect Dao.' Therefore enter the essential stillness of being, and spirit will be 'without bent'." The latter expression is from the *Zhuangzi* (44/17/44).

of spirit is what we call cultivating Dao. No more unsteady floating [through the realms of rebirth]—but "mystical harmony with Dao" [*Huainanzi* 7.1a]. **[3b]** Resting calmly within Dao is called "returning to the root" [DDJ 16]. Guarding the root and never leaving it is called stillness and stability.

When these increase daily, diseases are dispersed and original destiny is recovered. Continuous recovery leads to spontaneous knowledge of the eternal. "Knowledge" here means that nothing is left unilluminated, "eternal" means that nothing changes or perishes anymore. Any escape from the cycle of birth and death only comes from this. Following Dao and calming the mind therefore ultimately depend on freedom from attachment. As the *Daode jing* has it: "All things flourish, but each returns to its root. This return to the root means stillness, it is called recovering original destiny. Recovering original destiny is called the eternal, and to know the eternal is called brightness" [16].

Yet again, any hold on one's mind while abiding in emptiness means that there is still some place, and this cannot be called nowhere. Whenever one abides in some place, one causes the mind to be labored [YQ: and the breath to speed up]. Consequently it is not united with universal order, but on the contrary will keep producing disease. Only a mind fully detached from all things and in a state of immobility can be the proper foundation of perfect stability. Stability on such a basis will make mind and *qi* work harmoniously, and, in the long run, lightness and alacrity will increase. Only then one will be able to distinguish the "proper from the wayward" [XSJ 7]. When all mental arising is annihilated and no more difference is made between "right and wrong" [ZZ 2], one can forever discard awareness and knowledge and enter the state of blind stability. **[4a]**

However, if one gives free rein to all mental arising and does not attempt to tame and control it, then one is not really different from ordinary people. If one only annihilates the judgment of good and evil without giving the mind a direction for return, lets it float and wander around in dissolution and relies on stability to come naturally, one only deceives oneself. On the other hand, if one goes on attending to all one's affairs and yet claims to be free from defilements, then this reveals great goodness [YQ: beauty] in words, but highest [YQ: strong] error in deeds. All serious students should therefore be especially warned against this. The key here is to put confusion to rest without destroying the radiating mind, to guard stillness without getting attached to emptiness. Practicing like this continually will bring about the natural attainment of perfect vision.

If there is some ongoing affair to attend to or some important doubt about the method, one should rely on intelligent reasoning to resolve the situation or allay one's doubts. This will enhance awakening. It will also give rise to insight and further strengthen the basis of practice. Once awakening is reached, one must not produce thoughts any longer.[10] This is because thoughts will cause wisdom to harm stillness, i.e., make the offshoot injure the root. Though one may hasten to gain an hour's superiority, one will thereby get involved with another myriad generations of karma.

Any confused deviance or disturbing fantasy should be eliminated as soon as one becomes aware of it. [4b] Upon hearing slander or praise, or anything good or bad, one should just radically cut it all out and not admit it into the mind at all. This is because if anything is taken in, the mind will be full. With a full mind, Dao has no place to go. Whatever one may see or hear, it should be like one had not seen or heard at all. Then right and wrong, good and evil cannot enter the mind.

When the mind does not receive anything from the outside, we call it an empty mind. When it does not pursue anything on the outside, we call it a mind at peace. In a mind at peace that is always kept empty Dao will come to stay of itself. As the *Neiguan jing* has it: "To someone who can maintain an empty mind and nonaction, even without wishing for Dao, Dao will return of itself" [5a]. On the inside there is nothing the mind is attached to, on the outside there is nothing one would actively do. One is no longer pure or defiled, which is why slander and praise no longer arise. One is neither wise nor ignorant, which is why profit and loss no longer appear. If things are fixed one remains constant within their order. If circumstances are shifting one moves with the times. Such is the basic wisdom of avoiding attachments.

However, if someone at improper times and in inappropriate situations subdues his thinking and acts forcefully, yet calls himself unattached, then he is not really a student of perfection [YQ: truly aware]. Why? Well, the mind is like the eyes.[11] When only a tiny speck of dust enters them, they are no longer still. Likewise when a minor affair concerns the mind, it becomes agitated and confused. And once there is the disease of agitation, it is very difficult to enter a state of stability. [5a] Therefore the central point in cultivating Dao lies in the extinction of such diseases. As long as they are not eradicated any real stability of mind remains hard to attain.

It is just like a fertile field. As long as thorns and brambles are not cut down, one can sow as many seeds as one wants, but fresh shoots will not grow. Love, sight, thoughts, and worries are the thorns and brambles of the mind. As long as they are not cut down, stability and insight cannot grow. Again, as long as one lives in wealth and high esteem or is a scholar of the classics and histories, one may very well speak with "compassion and restraint" [DDJ 67], but one's

---

[10] YQ: "Once the affair is settled, it is over. No need to have many thoughts" (5a).
[11] See Wu Yun's essay below.

actions will be full of greed and oppressiveness. Eloquent enough to disguise falseness, powerful enough to awe others, someone like this will credit successes entirely to himself, while blaming all failures on others. A disease like this is very serious and study alone will not help. Its underlying cause is self-righteousness. [12]

As the mind has always been in the realm of dependence, it is entirely unaccustomed to standing alone. If it suddenly finds itself without support, it will hardly feel peaceful in itself. Though then peace may be found for a short time, the mind will fall back again into vagueness and confusion. Whatever arises in the mind must be controlled, one must by all means bring it to a state of immobility. Then—after a long time—it will eventually comply and naturally attain peace and repose. Independent of day or night, of walking, standing, sitting, lying down, or attending to one's duties, one must constantly remain intent of keeping the mind at peace. **[5b]** Once the mind is established in stability, it [YQ: merely] has to be nourished calmly. As there are no more irritations or arousals and as one has attained a minor level of stability, a feeling of spontaneous happiness will arise. Very gradually the mind becomes compliant and docile, always increasing in [YQ: aware of] limpidity and remoteness. What it loved dearly [YQ: valued highly] in its worldly life, it now resents as low and vulgar [YQ: superfluous]. How much closer, as stability has arisen and insight deepened, has it come to distinguish between perfect and apparent reality?

Oxen and horses are domestic animals. When they are left to themselves and not tamed, they soon develop stubbornness and never accept being harnessed and used for chariots [*Neiguan jing* 2b]. Goshawks and merlins are wild birds, but if they are tied and fettered by people, close to the hand every day, they naturally get used to it. How much more than these does the mind, when allowed to run wild and not controlled, increase in coarseness and crassness? How could it ever be able to "observe the wondrous" [DDJ 1]? As the *Daode jing* puts it: "Rather than present large pieces of jade preceded by teams of four horses, one should kneel and offer this Dao" [62].

However, the subtleties of the technique are found only upon practice. They do not show in one's ability to talk but only in how good one's practice is. Once one engages in the practice, words regarding Dao are understood properly, but as long as one does not practice, they merely sound foolish. Our contemporaries in their studies value the difficult and scorn the easy. When someone discourses on [YQ: profoundly discusses] the technique, and at that occasion

---

[12] This echoes the *Benji jing* (DH 42, 5.53 and 115-25; Ōfuchi 1979, 319-320). The text describes self-righteousness as seeing oneself with an ego-centered mind and notes that the mina fault of such thinking lies in conceiving of goodness as right and of evil as wrong or vice versa, i.e., having any kind of fixed opinion.

elaborates on emptiness and nonbeing as that which thoughts and ideas can
never reach, which even practical application cannot make accessible **[6a]**, they
sigh and say that they cannot comprehend it, acknowledge their inferiority and
show their deepest respects.

On the other hand, when someone speaks "perfect words that are not beautiful" [DDJ 81], points straight to the object and explains things clearly [YQ:
makes his plea] in a way that the audience can understand him and follow his
instructions, then this is really amazing. But people will turn away considering it
shallow and simplistic and, with an attitude of contempt and indifference, [13]will
not believe it. As the *Daode jing* says: "My words are very easy to understand
and very easy to follow in practice. None in the whole world can understand or
practice them. It is because people do not understand this that they do not understand me" [70].

Again, there are those who maintain that fire is not hot or that a lamp does not
shine. They find wonderful meaning in this. Now, fire has heating as its function and a lamp has the effect of illuminating the dark. But these people talk at
any length about fire being not hot—yet they dispense with heating not even
for a moment. [YQ: They vainly say that] a lamp does not shine in the dark, yet
they certainly have a lamp burning throughout the night. Here words and actions contradict each other, theory and reality do not fit together. Theirs are
merely words negating the reality of the phenomenal world, but people—quite
to the contrary—regard it as a profound mystery. Even such an eminent dialec-
tician as Huizi was regarded by Master Zhuang as unbearable [ZZ 33]. Who of
these ignoramuses would ever be able to radically cut out such arguments? Students of perfection must never mind them! **[6b]**

Moreover, some people say that great Dao is attained by living among things,
but never letting one's mind be defiled, by remaining within active life without
ever confusing one's spirit. There is "nothing that is not done" [DDJ 48]; there
is no moment without serenity. On the other hand, if one now avoids affairs
and prefers repose, leaves the active life and pursues stability, one will take
great pains to remain in control. There will be a dichotomy of agitation and
repose, and one will be hampered by the effort of holding on to one state of
mind, thereby giving rise to the disease of accepting one and rejecting another
without ever being aware of any [DZ: outward] entanglement. Despite of this,
one will say that one has attained some stage of Dao. What a terrible hypocrisy
is this?

But I answer: What unites all things is called great. What pervades all things is
called Dao. Verily, remaining among things without defilements, living in the
world without being agitated, this truly is great! This is fully subtle! But I say

---

[13] The first part of this sentence is not contained in the YQ.

that your mirror, Sir, is not entirely clear. Why? Because you see only the gleam of pearly brocades, but are not aware of the plain silk threads it was originally made from. You only hear the cry of the crane soaring into the sky, but do you know that it was formerly provided for with regurgitated food? A tree trunk obscuring the sun grows from a wispy twig. Similarly the saintliness of a stable spirit comes from accumulation of practice. **[7a]**

Now, it is vain to learn to speak of sagely potency and not know what the sage considers his potency to be. This might be called "seeing an egg and seeking a rooster; seeing a crossbow pellet and seeking a roast dove" [ZZ 6/2/76]. Why such a flurry? The *Daode jing* says: "Mysterious potency becomes deep and far-reaching, and with it all things return to their original natural state. Then complete harmony is reached" [65].

4. Detachment from Affairs[14]

The life of people is always governed by affairs and things. Affairs and things come in myriads, yet they can be given up by the individual. Thus, nesting on one branch of wood, a bird seems neglectful of the thicket reeds. Drinking a bellyful of water from a river, the beast is not stingy about the flooding billows. On the outside, one should strive for things among others, but on the inside one should "clarify one's needs to oneself" [ZZ 62/23/35]. Knowing that life has allotments, one should not be concerned with what one is not allotted. Recognizing that affairs have what is appropriate, one should not engage in what is inappropriate for a given situation. When one's affairs are dealt with inappropriately, one harms wisdom and strength. When one's concerns go beyond one's allotments, one suffers in body-form and spirit. **[7b]** If one has no peace within oneself, how could one ever [YQ: aspire to] attain Dao?

Therefore, anyone who is cultivating Dao must gain detachment from affairs and give up things. Knowing what is marginal and what essential about them, he can measure their importance. Recognizing that one has to accept or reject them, he finds no importance or necessity for himself and duly abandons them. For instance, eating meat and drinking wine, dressing in gauzy cloth and fine silk, having a high personal reputation and official position, or possessing fine jades and money are totally superfluous gratifications of passions and desires. These things are not at all good medicines to enhance life. The masses hanker after them and bring death and defeat upon themselves. Coming to think of them calmly, aren't they terrible delusion?

---

[14] The contrast between detachment from affairs (*shijian* 事簡) and entanglement in affairs (*shilei* 事累) is also outlined in detail in *Dadao lun* 20b.

The *Zhuangzi* says: "He who has mastered the perfect nature of destiny does not labor over what destiny cannot do" [48/19/1]. By "what destiny cannot do" are meant the things outside one's allotment. Vegetarian food and old clothes are good enough to nourish [YQ: extend] inner nature and original destiny, so why depend on wine and meat, gauze and silk, and only with them consider life complete? Therefore, whatever is not fundamentally necessary to sustain life has to be given up, and whatever of the necessary things is too many has to be abandoned. Wealth is harmful to the *qi*, and if it accumulates the whole body will suffer. [8a] Even in small quantities it is a worry, how much more so when there is a lot of it? Now, "if one takes the Lord of Sui's pearl to shoot at a thousand fathom high sparrow, some will find this ridiculous" [ZZ 77/28/29; *Huainanzi* 12]. How much more ridiculous, then, is one who turns his back on Dao and inherent potency, disregards inner nature and original destiny, and continues to pursue the unnecessary, thereby causing destruction for himself?

Comparing reputation and position to Dao and potency, one finds the former are false and petty, whereas the latter are perfect and noble. Once one is able to recognize pettiness and nobility, one must accordingly accept or reject them. In any case, one should never let reputation harm one's body-self or position change one's determination [DDJ 44]. The *Zhuangzi* says: "Who enhances his reputation and thereby loses himself is not a perfect knight" [12/6/12]. The *Xisheng jing* has: "I embrace the primordial source and guard the One, go beyond all and attain spirit immortality. You cannot guard it as long as you are still established in honor and official position"[7.13-14]. If one does not gain aloofness and detachment from bondages and affairs, they will exhaust the mind [YQ: body-form] and confuse wisdom. Thus the cultivation of Dao will be neglected. If one lives in the midst of action full of serenity, remains among people without any attachments, then one can count oneself among the accomplished. However, one who has not actually accomplished this and merely talks about not being attached only deceives himself. [8b]

5. Perfect Observation

Perfect observation is the foremost mirror of the knight of wisdom, the quality examination of the people of ability. Probing good and bad fortune which chances to come, divining the blessings and calamities inherent in activity and stillness, he succeeds in seeing ahead of life's motions and arranges his acts accordingly.[15] Deeply praying and maintaining sufficiency [YQ stability], hum-

---

15 This seems rather different from the *Daode jing*, which says: "Foreknowledge is an extraneous ornament of Dao and marks the beginning of stupidity" (38).

bly [YQ: meritoriously] serving the completeness of life, there will never be action in attachment from beginning to end, neither will one's principles contradict one's actions. Then one can speak of "perfect observation."

One bite of food or a wink of sleep usually become the source of some gain or loss, one step forward or one word spoken quite possibly lay the foundation for good and bad fortune. Though one might still cleverly restrain the results, it is much better to stolidly be on one's guard against the origins. By observing the root, the branch is known. However, one must first be free from impatient, struggling emotions. This is why we practice taming the mind and detachment from affairs. Daily diminish outward actions, bring the physical structure to stillness, and let the mind rest in leisure: then you can truly observe [YQ: and envision] the wondrous [YQ: cosmic order of perfection]. As the *Daode jing* has it: "Let there always be no desires so that the wondrous may be observed" [1].

Nevertheless, even while cultivating Dao the body-self must be provided with food and clothing, there are affairs that cannot be given up or things one cannot leave alone. Those have to be cared about with humility and should be attended to with clear perception. Don't let them become an obstruction or allow your mind give rise to anger and impatience. **[9a]** As soon as you give rise to anger and impatience because of some affair [YQ: you see affairs as affairs], the mind will be sick with agitation. How then can it be called a mind at peace?

All human affairs, all food and clothing of people are merely a boat. If I want to cross an ocean, I need a boat. After the passage is completed, the reason for the boat is no longer there.[16] But why should one abandon it before even having gone on the voyage? Food and clothing in themselves are empty illusion and without actual value. But as a means to free oneself from empty illusion, one must obtain provision with food and clothing. One should therefore never have any feelings of gain or loss about them. Whether involved in affairs or free from affairs, the mind should be constantly calm and at peace![17] Join others in seeking but not in coveting, in attaining but not in hoarding. No coveting means being free from worry; no hoarding means never experiencing loss. In deeds be like others, but in mind always remain aloof [*Huainanzi* 1.11b; DDJ 65]. This really is the most essential point of practice. Work on it very hard!

Despite a growing detachment from affairs there might still be some disease hard to eradicate. In that case just rely on the divine law and observe it. For example, you may suffer from a strong case of sensual involvement: observe

---

[16] This echoes the Buddhist parable of the raft found in the *Mādhimanikaya*. See Horner 1977, 1:173-74.

[17] This echoes a similar statement in the *Dingguan jing*: "Whether involved in affairs or free from affairs, constantly maintain no-mind!" The expression used here is *antai*, which literally means of "inner and cosmic peace."

the fact that all defiling sensuality arises merely from your imagination. If you do not allow imagination to arise, there cannot be any sensuality. Understand therefore that sensual imaginings are empty on the outside while sensual feelings are mere delusion within. **[9b]** As they are nothing but deluded feelings and empty imaginings, who would be the master of sensuality? The *Dingzhi jing* 定志經 [Scripture on Stabilizing the Will] says: "Sensuality is entirely imaginative. All imagination is ultimately empty. How can there be something like sensuality?"[DZ 325, 2b].

Also, consider that the beautiful sensuality of attractive women is even more dangerous than that of fox fairies. When fox fairies seduce men they arouse loathing and distress, hence at the death of the body-self they do not fall into the bad realms [of rebirth]. Loathing and distress keep them forever away from waywardness and debauchery. Human beauties, however, beguile men, make them fall in love and get attached to them. To the end of their lives in this body-self they hanker after them and get deeply steeped in wayward thoughts, then—after death—proceed to fall into the hells. [YQ: Forever they will have turned away from birth in the realm of people and from the road to happiness]. The *Shangpin jing* 上品經 [Scripture of the Highest Rank] says: "Why is it that people of one mind and joined as husband and wife in this world after death do not attain the human state together again? It is because of depraved thoughts" [DZ 344, 2a].

Then again, why—if sensual attraction ultimately comes down to beauty—do fish upon seeing such beauty enter deeper into the water, and birds fly off into the sky?[18] Immortals recognize sensuality as defilement and [energetic] turbidity, wise ones compare it to knives and axes of punishment.[19] In the couse of a destined life on earth, not eating for seven days will cause death, but a hundred years without sensuality will avert untimely departure. **[10a]** See, then, that sensuality is not essential or appropriate for the body-self or the mind, but an enemy and thief to inner nature and original destiny. Why must you be subject to entanglement and attachment, yourself inviting calamity and destruction?

To see another do evil and give rise to enmity and hatred in one's own mind is just like seeing someone kill himself and promptly stick out one's own neck to accept the other's blade and get killed oneself. The other person commits evil by himself, he does not ask me to do likewise. Why then should I reach out to take in another's negativity and make myself sick? If one can feel enmity upon seeing someone perform evil, then one must also react with negativity upon

---

[18] See *Zhuangzi* 1 (Watson 1968, 46) for these and other examples of the same idea, that beauty is in the eye of the beholder.

[19] This reflects a statement commonly found in medieval longevity literature about sensory involvement and excesses. See Kohn 2010, 7-8, 11.

seeing someone do good. Why is that so? Because in both cases Dao is obstructed.

Now, if one suffers from poverty, one should observe this and ask, "who made me poor?" Heaven and Earth are equable and regular, protecting and supporting without personal aims. So if I am poor now, it is certainly not the fault of Heaven and Earth. When parents give birth to a child, they desire to see him in wealth and high esteem. So if I am poor now I cannot blame it on my parents. Other men, ghosts, and spirits don't even have the time to save themselves, how then would they have the strength to make me poor? Going back and forth, I cannot find anyone to blame for my poverty. Thus I cannot help but realize that it must be my own karma, my own Heaven-given destiny [ZZ 19/6/95-96]. **[10b]**

I produce my own karma, whereas Heaven provides me with the destiny of this life. Karma relates to destiny like shadow and echo follow form and sound.[20] They are not to be avoided or resented in any way. Only one who has wisdom can master them with skill. Delighting in Heaven and understanding destiny, there will be no need to lament over any eventual suffering through poverty.[21] Therefore the *Zhuangzi* says: "Karma enters and cannot avoided: it is your own karma."[22] Thus if poverty and diseases come, they cannot be stopped. The *Scripture* says: "Heaven and Earth cannot alter their routine, yin and yang cannot revert their tasks [*ye*]" [unclear]. Judging the matter from this angle, we know that one has a perfect destiny, not a mere mask. How could one resent it?

The situation we find ourselves in can be compared to the encounter of a brave knight with a band of brigands. Never feeling dread or fear, he brandishes his sword and rushes to the battlefront, fighting until the robbers flee. Having thus gained merit in his service, he is gloriously rewarded for the rest of his life. If now there are poverty and diseases, irritations and troubles in my life, then these are my robbers and brigands. With an upright mind I can be a brave knight. Examining them in wisdom and by observation I brandish my sword.[23] The battle is won when all irriatations and entanglements are eliminated. To be luminous and constantly happy—this is the glorious reward. **[11a]** But often,

---

[20] YQ: "Karma and destiny are basically like shadow and echo" (11a). On shadow and echo as being closely connected to form and sound, see *Liezi* 1.

[21] YQ: "One who has wisdom can follow his karma and act benevolently, delighting in Heaven and never even aware of the possibility that he might suffer from poverty" (11a).

[22] 13/23/47. The original text, of course, would not speak of "karma." Watson translates *ye* as "outside concerns" (1968, 255).

[23] The sword is a metaphor for insight, common in Buddhism. See *Dazhi dulun* 大智度論 (*Prajñāpāramitā śastra*, T. 25.169a). For more on swords in Daoism, see Fukunaga 1973; Schafer 1979.

when suffering or affairs come to harass us, the mind instead of using the method of observation gives rise to worry and anxiety. This then is like an encounter with brigands when one rather than gaining merit in service casts off one's weapons and turns one's back on the battlefield. One duly has to bear the guilt of desertion and defeat. Thereby one rejects happiness and invites suffering—how could there be empathy?

If there is suffering or disease, one should first understand through observation that it originates in the fact that one has a body-self. Without a body-self the vexations would have no place to dwell. As the *Daode jing* states: "If I had no body-self, what vexations would I have?" [13]. Next you should turn to observe the mind and find that there is no perfect lord. Even though you search for him inside out, "you can't find him anywhere" [ZZ 4/2/15]. All plans and thoughts arise only from a deluded mind. Thus when one "makes one's body like dried wood and one's mind like dead ashes" [ZZ 3/2/2] all the various diseases are eradicated.

Someone who is horrified by death, for example, should think of his "body-self as the lodge of spirit."[24] Thus as the body-self grows old and sick, as *qi* and strength decline day by day, it will just be like a house with rotting walls. Once it becomes uninhabitable, it is best to abandon it and look for another place to stay. The death of the body-self and the departure of spirit are then a mere change of residence. However, when "one hankers after life and loathes death," resisting the "natural transformations,"[25] one's spirit and consciousness will be confused and let into error, losing their right action [*samyakkarmanta*]. **[11b]** As a result, when one is entrusted to life again and receives the constituting *qi*, one will not lean toward the pure and refined, but end up with much turbid and disgraceful *qi*. Generally all those stupid and dull, dumb and greedy come into being like this.[26]

Only if one does not feel exhilarated when alive or full of aversion when facing death can one attain the equality of life and death and thereby produce good karma for the body-selves to come. By greedily craving for a myriad aspects of projected reality, on the other hand, one will end up with love and disease alternating. If even one limb is sick, the whole physical structure is in discomfort

---

[24] This is a common statement in traditional Daoist literature, e.g. ZZ 18/6/79; *Huainanzi* 2.2b; *Xisheng jing* 17.5.

[25] These two citations come from ZZ 10/4/44, 15/6/8, 49/19/35 and 17/6/45.

[26] See ZZ 42/17/9. The *Huainanzi* lists a series of different energies constituting basic tempers and dispositions (ch. 3), which is next taken up in Wang Chong's 王充 *Lunheng* 論 衡 (Balanced Discussions) (Forke 1972, 1:381). In a Daoist context, the same idea appears in Du Guangting's *Yongsheng jixian lu* (DZ 783): "A person of pure *qi* is clever, alert, wise, and intelligent. A person of turbid *qi* is unlucky, harsh, dumb, and foolish.(1.5b; Kohn 1989b, 92).

and unrest, how much more so when the one mind is full of myriads of diseases? Desiring eternal life in one body-self—how is possible? All craving and aversion arise from delusion. By accumulating delusion instead of expelling it one will obscure the vision of Dao. Thus relinquish all desires and abide in nonexistence! Be placid, pure, and well-rooted [YQ: cast off all desires and maintain a straightforward mind], and only then turn to observation! Whatever you loved before will now only cause weariness and disdain.

But if you try to observe projected reality with a mind attached to projected reality, you can never be aware of your negativities to the end of your days. Only with a mind utterly detached from projected reality can you observe projected reality itself and reach a perfect understanding of right and wrong. The process can be compared to a sobered man who now can see the drunkard's evil deeds the wrong of which he was totally unaware of as long as he was drunk himself.[27] The *Shengxuan jing* says: "I uproot and cast off worldly life and give up the world completely" [XSJ 7.12].[28] [12a] The *Xisheng jing* states: "Eyes and ears, sound and color keep one always in a state of tension. . .. Thus I cast off the ordinary, reject and leave the common world" [7.8, 12]. Accordingly Lord Lao gave up the world and cast off worldly life. Realizing now that smell and taste are to be given up as nothing but a steady flow of craving and desires, how could one regard the fishmonger's shop as stinking?

6. Stability of Cosmic Peace

The stability of cosmic peace is the ultimate point of leaving worldly life and the first firm foothold of reaching Dao. It represents merit perfected in the practice of stillness and is the end to affairs through attainment of inner peace. The body-form like dried wood, the mind like dead ashes, there are no more impulses, no more searches. One has reached the perfect contemplative state of serenity. With no-mind one settles in stability, thus there is nothing that is not stable. The *Zhuangzi* says: "He whose inner being rests in the stability of cosmic peace will spread a heavenly radiance" [63/23/41]. Here "resting" refers to the mind, whereas "heavenly radiance" means insight coming forth. The mind is the vessel of Dao. When this is utterly empty and still, Dao can reside there and

---

[27] This evaluation of drunkenness rather conforms to the Buddhist usage of the metaphor. The *Zhuangzi*, on the other hand, sees drunkenness as comparable to the state of oblivion, the ideal mental state of the sage. It gives the example of the "drunken man who falls off a carriage," but remains unhurt because his mind is utterly "unknowing" (48/19/12; Watson 1968, 198).

[28] The *Shengxuan jing* and the *Xisheng jing* are often cited interchangeably in medieval texts. See *Xiaodao lun* 笑道論 (Laughing at the Dao, T. 52. .143c-152c), sect. 34 (Kohn 1995, 146). The same statement also appears in *Daojiao yishu* 1.7a.

insight arises. This insight comes from inner nature and does not depend on present circumstances. Thus we call it "heavenly radiance." **[12b]**

However, if greed and love disturb and confuse it, there will be only darkness and delusion. By cleansing the mind to "snow-white clarity" [ZZ 58/22/29] and by softly stretching it out, one recovers purity and returns to stillness. The spirit and consciousness of original perfection softly and gradually comes to shine of itself. This is not to say that at that moment an entirely alien insight is born. Rather, it is an insight arising from one's very self and as such it should be held very precious.

One should never jeopardize stability by too much knowledge. It is generally not difficult to give rise to insight, but very hard indeed not to use it. Ever since, people who forgot their body-form were numerous, but those who forgot their reputation were few. And having insight without using it means to forget all about one's reputation. Rarely have people like that been found in the world. Thus we say it is hard to practice this. Being noble without pride, rich without indulgence in luxury is not tempting worldly luck.[29] People like that are able to keep their wealth and high esteem for a long time. Remaining in stability without movement, full of insight without using it is not tempting Dao. It allows the attainment of deep purity and perfect constancy. The *Zhuangzi* says: "To know Dao is easy--to keep from speaking about it is hard. To know and not to speak, this gets you to the heavenly part. To know and to speak, this gets you to the human part. Men of old looked out for the heavenly, not for the human" [89/32/17].

By insight one can know Dao but one cannot attain it. People know the advantages of gaining insight, but they don't know the benefit of attaining Dao. **[13a]** Whereas insight illuminates universal order, lively argumentation is only used to influence the feelings of others. The mind is stimulated and involved in affairs and thus grows ever more attached to categories. Yet someone may say: 'I am in the midst of all this activity, yet I remain constantly serene.' How can there be understanding of serenity as long as it still depends on things? Such an attitude and such claims have nothing in common with the stability of cosmic peace. Such wisdom, though certainly beyond the ordinary, is yet nowhere near Dao. It is like setting out with the intention of hunting a deer and returning only with a hare, a very insignificant catch: crooked and petty!

The *Zhuangzi* says: "Those of ancient times who practiced Dao employed tranquility to nourish wisdom. Wisdom arose, yet they did nothing for its sake. So

---

[29] "Tempting" translates *guo* 過, lit. "go beyond." In other words exceeding the limits of one's allotment and destiny. The statement echoes DDJ 9: "To be proud with nobility and wealth is to cause one's own downfall." The idea is prominent in later writers, notably Guo Xiang and Sun Simiao.

they may be said to have employed wisdom to nourish tranquility. Wisdom and tranquility took turns nourishing each other, and harmony and universal order emerged from inner nature" [41/16/1]. What Zhuangzi here calls "tranquility and wisdom" is stability and insight. "Harmony and universal order" are Dao and inherent potency. By having wisdom and not using it, by calmly resting in stillness, thus strengthening it over a long period, Dao and potency will naturally be perfected.

But let us ask: By what actions does one attain this stability? On the one hand, whenever you recognize an advantage, make sure you always note the disadvantages. And whenever you feel anxiety about misfortune calm the mind. On the other hand, keep on diminishing, forsaking, purifying, and cleansing—always continue in the practice and the mind will mature. These measures applied together will certainly lead you home to stability. You will then accept it as a completely natural state. [13b] Even sudden clasps of thunder or the tumbling down of a mountain will no longer startle you.[30] Even the crossing of bare blades won't bring about any fear. Reputation and advantages will seem transient as if "passing a crack" [ZZ 82/29/51] life and death will appear as the mere "bursting of a boil" [ZZ 18/6/68]. Thus you realize that as long as application of the practice and your determination to continue are not divided, you will harmonize them in your spirit.

The vacuity and mystery of the mind cannot be fathomed indeed. It really is a strange thing: if you approach its substance it does not seem to exist, if you pursue its application it certainly is there. "Without haste it is swift, without being summoned it arrives" [DDJ 73; ZZ 26/11/17]. In a state of anger it will hit the center of a stone, arrow and feathers.[31] In a state of grudge it will make it freeze in the heat of summer. Unleashing hatred it gets near the nine realms of darkness. Accumulating benevolence, how could it be far off the Three Heavens?[32] It comes and goes abruptly, whether agitated or calm cannot easily be told. Sometimes it's there, sometimes it's gone. Neither milfoil nor tortoise shells could divine it. How could one compare the difficulty of taming and controlling the mind with mere deer or horses?

Lord Lao promotes constant benevolence in order to save people, he ascends to the Numinous Terrace and displays the subtle. He outlines cause and effect

---

[30] This echoes *Huangting neijing jing* 3.7, comm. Also Wu Yun's *Xinmu lun* (see below).

[31] The allusion is to a story of a man who thought he was shooting a wild bull but in fact hit a stone. the power of his shot was so strong that the arrow entered the stone all the way to the feathers. See *Lüshi chunqiu* 9.5.

[32] The nine realms of darkness (*jiuyou* 九幽) are the hells or earth prisons (*diyu* 地獄) in the underworld. The Three Heavens (*santian* 三天) are the original levels of creation, mysterious, primordial, and beginning (*xuan yuan shi* 玄元始) *qi*. Kohn in Pregadio 2008, 851-52.

of the Three Vehicles and expands on the spontaneous nature of the myriad things.[33] He makes people gradually, day by day, diminish their deliberate actions and suddenly attain the return to unknowing. As a metaphor we speak of it as of drawing a bow and piercing the aim with an arrow. As a method **[14a]** we describe it as blunting the sharpness and untying the knots.[34] If you maintain the constancy of [YQ: follow the path of] cultivation you will by practice perfect your inner nature. Smash up your limbs and body, drive out intellect and perception and experience detachment and oblivion. Unmoving in the stillness, you will imperceptibly and subtly enter clarity of spirit. Those who take steps in any other direction will never understand what I mean. But those who go along with this Dao can be certain to see the subtle. Small effort—high rewards! It is essential! It is subtle!

7. Attaining Dao

Dao is a spiritual and wonderful thing. It is numinous and yet has inner nature; it is empty but without any symbol. Following or meeting it, it cannot be fathomed. Neither its shadow nor its echo can be pursued [DDJ 14]. Without knowing why it just is, pervading all life.[35] Yet it is never exhausted. This is what we call Dao.

Utmost sages have attained it in antiquity, and thus the wondrous divine law has been transmitted to us today. Following descriptions, probing into principles, we find it completely real. Worthy knights of pure faith have overcome their selves and practiced it diligently. Once the mind is emptied and the "spirit like a valley" [DDJ 6], Dao alone will come to assemble. Once Dao has become strong [YQ: of utmost strength], it imperceptibly [YQ: softly] works changes in body-form and spirit. **[14b]** The body-form aligned with Dao and pervading spirit is what constitutes a "spirit person."[36]

His spirit and inner nature are empty and fused into one. His physical structure no longer changes or decays. His body-form is united with Dao, he no longer experiences life and death. Withdrawn from life, his body-form merges with

---

[33] The concept of the Three Vehicles (*triyāna, sancheng*) is of Buddhist origin and designates different paths to enlightenment: listening (*srāvaka*), cultivating oneself (*pratyekabuddha*), and striving for universal salvation (*bodhisattva*). In Daoism, is signifies the three major school of the middle ages, Highest Clarity, Numinous Treasure, and the Three Sovereigns together with the Celestial Masters

[34] The last two sentences contain allusions to DDJ 48, 65, 77, and 56.

[35] YQ: "Not knowing why it is not so, yet it makes everything be" (15a). See also *Benji jing* 4.166 (Ōfuchi 1979, 315); and Wu Yun's *Xingshen kegu lun* (DZ 1051, 2.20a).

[36] See ZZ 2/1/22, 12/4/79.

spirit; apparent in the world, his spirit merges with his *qi* [YQ: body-form]. Therefore a spirit person can step into water or fire without suffering harm. He can stand in the sunshine or the moonlight without throwing a shadow. Survival and destruction resting with himself, he passes in and out of the spaceless.[37] If even the coarse substance of his body-self becomes like the empty and wondrous [Dao], how much more should his numinous wisdom excel in depth and remoteness? The *Shengshen jing* 昇神經 [Scripture of Ascension to Spirit] says: "When body-self and spirit are unified the perfect body-self is born" [unclear]. The *Xisheng jing* has: "Body-form and spirit merged in harmony means eternal life" [29.5].

The way of emptiness and nonbeing [YQ: of an empty mind] can be deep or shallow. When it is deep it covers both, including [the mind and] also the body-form. When it is shallow it goes only as far as the mind. When it covers both including the body-form, one is a spirit person. When it only goes as far as the mind, one only attains insight and awakening, but the body-self will not be spared. Why is this? Insight is the activation of the mind, and when the mind [YQ: body-self] is active a lot, it will be labored. When one first attains a little bit of insight, one is delighted and deliberates a lot. Thereby spirit and *qi* are drained away and, as no numinosity enriches the body-self, one's clarity [YQ: life] will be extinguished very early. [15a] Thus it is very difficult to perfect Dao. This is what the scriptures call "deliverance from the corpse."[38]

Thus the great man retains his radiance and stores his brilliance in preparation of complete fulfillment. He concentrates his spirit and treasures his *qi*, studies Dao and makes his mind no-mind, so that his spirit can merge with Dao. This truly is realizing Dao. The *Daode jing* says: "He who is identified with Dao—Dao is also happy to have him" [23]. And "Why did the ancients highly value Dao? Did they not say, 'Those who seek shall have it and those who sin shall be freed'?" [62].

When a mountain contains jade its grasses and trees will not wither. When someone embraces Dao, body-form and bones will never get rigid. Daily increasing in material subtlety, one's disposition unites fully with spirit. By refining the body-form to enter the subtle, one merges with Dao into one. Upon dispersal, the body-self turns into a myriad concrete manifestations [dharmas], just as the myriad manifestations when joining together combine to form the body-self.

---

[37] The idea of survival and destruction depending on the person rather than on heaven appears in ZZ 15/6/5 and 44/17/49, and later in the *Baopuzi* (2.4a, 4.11b, 6.6a). For Dao as spaceless, see DDJ 43, ZZ 28/11/65.
[38] The method of transcendence that requires a token object (staff, sword) to be left behind. See Robinet 1979a; Cedzich 2001.

Wisdom radiates boundlessly, the body-form goes beyond all limits. Comprehending the emptiness of all sensory forms one is active [in the worlld]. "Harboring both creation and change" [ZZ 17/6/55], one generates merit. Perfectly in accordance with the bentless, one is nothing but Dao and potency. Thus the *Xisheng jing* says: "Join your mind with Heaven and there will be no more knowledge. Join your body-self with Dao and there will be no more physical structure. Then the Dao of Heaven will be perfected" [XSJ 25.4-6]. **[15b]** "Perfected" here means that one has indeed attained the ultimate. Again it says: "When spirit does not leave my body-self, I am forever one with Dao" [26.2].

Body-self unified with Dao means that one will survive forever. Mind unified with Dao means that all manifestations are pervaded. Ears unified with Dao means that all sounds will be heard. Eyes unified with Dao means that all sights will be seen. Perfect inherent potency of the six senses only comes from this.

[DZ] Recently it has become the general habit not to know the more esoteric parts of the doctrine. People just hear of a Dao of "casting away the body-self" and never accept that this ultimately refers to the mystery of identifying one's body with Dao. Without shame for their shortcomings imitating others' wrongs, such people are like summer insects who don't believe in icy frost or like fruitflies entirely without knowledge of Heaven and Earth [ZZ 56/21/37]. Their ignorance is so incredible—how could one enlighten them?

[YQ] There is a profound and deep advantage in perfectly discussing the mysterious teaching. In an attempt to put it into words I therefore tried to formulate the ultimate principle. The esoteric mystery of Highest Clarity is found in applying essential cultivation to deluded conventional thinking and in using the methods of the divine elixir to refine the body-form. Thereby knowledge and consciousness become pervasive and reach oblivion. A zealous faith in Dao and inherent potency develops.

Only by unifying one's bodily constituents with Dao and by emptying one's mind completely are all the bondages dissolved. As soon as the cultivation reaches as far as the bones of the body, the latter will no longer cast a shadow. When skillful means and benevolent ingenuity come together, the spring of Dao and one's mind and body-form will nourish one another. Universal order far exceeds its carriage or habitation: it enters from without. Yet even though these two [i.e., order and habitation, Dao and people] are on different levels, they ultimately return to the same goal. They both ought to reach out to the deep and abstruse.

Neither talk nor silence can ever attain the subtlety of these two. Thus they could never even be touched upon by Confucius or the Buddha. Even I know only this much of which I've given an approximate outline.

Text Two

Inscription on Oblivion[1]

→ I have heard my old teacher explain: Sitting in oblivion is the foundation of long life. Thus we engage perfection to refine the body-form, and once it is pure we merge it into *qi*. We retain Dao to refine *qi*, and once it is clear we merge it with spirit. The physical structure unified with Dao: this is "attaining Dao." ← As Dao is without ultimate, how could the immortal ever die?[2]

→ Perfection is the prime of Dao, thus we cleanse spirit to match perfection. Zhuangzi says: "I smash my limbs and physical structure, drive out intellect and perception, cast off body-form, do away with knowledge, and become one with Great Pervasion" [ZZ 19/6/92]. This is exactly what we mean. Zhuangzi also says: "Wisdom and stillness take turns cultivating each other, thus harmony and order emerge from still inner nature" [41/16/1]. This is just it. And he says: "He whose inner being rests in the stability of cosmic peace will send forth a heavenly light" [63/23/41]. Here "resting" refers to the mind, while "heavenly light" means the radiance of insight. As you stabilize your mind, the radiance of insight develops within. By this radiance you can then see the myriad aspects of projected reality, and in emptiness and oblivion you will merge mentally with the realm of boundless serenity. This is what we call "sitting in oblivion." ←

---

[1] Carved in 829 at Mount Wangwu, this inscription relies on the oral transmission brought from Mount Tongbo by a certain Mr. Xu, of whom we know nothing (Wu 1981, 47a, 48a). The text of the inscription is found in an abbreviated and slightly altered version in the *Daoshu* (2.7a-8a). This translation follows the text of the inscription as given in Wu 1980 and indicates *Daoshu* variants in the annotation. Certain items are not specially mentioned, notably particles in the *Daoshu*, such as *qi* 其, *yi* 矣, and *zhe* 者, and its usage of *wu* 吾 instead of *yu* 余 for "I." To create easier access to this mix of editions, I insert forward and back arrows (→,←) when sections also found in the *Daoshu* begin and end.

[2] After the first sentence, this paragraph also appears in *Shenxian kexue lun* 11b.

People nowadays train in popular studies and acquaint themselves with many teachings, yet they are unable to attain the essential points of these teachings. → For example, there recently was Daoist Zhao Jian who compiled a treatise on sitting in oblivion in one *juan* and seven sections. Covering a broad subject matter in intricate language, he explains a simple essential idea in extensive arguments.[3] ← He thus presents the tradition of one school, yet he is far from matching the truly mysterious. → Thereby he makes the reader only think of his chapters and phrases, tempts him to merely memorize his outward arrangements [lit. doors and windows] and textual layout. This one may call sitting with a "madly racing mind" [ZZ 9/4/32], but never really sitting in oblivion. ←

Rather, when sitting in oblivion, what would there remain unforgotten? Only then can one say: Sitting in oblivion is the gate to long life. → Laozi says: "If I did not have a body-self, what vexations would I have?" [DDJ 13] ← But if one does not have a body-self and thus returns to annihilation [*nirvāna*], shouldn't that be called the loss of the basis of eternal life? Yet I answer: What you would call → "not having a body-self" does not refer to not having this particular physical body. It rather means that the physical structure is unified with the Great Dao, that one is never influenced by glorious positions[4] and does not seek after speedy advancement. Being placid and without desires, it means to forget that there is this body-self dependent on all kinds of things. ← If the sage therefore urges us to refine spirit and merge with Dao, ascend into the formless and unite with Dao to become one, then this is exactly the meaning of "casting off body-form, doing away with understanding, and smashing up one's limbs and body."

→ [What is highest] in eternal life is that spirit and body-form are joined in completeness. Thus it is said: "The trigrams *Qi* an and Kun constitute the pattern of the changes. If *Qi* an and Kun were destroyed, one could no longer feel any changes. Thus the body-form is a vessel, it is the storehouse of inner nature. If it is destroyed, inner nature has no place to reside. ← If inner nature had no place to reside, where in me would it be?"[*Shenxian kexue lun* 11a]. Thus what we value highest about body-form and spirit is their being joined in completeness. One who only → nourishes spirit without nourishing the body-form is like a man who destroys his house and lives out in the open. ←How could spirit ever rest peacefully? Rather, consciousness would continue to be transformed in the different realms and would eventually take residence in another family. Thus it is said: "The wandering of the consciousness-soul produces transformations" [*Shenxian kexue lun* 11b-12a]. This is just it.

---

[3] The *Daoshu* presents this in a different order, placing the last sentence in the beginning of the paragraph.

[4] From "unified with the Great Dao," this section is missing in the inscription.

Yet someone may say, "When at the end of life one observes one's mind and consciousness properly, then spirit will transcend the world and enter the realm of perfection. It will never again fall into the evil realms of existence." But these words are only spoken for comfort, they → are not words of perfection and propriety. Now [today] there are wise men of lofty potency ← who either excuse themselves and rest outside of worldly involvement and mundane grime or who bustle around at court and in the city and yet → say that they are entirely oblivious of themselves and others and never make any distinction between right and wrong. Yet, when these men see someone do evil, they inevitably knit their brows and make a face. When they see someone do good, they in all cases brighten up and smile happily. ←

When spirit is pure and *qi* vigorous → then one is deluded by this fact and considers it either good or bad,[5] but how much worse will the delusion get once the end of life is drawing closer? ← And how will one ever be able not to be enticed by the manifold false impressions? The mind. . . . [text illegible] will be split. → Thus, if existing consciousness is transformed into nonconsciousness ← or human consciousness into animal consciousness, how could one explain this? For example, → the Lady of Qin was turned into a stone ←, which is a case of existing consciousness being transformed into nonconsciousness. → Mrs. Huang was changed into a turtle ←, which exemplifies the situation of human consciousness being transformed into animal consciousness.[6] → Seen from this angle, mind and consciousness are understood as being molded entirely by yin and yang. How could they ever be stable in themselves? This is precisely why Daoists highly value body-form and spirit in joined existence [DS: completeness]. ← And how could it not be absurd and fantastic to speak of observation while abandoning the body?

Nowadays there are frequently people → who know that glorious positions are worthless and vain, and who understand that life and death are one whole [DS: track]. Yet when the end approaches they will seek out doctors and pray to the demons. ← To these people the sages say: "He who dies but does not perish enjoys long life" [DDJ 50]. How could this be empty talk? Therefore, when one wants to attain some level of Dao, one must first of all practice sitting in oblivion. → [Sitting in] oblivion means the annihilation of the myriad states of projected reality.

For this one must first understand that one holds countless deluded assumptions. Next, one must stabilize the mind. Above the stable mind everything must be free, open, coverless. Beneath the stable mind everything must be wide,

---

[5] This part, from "one is deluded," is not found in the inscription.

[6] See *Soushen ji* 搜神記 (In Search of the Supernatural), dat. ab. 350 (see Bodde 1942; Campany 1996), ch. 14.

spacey, bottomless.[7] If you just continue to remain in this state and do not move, ← you will unite with Dao into oneness. This we call entering the state of great stability. Once this is established, insight will arise by itself. → When insight first arises, ← make sure you do not labor stability. If you just continue to observe your deluded assumptions, you will certainly attain the perfectly wondrous. → However, as this body-self has not escaped the molding through yin and yang and revolves through the grime of the world [lit. "wheel mud"], one must rely on gold and cinnabar to undergo the metamorphosis of wings [*Shenxian kexue lun* 12b]. ←

Only then can one ascend and → enter the formless, to go beyond the remotest points of all transformation. ← Entering the gate of the boundless, one becomes fully one with Dao. This is called "attaining Dao." → Only after that will yin and yang be fully controlled. ←

---

[7] *Dingguan jing*, line 29. See below.

Text Three

Stability & Observation[1]

[YQ 6b] "Numinous" means spirit. Part of Heaven, it is called numinous. "Treasure" means valuable. Part of Earth, it is called treasure. Heaven's numinous transformations and spirit activations are immeasurable, thus it broadly covers everything without bounds. Earth's host of treasures and supportive nourishing come in a wide variety, thus it amply supports the myriad things.[2] This scripture is like Heaven and like Earth. **[7a]** It covers and supports; it is numinous and valuable. Its merit and inherent potency are without bounds; it is attained only by the mind directly. Therefore it is called a "numinous treasure."

"Stability" refers to the stabilization of mind, a state as immovable as Earth. "Observation" is the examination of things by insight, it means that one remains constantly radiant like Heaven. Stabilize the physical structure and be free from all activity of mind, then insight will radiate without bounds. Stability and insight jointly enhance cultivation, thus it is called "Stability and Observation."

The Heavenly Worthy told the Mysterious Perfected on the Left

"Left" here stands for stability, while "mysterious" means deep and wondrous [DDJ 1]. "Perfected" refers to purity, to oneness without contamina-

---

[1] This translates the *Dingguan jing* from YQ 17.6b-13a, identical with DZ 400. A slightly variant version appears in the appendix to the *Zuowang lun* (DZ 1036; 15b-18a) which also adds two sections: a paragraph reviewing the fundamental concepts of the *Zuowang lun* after the first third; and the five phases of the mind before the seven stages of the body. Differences are marked in the text under the abbreviation "ZWL." Further variants are found in: *Guanmiao jing* (DZ 326); *Daode zhenjing guangsheng yi* (DZ 725, 49.8ab); *Daoshu* (DZ 1017, 2.2b-3b); *Xuanzhu xinjing zhu* (DZ 574, 6b & 9b-10b); *Chuzhen neidan jiyao* (DZ 1258, 2.3a-4a); *Nenggai zhaiman lu* 5.24ab. Major discrepancies are described in the footnotes.

[2] See *Zhuangzi* 19/6/89, 34/13/15, 92/33/43.

tion. Among human beings, such a person pervades and fulfills inner nature. "Told" refers to the act of speaking.

Now, if you want to cultivate Dao,[3] first give up all affairs.

> Having a mind progressing forward is called "cultivate Dao." Being completely free from defilements is being "giving up affairs."

Once all outer affairs are eliminated, they make no more trouble for the mind.[4]

> [7b] The six sensory impurities [gunas] are what the text means by "outer affairs." You must push them far away. The six are: sight, sound, smell, taste, touch, and thought [dharmas]. Not being defiled by or attached to them, we say that they are "all eliminated." Then projected reality no longer causes trouble for the mind and there are no more irritations [kleśas]. The mind produces no more defilements; projected reality can no longer create irritations. Mind and projected reality both forgotten, there are neither afflictions nor irritations. Thus the text speaks of "no more trouble for the mind."

Only then can you sit at peace.

> Having controlled and cleansed all afflictions and irritations is called being "at peace." The non-arising of any state of mind is called "sit."

In inner observation see a mind arise.[5] If you become aware of a thought arising, immediately eliminate and destroy it. [ZWL: As it arises, so you eliminate it.] That will allow you to find peace and stillness.

> A mind of insight radiating within is called "inner observation." As long as impure thoughts have not been eliminated, we say "a mind arises." First a thought suddenly arises, then you become aware of it and follow it. When the mind that has arisen has passed away, awareness and radiance. are also forgotten. Thus the text says "eliminate and destroy." The utter non-arising of any mind is called "peace." The awareness of inner nature without agitation is called "stillness." Thus the text says "peace and stillness."

---

[3] The *Guanmiao jing* here has "observe the mystery."

[4] The *Guanmiao jing* has: "Only when all outer affairs are eliminated can one purify and calm the thoughts in the mind." The *Daoshu* says: "Outer affairs should not disturb the mind."

[5] The first few lines of the text, in the ZWL version, read: "To cultivate Dao and complete perfection, first get rid of depraved and bad behavior. Once all outside affairs are eliminated, there is nothing to concern the mind. Only then can you sit upright to practice inner observation and right awareness" (15b).

Next, whether containing greed or attachment or not, all floating [mental] wanderings and confused imaginings should be driven out completely.

> When multiple minds do not arise, when deluded thoughts are entirely forgotten, when no confused imaginings appear—what greed or attachment could there be? Thus the text says they are "driven out completely."

Practice diligently night and day, never stop for even a short moment!

> "Day" here stands for a clean state while "night" means impurity. Both have to be forgotten completely, there should be no distinction made between them. Thus the text says, "never stop!"

Only destroy the agitated mind, don't abandon the radiating mind![6]

> Deluded imaginings and all kinds of distinctions are what make up the "agitated mind." By awareness and radiance you get rid of them, thus the text says "destroy." Insight and radiance should always be bright, without the interruption of even an instant. Thus it says, "don't abandon the radiating mind!" **[8b]**

Only gather in [ZWL: merge] the empty mind, never collect the dwelling [ZWL: being] mind.[7]

> A mind of utter non-arising is called an "empty mind." Remaining altogether free from attachments is what is meant by "never collect the dwelling mind."

Never rely on even one concrete manifestation [ZWL: thing], and the mind will always be dwelling [in itself].

> Taking in even one concrete manifestation is called having attachment to the phenomenal world. A mind that does not take in even one concrete manifestation is therefore "not relying." Radiant and constantly serene, it is "always dwelling [in itself]."

[ZWL 16a →] This method is mysterious and wonderful, its advantages and gains are extremely profound.

It does not entirely depend on a former existence's good karma or faith yet lacking these two, one ultimately will not have perfect faith.

---

[6] The *Zhuzhen neidan jiyao* comments: "Always knowing, always aware: when you don't abandon the radiating mind, stability and insight are full and complete."

[7] The *Xuanzhu xinjing zhu* comments: "Before one's father and mother were born, there was no mind, there were no things. Thus one's being was not fixed at all. Inner imaginings do not leave, outer fantasies do not enter." The last sentence also appears in the later *Liaoshen jing* 了身經 (Scripture of Realizing the Body-Self , DZ 25), 1a, 3b.

And even thorough knowledge and frequent recital of this text will be no substitute for a perfect understanding of its veracity.

Yet, if you have this—how could sights or sounds disturb your mind, evil and slander touch your ears?

If I see my inner nature in relation to my ego and to other people, my sickness is very serious indeed.

As long as the mind is separated from Dao, it is hard to awaken to cosmic order.

But if the mind is to return to perfect Dao, full of profound nature and faithful longing, it must first of all receive Three Precepts:

1. Detachment from karmic conditions

> This means that one selects what is essential and abandons all potentially disturbing things. The *Daode jing* says: "To have little is to possess, to have plenty is to be perplexed" [22].[8]

2. Freedom from desires[9]

> This means that one should get rid off all craving and searching. The *Daode jing* [1] says: "Let there always be no desires so that the subtle may be observed."

3. Stillness of mind

> This means that one should stop and intercept all the ups and downs of mental activity. As the *Xisheng jing* says: "Get rid of all defilements, intercept all thoughts, calm the mind and guard the One!" [39.10]

If one diligently practices in observance of these precepts, never being lazy or lax about them, then one will pursue Dao with no-mind and Dao will naturally come to stay.

> The *Xisheng jing* says: "If human beings are empty, latent, and free from action, they may not desire Dao, yet Dao naturally returns to them."[10] [36.10]

Seen from this angle, the method of detachment and profundity can really be trusted! Can truly be esteemed! [← ZWL 16b]

---

[8] The commentary to these precepts comes from *Daoshu* 2.3a. It is not found in the *Zuowang lun*.

[9] This is also one of the basic nine precepts according to the *Xianger zhu*. See Kohn 2004, 59.

[10] This is an allusion to *Daode jing* 23: "Who joins Dao, Dao will also join. Who joins inherent potency, inherent potency will never leave."

Yet, the normal mind is hasty and competitive. First learn to calm this mind—it is very hard. Calmness may not be found, or it arrives [ZWL: is attained] for an instant and is lost again.

> This means that in working with inner nature, afflictions and irritations are very hard to destroy. The power of stability not established yet, so "it comes for an instant and is lost again." **[9a]**

Drive out all remaining interactions and struggles [of the mind], which makes all parts of the body flow about [ZWL: sweat profusely].

> The mind gives rise to defiled visions of projected reality which in turn imprison it. Mind and projected reality duly come to defile each other. This is what is meant by "interactions and struggles [of the mind]." If deluded imaginings do not stop, all sorts of wrong ideas come forth, which is when "all parts of the body flow about."

For a long time practice meditation [ZWL: train it gently], and eventually the mind will adjust and mature. If you cannot hold it in even for an instant, you will forfeit the training of a thousand lives [ZWL: your whole life].

> A stabilized mind in a state of non-arising is aligned with perfection and constancy. If even one thought is not held in, it means another thousand lives.

Once you have attained a little self-purification, continue the practice walking, staying, sitting, lying down.

> The initial achievement of clarity and purity does not yet mean the arising of right insight. Thus it says, "attain a little." Thus practice self-purification in all four periods of dignified observances.

Whether in a spot of excitement or in a situation of upheaval, always create an intention to be at peace [ZWL: intentionally make it peaceful].

> Seeing all sorts of phenomena means "a spot of excitement." The arising of various states of mind is "a situation of upheaval." Calming confusion and returning to serenity is "creating an intention." Attaining a space of complete tranquility means being "at peace." **[9b]**

Whether involved in affairs or free from affairs, constantly maintain no-mind! Whether in stillness or upheaval, your will be one only!

> Existence and nonexistence dismissed alike, serenity and activation both forgotten, the myriad concrete manifestations seen as nondual—this is called "one only."

If you tie the mind down too tightly, you will produce disease. The breath becomes irregular and crazy: those are its symptoms.[11]

> Using a lopsided mind to clutch stillness is called "tying down the mind." The mind seeing phenomena on the outside is called "crazy."

Should the mind be completely immobile, let it go to respond [to things]. As you attain the right spot between laxity and tension, it naturally adjusts and entrains.

> When insight arises from stability, we speak of "letting the mind go to respond [to things]." Stability and insight in equal measure is "attaining the right spot." An imbalance in favor of stability is called stupidity [dullness of mind]. A lopsidedness toward insight means craziness [hyperactivity of mind]. The measured functioning of stability and insight is "adjusted and entrained." [10a]

Controlled yet unattached, free yet not agitated [ZWL: unattached], in upheaval without negativity [ZWL: agitation], in excitement without afflictions: such is perfect stability![12]

> Serene yet steadily radiant, radiant yet constantly serene, empty yet steadily functioning, functioning yet constantly empty—this is the attainment of original and primordial serenity, thus described as "perfect stability."

If you don't develop afflictions when met with excitement, don't set out in search of more excitement! If you don't give rise to negativity in times of upheaval, don't increase it by intention![13]

> Restrain your inner nature in contact with the impurities and hardships of the world. Always keep it under tight control and never let it break loose.

Rather, make freedom from affairs your perfect home [ZWL: stability], and when there are affairs, just go along with their outward manifestations [lit.: traces].

> See how your original inner nature is empty and serene and make it "your perfect home." See how insight functions without limits and "just go along with the traces." [10b]

---

[11] The *Daoshu* reads: ". . . brings disease and a crazy mind."

[12] The *Daoshu* adds: "Having reached this, do not presume on it!"

[13] The *Guanmiao jing* summarizes the following section: "Rather, stabilize the spirit in stillness for a long time, and the heavenly light will begin to radiate of itself. Never forcefully or hastily try to make it shine because that would only injure essential nature. In a state of stillness, see that there is nothing to grasp. Because if there still is something you could grasp, this would pervert and disturb perfection."

Like a water mirror reflects everything so you should go along with things and reflect their forms.

> Original mind is as clear and pure as "a water mirror." Its radiance functions without obstruction, so the myriad things all appear in it. Thus the text says, "reflect their forms."

Beneficent skillfulness and expedient means are used to enter stability.

> All concrete manifestation are empty in their inner nature, so serenity does not arise from anything. Thus it speaks of "entering stability."

Insight will arise sooner or later, yet it never comes from human [efforts]. So never in stability get nervous in your efforts toward insight!

Being nervous and tense only injures inner nature [ZWL: stability]. Once there is such injury, there is no chance of insight.

> Nervously pursuing the knowledge and vision of perfect stability causes deluded greed for and attachments to the phenomenal world. Thus the text says: "no chance of insight."

In stability never actively pursue insight. Insight will arise naturally, and only then it is perfect insight. [14]

> Physical structure and mind serene and still, they function wondrously without bounds. This is called "perfect insight." **[11a]**

Having insight without using it is being wise in fact but ignorant in appearance.

> Never allowing any distinctions in the mind is what is meant by "not using insight." Shading one's light and hiding one's traces is being "ignorant in appearance."

Stability and insight thus increase and develop into unmatched beauty.

> Serenity and radiance in equal measure—both reach "unmatched beauty."

However, if in a state of stability there are thoughts and fantasies, manifold delusions and a host of evils, then specters and wicked spirits will appear accordingly.

> The images taken in by the mind come to life and all the wicked spirits vie with each other to raise confusion.

---

[14] The *Daoshu* has: "In stability, when you actively pursue insight, this will injure your stability. Stability will then persist without insight."

But when you see the Heavenly Worthy, the host of immortals or perfected, this is an auspicious sign.[15]

> Yet, since these are mere phenomena as well, make sure not to develop any attachment to them.

Just watch out: above the stable mind everything is free and open and coverless; beneath the stable mind everything is wide and spacey and bottomless.[16] **[11b]**

> No thought of the past: "coverless." No thought of the future: "bottomless."

Old karma diminishes daily [ZWL: forever], new karma is never produced.

> Old deeds being used up, that's "old karma diminishes daily." No rise given to any state of mind, that's "new karma is never produced."

No more bondage or obstructions—you are free from fetters and defilements.

> Being utterly free from attachments is having "no more bondage or obstructions." Being totally liberated and without any ties is being "stripped free from all fetters and defilements."

Practicing on and on for a very long time, naturally you attain Dao.

> Insight radiating continually without interruption is "practicing on and on for a very long time." The state which duly arises of alignment with cosmic order, of harmony with truth, is called "realizing Dao." **[12a]**

Those who attain Dao typically undergo [ZWL: five phases in their mind and] seven stages in their body-self.[17]

[ZWL 17b →] The Five Phases of the Mind are:

1. Much agitation, little stillness.

2. Agitation and stillness in balance.

3. Much stillness, little agitation.

4. Still in times of leisure, upon involvement return to agitation.

5. The mind fully at one with Dao, no agitation even in involvement.[18]

---

[15] The ZWL here has: "But when you see perfected or Lord Lao, divine wonders and amazing sights, this is an auspicious sign" (17a).

[16] The imagery of this verse is taken from the "Yuanyou" (Far-off Journey) in the ancient *Chuci* (Songs of the South): "In the sheer depth below, the earth was invisible; in the vastness above, the sky could not be seen" (Hawkes 1959, 86).

[17] The *Daoshu* adds: "These are arranged according to increasing depth."

Only upon reaching this level can the mind experience peace and happiness.[19] All guilt and defilements have passed away completely, and there are no more contaminations nor afflictions.[20] [← ZWL 17b]

The Seven Stages of the Body are:

1. The mind attains stability with ease and is constantly aware of all defilements and outflows.[21]

2. Diseases inherited from former lives [ZWL: and nervousness] gradually diminish, body-self and mind become light and clear.

> Perfect *qi* and embryo respiration heal all diseases. Embodying Dao, at one with perfection, the body-self is light and does not age.

3. Forestalling the tendency of untimely death, one returns to one's years [ZWL: to the prime] and recovers destiny [DDJ 16].[22]

> Bones and filling strong and full, one can "forestall the tendency of untimely death." Youthful appearance never changing, "one returns to one's years and recovers destiny."

4. Extending life to several [ten] thousand years: be called an immortal. [12b]

> Living forever and never dying, extending life for several ten thousand years: this is called being enrolled in the immortals' registers. Thus one is "called an immortal."

5. Refining the body-form to *qi*:[23] be called a perfected.

> Attaining original, primordial *qi*, this is "refining the body-form to *qi*." Maintaining an upright inner nature and being without falsehood: this is "a perfected."

---

[18] The *Xuanzhu xinjing zhu* offers the variant: "Whether at leisure or in excitement, there is no agitation even in involvement."

[19] The *Xuanzhu xinjing zhu* adds: "Embracing the prime and guarding the One, body and spirit are empty and at rest. Yet there is still a will. Only later awareness is aroused, and the functioning of Dao is daily new."

[20] Du Guangting in his *Daode zhenjing guangsheng yi* changes the final line to read: "This is the ultimate freedom from defilements." He adds: "The five phases [of the mind] are different manifestations of the practice of Dao. The seven stages [of the body] are its result. They are only attained through continuous practice."

[21] ZWL: "All conduct and activity in line with the occasion, appearance and complexion are in harmony with inner joy." Du Guangting has: "The mind realizes full stability and awareness; there are no more impurities."

[22] The *Xuanzhu xinjing zhu* adds: "The limits of normal existence are transcended; in appearance one gains a youthful complexion."

[23] The *Xuanzhu xinjing zhu* here uses "body-self."

6. Refining *qi* to spirit: be called a spirit person.

> As perfect *qi* you pervade spirit, [one with] yin and yang unfathomable: be called "a spirit person."²⁴

7. Refining spirit to join Dao: be called an utmost being!²⁵

> Perfect spirit matching Dao: this is the "utmost being."

Upon this [transformation] the power of reflection grows the higher the brighter.²⁶

> The "power of reflection" means being constantly radiant without stopping. "Grow brighter" means it sparkles and glitters without interruption.

Fully having attained utmost Dao, insight is also full and complete. **[13a]**

> If you have realized original inner nature, this is "having attained utmost Dao." "Insight full and complete," the myriad concrete manifestations all merge.

However, if someone has studied stability of mind for a long time, yet has not achieved even the first of the [ZWL: Five Phases or] Seven Stages in his body-self, is thus growing older in defilement and obstruction, loses vigor and eventually dies [ZWL: says of himself that he possesses insight and awareness],²⁷ and maintains that he has completed Dao ZWL: striven to pervade cosmic order, but has not in fact done so—then one must call him a cheat.]—if there is such a one, then one must know that he is not in fact pursuing the perfect principle of Dao.

> Pervading spirit and at-one with Dao, the body-self has attained Dao and perfection. However, if the mind experiences [Dao], yet one dies in one's body-self, then one will not leave the realm of birth and death. The *Xisheng*

---

²⁴ See *Yijing*, Xici I.5: "Yin and yang unfathomable is called spirit."

²⁵ Du Guangting here has "sage" instead of *zhiren* 至人. The *Xuanzhu xinjing zhu* has a different version of this stage, closer to that found in Sun's *Cunshen lianqi ming*: "Going beyond the Three Worlds, one is ranked as an emperor of emptiness, a lord of great brilliance of the Great Dao. As such one pervades all spirit and numinosity while one's wisdom encompasses the myriad things."

²⁶ The *Xuanzhu xinjing zhu* has: "The higher you ascend in these stages, the brighter your mirror becomes."

²⁷ The *Guanmiao jing* concludes this differently: "Wanting to attain perfect Dao in this way—I have never heard of that!" The *Xuanzhu xinjing zhu* gives yet another variant: "But people nowadays may study Dao to the end of their days, yet don't even achieve the first stage. Instead they grow older in defilement and obstruction, lose their vigor and eventually die. Yet they maintain they have attained Dao and penetrated . That this could be true I have never yet heard!"

jing says: "If you have lost the root of life, how can you know the primordial source of Dao?" [8.11]

The Heavenly Worthy concluded by reciting the following *gatha*:[28]

> Knowledge arises from projected reality;
> Burning comes from karmic conditions;
> Each has the tendency to agitate inner nature
> And going along with them means losing the source of Dao.
>
> Giving rise to a mind full of desire to stop knowledge,
> This mind will give rise to knowledge and increase afflictions.
> Only by fully knowing that inner nature is originally empty
> Can knowledge lead to the "gate of all wonders."

---

[28] This appears only in the *Dingguan jing* version of the text.

Text Four

Refining Qi [1]

Sun Simiao

[DZ 1a]The body-self is the habitation of spirit and *qi*. As long as spirit and *qi* are [made] present, the body-self is strong and healthy. As soon as spirit and *qi* scatter, the body-self dies. Therefore, if you want to keep your body-self present, first see that spirit and *qi* are at peace. *Qi* is the mother of spirit, thus spirit is the son of *qi*. Only when both are together can you live forever and not die.

Now, to pacify spirit, first refine primordial *qi*. When this *qi* resides in the body-self, spirit is at peace and *qi* is like an ocean. If this ocean of *qi*[2] is full to overflowing, the mind is at peace and spirit stabilized. When this inner stability [YQ: spirit and *qi*] is not lost, body-self and mind are gathered in stillness. Stillness then grows further into stability, and the body-self continues to exist for years eternal.

Dwell constantly on the source [YQ: prime] of Dao, and naturally you become a sage. *Qi* then pervades spirit and projected reality, while spirit pervades insight and original destiny [YQ: inner nature]. Destiny settled and the body-self

---

[1] *Cunshen lianqi ming* (DZ 834, YQ 33.12a-14b). The main part of this text, the five phases of the mind and the seven stages of the body, form an important section of the *Dingguan jing*, which appears as appendix to the *Zuowang lun* and is translated below.

[2] The Ocean of Qi (*qihai* 氣海) is the lower elixir field, located deep inside the body slightly beneath the navel. It is the energetic center of the person, especially in men—equal to the Cavity of *Qi* (*qixue* 氣穴), the middle elixir field, in the chest in women. In Daoist body lore, it is the seat of a second Mount Kunlun, the first being in the head. In medicine, it is an acupuncture point on the Conception Vessel (CV-6) as well as on the Belt Vessel.

fully present, you reach harmony with perfect inner nature. Thus you attain an age as old as the sun and the moon. Dao perfected, you reach the ultimate realm.

If you want to learn the technique of refinement of *qi* as described here, you must first of all stop eating grains. Then focus your mind peacefully on the Ocean of *Qi*, [1b] visualize spirit in the elixir field, control the mind, and quiet your thinking. Once the Ocean of *Qi* is replenished, you always feel satiated naturally.

In the cultivation of mental one-pointedness, a hundred days mean a minor achievement, whereas three hundred days bring a major level. Only after this can you enter the five phases [of the mind]. Having passed through these, you undergo the seven stages [of the body]. As pure spirit and numinosity you then go on changing, naturally present through all arising and passing away. Whether confronting a steep cliff or a thousand miles' distance, you go or stay without obstruction.

As long as *qi* does not disperse and the Ocean of *Qi* is full, spirit calmly rests in the elixir field and body-self and mind are continually firm. Naturally a youthful complexion will return and stay on despite changes occurring in your physical structure. Once immortality is perfected, appearing and disappearing from the common world will merely be a free passage of numinosity throughout the changes. This, then, is what we call "going beyond the world." One who accomplishes this is called a "perfected." Aligning his years with Heaven and Earth, he grows to be as old as the sun and the moon.

In this technique there is no need to absorb *qi*, swallow saliva, or undergo hardships. Eat when you need to, rest when you feel tired.[3] Spontaneously present and naturally free, you are without hindrance, without obstruction. Pass through the five phases and seven stages to enter the very center of stabilization and observation. Studying Dao like this, you first attain

---

[3] This attitude goes back to the *Zhuangzi*, and is found expressed most clearly in Zhi Dun's commentary to the first chapter: "When I'm hungry, I still my hunger. When I'm thirsty, I drink my fill." It is also common in Chan/Zen literature, e.g., the *Linji lu* (see Schloegl 1976).

The Five Phases of the Mind[4]

1. The mind experiences much agitation and little stillness. Thinking is conditioned by a myriad different aspected of projected reality, accepting this and rejecting that without any constancy whatsoever. [2a] Dreads and worries, plans and calculations keep racing on inside like wild horses. This is the normal mind.

2. The mind experiences a little stillness and much agitation. One controls agitation and enters stillness [YQ: entering the mind], yet the mind at once is scattered again. It is very hard to control and subdue, to curb its agitation and entanglement. This is the beginning of progress toward Dao.

3. The mind experiences half agitation and half stillness. The quiet state of mind is like that of a controlled mind already, but this state cannot be maintained for long. Stillness and scatter-brain are about equal, one makes the mind care about its own agitation and entanglement, thus it gradually gets used to stillness.

4. The mind experiences plenty of stillness and only occasional agitation. One becomes gradually versed in controlling the mind, thus any agitation that arises is checked at once. The mind is fully one-pointed and when one-pointedness is lost it is immediately recovered.

5. The mind is turned entirely toward clarity and stillness. Whether involved in or free from affairs, there is no agitation at all. From an efficiently controlled mind, firmness and solidity arise [DZ: dispersing tendencies are stabilized] and stability develops.

Only after one is firmly established in this can one enter the seven stages. Just leave all to the natural process and let it find spontaneous attainment. There is nothing to be actively done. [2b]

---

[4] These phases match those listed in the *Dingguan jing*, except that it omits Phase 2 here and instead adds as Phase 4: "Stillness in times of leisure, upon involvement return to agitation."

The Seven Stages of the Body[5]

1. The diseases inherited from former lives diminish, the body-self grows light and the mind translucent. The mind is now totally at rest within, spirit is still, and *qi* at peace. The four elements [of fire, water, earth, and air] are joined in harmony, the six types of sensations [through seeing, hearing, smelling, tasting, touching, and thinking] are deeply serene. With the mind at peace in the mysterious realm, continue to embrace the One and guard the center. Joy and exultation daily new: this is called "attaining Dao."

2. Going beyond the limits of ordinary life, you recover a youthful complexion. The body-form in a state of joy, the mind constantly at peace, you pervade numinosity and gain penetrating vision. Best move to a different part of the country, choose a spot and settle down. It is better not to be a too old acquaintance with the local folk.

3. Extending your years to a thousand, be called an immortal. Travel extensively to famous mountains, flying or walking, spontaneously present; you have azure lads as guards and jade maidens for entertainment. Stepping high on mist and haze, colored clouds support your tread.

4. Refining your body-self to *qi*, *qi* becoming your body-self, be called a perfected. [3a] Appearing and disappearing in spontaneous presence, your glittering light radiates of itself, night and day in equal brightness. Traverse through grottos and palaces [in ecstatic flight] with immortals in attendance.

5. Refining *qi* to spirit, be called a spirit person. Changing and passing on in spontaneous presence, your activities and functions are without bounds. Your inherent potency can move Heaven and Earth, remove mountains and drain the sea.

6. Refining spirit to unify with the world of form, be called an utmost being. Your spirit pervades numinosity, your appearance and body-form are no longer definite. You change according to occasion and go along with things to appear in different forms.

7. Going [YQ: Rising high] beyond all things in your body-self, whirl out of all relations and reside next to the Jade Emperor of the Great Dao in the Numinous Realm. Here the wise and sagely gather, at the farthest shore and in ultimate perfection. In creative change, in numinous pervasion, you reach to all things. Having taken your cultivation this far, you have reached the source of Dao. Here the myriad paths come to an end. This is called the ultimate realm.

---

[5] The DZ edition does not have this title. The *Dingguan jing* version adds a preliminary first stage and leaves out the highest, seventh level.

People nowadays study Dao less and less every day, and as they don't even achieve the first stage, how would they ever attain numinous pervasion? **[3b]** Rather, they continue to preserve their stupidity and passions, they determinedly hold on to their defilements and personal dispositions. With the four seasons moving on in their course, their bodies and appearances falter until the physical structure collapses and they return to nothingness. Someone who calls this realizing Dao certainly is a hypocrite.

On the other hand, the combined methods of embryo respiration and introspective observation allow keeping of spirit and preserving of the body-form. [YQ: Original patriarchs of old have handed these methods down to us today, but in their first beginning they were conceived and transmitted by perfected.]

The methods were preserved only through oral transmission and never put down in writing. If a virtuous person of perfection [YQ: a man of inherent potency and determination] by chance comes into contact with them, he must by all means be very diligent and careful about them. He must preserve and follow them without harboring any doubts. It will be only the wise and the worthy who will encounter this sagely text.

Text Five

Inner Observation[1]

Lord Lao said:

[1b] Heaven and Earth mingle their essences; yin and yang engage in interchange. Thus the myriad things come to life, each receiving a particular karmic destiny: yet all one in that they share in numinous Dao.[2] When father and mother unite in harmony, human beings receive life.

In the first month, essence and blood coagulate in the womb.
In the second month, the embryo form begins to take form.
In the third month, the yang-spirit rouses the three spirit souls to life.
In the fourth month, the yin-numen settles the seven material souls as guardians of the body-form.
In the fifth month, the five phases divide among the organs to settle their spirits.
In the sixth month, the six pitches stabilize in the six intestines to nourish numen.
In the seventh month, the seven essential stars open the orifices to connect to cosmic light.

---

[1] This translates the *Neiguan jing* as found in DZ 641 with variants in YQ 17.1a-6b indicated in brackets. Passages also found in the *Chuanshou jingjie falu lueshuo* (DZ 1241, 2.5b-7a) of 713 are marked at their occurrence with "CS →" and "←".

[2] This echoes Guo Xiang: "Though beings may be big or small . . . in that they all have a share [in Dao] they should go along with in a state of free and easy wandering, they are all alike" (DZ 745, 1.1a).

In the eighth month, the eighth phosphors spirits descend with perfect numen.[3]
In the ninth month, the palaces and chambers are properly arranged to stabilize essence.
In the tenth month, *qi* is strong enough and the image is complete.[4]

[Throughout] Primordial harmony never stops its feeding and support.

The Lord Emperor of the Great One resides in the head. He is called the Lord of Niwan [Palace]. Radiating vitality, consciousness, and all spirits, he is people's [central] soul. **[2a]** The Ruler of Destiny resides in the heart. He regulates the prime energies of life [YQ: source of the mind]. Wuying occupies his left, from where he manages he three spirit souls. Baiyuan occupies the right, from where he organizes the seven material souls. Taohai resides in the navel, from where he preserves the root of the essence. Irradiating all the hundred joints, they give life to the hundred spirits.[5]

Because of their presence throughout the body, spirit is never vacuous. Primordial *qi* enters through the nose and reaches the Niwan [in the head], so spirit shines forth and the body-form is firm and at peace. For all movement and rest, however, it fully depends on the mind. This is how life first begins.

Look at this carefully in inner observation. [CS →] The mind is in control. As the ruler of the body-self it can prohibit and control everything, making sure that body-form and spirits do not become wayward. [YQ: It limits and controls the body spirits]. "The mind is spirit" [ZZ 48/19/11]. Its changes and transformations cannot be fathomed and does not have a stable form [see ZWL 2b-3a, 13b]. In the five organs, the following spirit manifestations reside:

---

[3] The seven essential stars (also called primes and luminants) are the five planets (Mars, Venus, Jupiter, Mercury, and Saturn) plus the sun and the moon. Already in the commentary to the *Huangting neijing jing* 17:3 they are associated with the body orifices. The eight phosphors are described as the chiefs of the twenty-four gods presiding over the constructive and defensive energies in the human body (commentary to *Huangting neijing jing* 23:8). See Strickmann 1979, 173; Robinet 1979, 94.

[4] The same passage describing the development of the human embryo is also found in the *Hunyuan shubing pian* (YQ 29.1ab). An earlier version is contained in the *Yinyuan jing* 因緣 經 (Scripture of Karmic Retribution, DZ 336), 8.1b-2a. An early description of the development of the human embryo appears in *Huainanzi* 7.

[5] Niwan is the upper elixir field and one of the nine palaces in the head (*Huangting neijing jing* 21.14, comm.) and the god of the brain in (7.4), as which he governs the gods of the face (7.10). The other gods named here are princes of the Great One (15.11). Wuying especially is described as residing on the right (11.7). Taohai is also known as Daogeng or Bodao; he resides in the lower elixir field or in the navel (15.10). See also *Laozi zhongjing* (YQ 18.16b-17b). The passage lists the same deities also described in *Chuanshou lueshuo* 2.4b.

> spirit soul in the liver;
> material soul in the lungs;
> essence in the kidneys;
> intention in the spleen;
> spirit in the heart.[6]

Their appellations vary in accordance with their respective positions. The heart belongs to the phase fire. Fire is the essence of the south and of greater yang. Above it is governed by the planet Mars, below it corresponds to the heart. [2b] Its color is red and it consists of three valves that resemble a lotus leaf. As the light of pure spirit is rooted there, it is named thus.[7]

Spirit is [YQ: neither black nor white], neither red nor yellow, neither big nor small, neither short nor long, neither crooked nor straight, neither soft nor hard, neither thick nor thin, neither round nor square.[8] It goes on changing and transforming without measure, merges with yin and yang, greatly encompasses Heaven and Earth, subtly enters the tiniest blade of grass [Xisheng jing 7 and 17]. Controlled it is straightforward, let loose it goes mad. Clarity and purity make it live, turbidity and defilements cause it to perish. [Qingjing jing 2a]. Fully bright, it radiates to the eight ends of the universe. Darkened, it confuses even a single direction. Keep it empty and serene, and life and Dao will spontaneously be constant. Maintain it in nonaction, and the body-self will prosper. [YQ: The world thinks that] Because spirit is formless, nobody can give it a fitting name. All good and bad fortune, all success and failure only come from it. [←]

Thus the sage establishes rulers and minister, clarifies rewards and punishments, sets up officials and adiminstrators, and arranges laws and regulations to properly instruct people. People having a hard time submitting to these is because of their minds. When the mind is clear and pure, the myriad misfortunes do not arise.[9] All ups and downs, life and death, all vicissitudes and evils arise from the mind. [3a] All delusion and fantasy, love and hate, all accepting and rejecting, coming and going, all defilements and attachments, as well as all entanglement and bondage arise gradually from becoming involved in things. Madly turning hither and thither, tied up and fettered, one is unable to get free. Thus one is bound for peril and destruction.

Oxen and horses when led properly can easily wade through the marsh [see ZWL 5b]. When let loose, however, they will sink in deeper and deeper and can

---

[6] These correspondences are classic in traditional Chinese medicine. See *Huangdi neijing lingshu* (DZ 1020, 2.4ab). For more details, see Ishida 1982, 3; Kohn 2005, 43.

[7] This explanation of the phase-correlations of the organs is left out in CS.

[8] Cited in *Dadao lun* (DZ 1037), 17b.

[9] Already Guo Xiang notes that the perfect man will "always step into good fortune" (ch. 8) and "will never be befallen by calamities" (ch. 1; Knaul 1985, 30; Robinet 1983).

never get out again by themselves. So they have to die. People are just like this: when first born their original spirit is clear and still, translucent and unadulterated. Then, however, they perceive that they have a body-form. This body form causes defilements through the six senses:

> If there are eyes, one will covet color.
> If there are ears, one will block out noise.
> If there is a mouth, one will indulge in flavors.
> If there is a nose, one will take in smells. [cf. DDJ 12]
> The mind intent on [YQ: embraces] refusing and coveting,
> The body-self desires to be fatter or slimmer.

From all these ups and downs no one is can wake by himself. [ZWL 8a]. Thus the sages with compassionate consideration established the doctrine to teach people to reform. They made them use inner observation of self and body in order to purify the mind.

Lord Lao said:

Now observe that your body-self has arisen from emptiness and nonbeing in accordance with karmic conditioning and opportune encounters. An accumulation of essence and an assemblage of *qi*, a coming down of florescence [YQ: karma] and a descent of spirit—when all these come together, one receives life. **[3b]**

Patterned on Heaven and symbolizing Earth, inhaling yin and exhaling yang, you share in the five phases and go along with the four seasons. The eyes are the sun and the moon. The hair is the stars and the planets. The eyebrows are the flowery canopy [Cassiopeia]. The head is Mount Kunlun.[10] An array of towers and palaces keeps essence and spirit at peace.

Among the myriad things, humans are most numinous. Their inner nature and destiny being in harmony with Dao, they should always love them and practice inner observation of their body-self. In all creation only human beings are truly [YQ: who would be more] venerable, yet they do not think of themselves as noble. Foolishly defiled by the grime of the world, they reek of impurity [YQ: agitation]. Disturbed and confused in body-form and spirit, how could they observe themselves and others and judge which is dearer and which more distant? Preservation of Dao and long life are attained by doing good and preserving perfection. But people of the world are ignorant and keep themselves busy with trifles, thereby bringing hardship and misery upon themselves.

---

[10] The concept of an anthropomorphic cosmos is reflected in the creation myth of the cosmic giant Pangu (Skt. Purusha; see Lincoln 1975), which has also been told about Laozi. It is found in YQ 3.15bb and 56.1b, with an earlier version in the *Xiaodao lun* (T. 52.144b; Kohn 1995, 54).

Lord Lao said: [CS→]

> The allotment people receive from Dao is called destiny.
> The body-form people are endowed with by the One is called inner nature.
> That by which people respond to things is called mind.
> That which the mind considers is called intention.
> That which results from intention is called will.
> The state where none among things is not known is called wisdom.
> The wisdom that encompasses the myriad things is called insight. [←]
> That which moves and regulates the body-self is called spirit soul.
> That which quiets and manages the body-form is called material soul. **[4a]**
> That which circulates through bones and flesh is called blood.
> That which preserves spirit and nourishes *qi* is called essence.
> *Qi* when clear and swift is called constructive.
> *Qi* when turbid and slow is called protective.[11]
> That which combines and manages the hundred spirits is called body-self.
> That which relays a vision among the myriad images is called body-form.
> That which keeps it clod-like and cohesive is called solidity.
> That which allows appearance to be measured is called physical structure.
> That which is arranged according to bigger and smaller is called physis.
> That which cannot be fathomed by the host of thoughts is called spirit.
> That which forever corresponds to transformations is called numen.
> That which happens when *qi* enters the body-self is called life.
> That which occurs when spirit leaves the body is called death.[12]

[CS →] That which pervades all life is called Dao. When Dao is there, it yet has no form. When it is not there, it yet has an impact [lit.: feeling; see ZZ 4/2/16,

---

[11] See *Huangdi neijing lingshu* 8.6b.
[12] The YQ gives a different list of psychological definitions:
The coming together of the *qi* of life is called essence.
The workings of essence are called numen or life-force.
The transformations of the life-force are called spirit.
The changes of spirit are called spirit souls.
The force that follows the workings of spirit souls is called consciousness.
The coming and going of essence is manifest in the material souls.
The force that rules and organizes essence and the material souls is called the mind.
When the mind touches something, there is sensual perception.
What arises from sensual perception is called intention.
When intention is directed towards an aim, it is called the will.
When the will becomes clear, there is a thought.
Thoughts regarding distant objects are called plans or ideas.
Ideas that can be applied in reality constitute wisdom.
It is through wisdom that consciousness arises. (14.13b)

16/6/29]. Changing and transforming, it cannot be measured; it pervades spirit and the host of living things. When residing in people's body-self, it is spirit light. This is called the mind.

Thus teaching people to cultivate Dao means to teach them to cultivate the mind. Teaching people to cultivate the mind means to teach them to cultivate Dao. Dao cannot be seen, so one must rely on life itself to clarify it. Life cannot be constant, so one must apply Dao to guard it. When life perishes, Dao is lost. When Dao is lost, life perishes. **[4b]** Only when life and Dao are combined in harmony will there be long life and no death. Undergoing the transformation of wings, one becomes a spirit immortal.[13] The reason why people cannot preserve Dao is because they do not practice inner observation of their minds. Practicing inner observation without stopping, life and Dao remain forever." [←]

Lord Lao said:

The reason why people float in and out of the evil ways [of lower rebirths] and continue to be immersed in vanities and defilements is that their six senses give rise to delusion and bring forth the six states of consciousness [sensory impurities, *Dingguan jing* 7b]. These six in turn bring forth divisions and distinctions,[14] fetters and bondage, love and hate, coming and going, accepting and rejecting, as well as defilements and attachments, afflictions and irritations. Thus people remain forever separate from Dao.

Thus people should practice inner observation of the karmic conditions and arising of the six states of consciousness. Where do the six forms of desiring consciousness arise? Consciousness arises from desires. Where do desires come from? Desires arise from consciousness. [YQ: Consciousness arises from the mind, the mind arises from ego, ego arises from desires].[15] Once deluded imaginings and perverted views come forth, there is consciousness.

He also said:

What we call spontaneity or nonaction is originally empty and still. It is fundamentally free from consciousness. But as soon as there is the consciousness of

---

[13] The expression "transformation of wings" is already used in the *Liexian zhuan* to describe the process of becoming an immortal. Immortals were thought to be transformed either through fire or by some inner means into light, ethereal substances or creatures that could fly. Thus one finds numerous images of immortals with feathers on Han dynasty bronze mirrors. In later mystical texts, the expression denotes the ultimate metamorphosis of an ordinary mortal into a celestial being. See *Daoshu* 2.8a.

[14] Already Guo Xiang points out that divisions and distinctions are the major symptoms of Dao loss. "If right and wrong were not there, Dao would still be complete. With the destruction of Dao emotions begin to be partial and love develops" (ZZ 2; Knaul 1985, 25).

[15] See also *Benji jing* 5, l.. 115-125 (Ōfuchi 1979, 320).

divisions and distinctions, wayward perspectives begin to arise. Once such wayward perspectives appear, people are engulfed by afflictions and irritations, involvements and entanglements, fetters and bondages, ups and downs, life and death. They are forever lost to Dao. **[5a]**

Lord Lao said:

Dao is free from life and death, but the body-form does undergo life and death. Thus we say that life and death are characteristics of the body-form, but not characteristics of Dao. The body-form only comes to life when it receives Dao. The body-form only dies when it loses Dao. Whoever is able to preserve life and guard Dao will live forever and not perish."

Lord Lao said:

To someone who can maintain the mind in clarity and stillness Dao will come and stay of itself [ZWL 4b]. When Dao comes to stay of itself, spirit shines bright and remain suffusing the body-self. When spirit shines bright and remains suffusing the body-self, life will not perish [XSJ 29].

People always desire life, but they are unable to empty their minds. People always hate death, but they are unable to preserve spirit. This is as if one desired nobility, but would not apply the proper way; craved for wealth, but would not pursue treasures. It is as if one wanted to make haste and never moved a foot, wanted to be fat and never ate one's fill. **[5b]**

Lord Lao said:

[CS →] Dao is attained by the mind; the mind is made bright by Dao. Once the mind is bright, Dao descends; Dao descended, the mind is all-pervasive. [*Tian-yinzi* 3]. The brightness of spirit in the body-self is like the light in a basin lamp. Light arises from fire, fire arises from burning. Burning in turn arises because of the oil, and the oil needs the wick and the basin lamp proper. Once those four [fire, burning, oil, and lamp] are gone, where would light come from?

That is to say, brightness karmically depends on spirit radiance; spirit relies on the mind being fully present; the mind exists only within the body-form; and body-form is only complete through Dao. Even one of these four being insufficient, how could there be brightness? Thus we say that spirit brightness makes the eyes see and the ears hear, the intention know and the mind be aware. All distinctions made between things and cosmic order, all knowledge of even the finest and subtlest ultimately comes from spirit being bright. Thus we speak of spirit brightness.

Lord Lao said:

> Empty your mind: let go of solidity!
> Make your mind no-mind: get rid of existence!
> Stabilize your mind: make it unmoving!
> Calm your mind: let there be no peril!
> Make your mind still: let there be no confusion!
> Make your mind upright: let there be no waywardness!
> Make your mind clear: let there be no turbidity!
> Make your mind pure: let there be no defilements!
> [cf. ZWL 4b] **[6a]**

Once you have achieved the elimination of all these, the following will appear:

> An upright mind: no more reversal!
> A balanced mind: no more high or low!
> A bright mind: no more gloom or darkness!
> A pervasive mind: no more hindrance to go!

These four minds will begin to radiate naturally [YQ: are so originally and naturally]. Words are too coarse to explain—imagine it for yourself! Students of Dao should ardently practice this! [←]

Lord Lao said:

> Knowing Dao is easy—trusting Dao is hard.
> Trusting Dao is easy—practicing Dao is hard.
> Practicing Dao is easy—attaining Dao is hard.
> Attaining Dao is easy—guarding Dao is hard [DDJ 70].
> Guarding Dao and never losing it—live forever!

Lord Lao said:

Dao is not to be transmitted by word nor attained by hearsay. Just empty the mind, still the spirit, and Dao will come to stay of itself. Ignorant people, not realizing this, labor their body-self and exhaust their mind. They exert their will and agitate their spirit. Yet thereby they push Dao further away and make spirit grow sadder and sadder. They oppose Dao in pursuit of Dao [YQ: is resenting Dao and not accepting its compassion]—be warned against this! **[6b]**

Lord Lao said:

Dao highly values long life, so preserve spirit and make the root firm [DDJ 16]. Never let essence and *qi* disperse, but keep them pure white and always together. Body-form and spirit merged with Dao, you can fly to Mount Kunlun, come to life before creation, continue living after creation, and forever pass in and out of the spaceless.

Yet, if you do not pass through this gate, you will waste yin and disperse yang, restrict the material souls and strangle the spirit souls. For millions of years you will be a family man, producing offspring for thousands of generations. The yellow grime of the world will surround you while the perfected astride his ox enters the golden halls and jade chambers of heaven, always giving up the old and welcoming the new.[16]

Lord Lao said:

The way of inner observation lies in stilling the spirit and stabilizing the mind. Confused imaginings do not arise, falseness wayward delusions do not encroach. Make the body-self firm within your surroundings, close your eyes and examine [yourself] mentally. Within and without become empty and serene; spirit and Dao subtle and profound.

On the outside, contain the myriad aspects of projected reality; on the inside, examine the one mind.[17] In the event, just shine forth in stillness—stillness and confusion both at rest. As thought follows upon thought, deep inside your root reaches ultimate peace. Deeply luminous and eternally steady, your obscurity and mystical fusion cannot be fathomed.[18] All sorrows and vexations forever extinguished, there is no more consciousness of right and wrong.

Lord Lao said:

[7a] I am not a born sage; I studied Dao to attain it. Thus, pursuing Dao I received it all: the thousand scriptures and the myriad methods, which are ultimately only in the mind.

---

[16] The sage depicted riding an ox while leaving for the west is Laozi. It is also part of the Laozi myth that he symbolizes a progress from the old toward the young—that is, a reversal of the normal human development. See *Guangsheng yi* 2.16a.

[17] See *Qingjing jing* 2a. The text adds a third category: observation of the distant. Within and without here indicate that one observes oneself from the positions of mind and body. Observation of others, then, is called "observation of the distant."

[18] Similarly, the *Dingguan jing* encourages adepts to be "like a water mirror" (10b).

Text Six

Heavenly Seclusion[1]

The path to spirit immortality is rooted in long life. The key to long life is to make nurturing *qi* a priority. Now, *qi* is received from Heaven and Earth, then harmonized by yin and yang. Yin and yang spirit and emptiness—this is the [nature of the] mind. The aspects of the mind that rule sleeping and waking during night and day are the spirit and material souls. Set up like this, people's body-self is never far from the path to immortality.[2]

I do not know where the Master of Heavenly Seclusion came from. He wrote this treatise in eight sections to encompass the secret and the wondrous. Things found here cannot be attained through study alone.

Now, [the methods of] cultivating and refining the form-body to pure *qi*, nourishing and harmonizing the mind to emptiness, in their "return to the root" [DDJ 16] go back to Boyang [i.e., Laozi], while their "bestowing inner radiance" is found with Zhuangzi. "Long life and eternal vision" [DDJ 59] also begin with these works.

I have practiced the techniques of Dao myself. Now I feel compassion for the people of the world. They often die prematurely and do not live to perfect longevity. Therefore I decided to transmit the teaching to fellow adepts of long life.

---

[1] This translates the *Tianyinzi* (Master of Heavenly Seclusion, DZ 1026). The text has been popular since its inception and appears, with minimal variants, in many collections, including the *Daozang jiyao* (dat. 1577; Weiji 7.27a-40b), *Ershi jia zishu* (dat. 1578), *Baizi quanshu* (dat. 1875), *Yimen guangdu* (dat. 1940), and *Qigong yangsheng congshu* (dat. 1990; #19). The main variants used in the annotation come from the *Daoshu* (abbr. "DS") and *Congshu jicheng* (abbr. "CS"), ch. 573.

[2] This first paragraph seems to be a later addition. Song bibliographies have the text start with the next section.

I have simplified it so that it can be practiced and referred to easily. From Boyang to the Master of Heavenly Seclusion, there has only been this teaching.

Respectfully submitted

1. Spirit Immortality

When a human being is born, he or she is naturally endowed with the *qi* of emptiness [DS: numinosity]. Essence and intellect are pervasive and awake, learning has no obstructions: this is what we call "spirit." Settle the spirit within and let its radiance shine without, so that you naturally become different from ordinary people: this is what we call a spirit immortal. Therefore even a spirit immortal is still a human being.

Just focus on cultivating the *qi* of emptiness and never get involved in worldly discussions and analyses. Follow your self in spontaneity and never let wayward views obstruct your path. Thus you reach success.

NOTE: Joy, anger, sadness, happiness, love, hate, and desires—these seven are [natural] emotional tendencies turned wayward. Wind, damp, cold, heat, hunger, satiation, labor, and idleness—these eight are *qi* turned wayward. Rid yourself of these manifestations of waywardness and reach immortality![3]

2. Simplicity

The *Yijing* says: "The way of Heaven and Earth is simple" [*Xici* I.1]. What does this mean?

The Master of Heavenly Seclusion says: "Heaven and Earth are above my head and beneath my feet. When I open my eyes I can see them. I can speak of them without complex devices. Thus I say: consummate simplicity is the inherent potency of immortality." [CS: Thus I speak of simplicity. Simplicity is an expression for spirit immortality.]

NOTE: The Scripture says: "Utmost Dao is not complex, the perfect man does not act" [cf. ZZ 58/22/18].

What path should one use to seek this?

He says: "Without seeking you cannot know; without a path you cannot attain. All students of spirit immortality must first attain simplicity. Teachings that are

---

[3] This paragraph appears as a note in DZ 1026, but has been integrated into the main text frequently. The seven emotions are first described in the "Liyun" chapter of the *Liji*. It has "fear" instead of "happiness."

intricate, artful, and attractive only lead people astray. They do not lead to "return to the root." They can never be my teaching."

NOTE: Some people in the world study immortality but are only deluded by it. Some study breathing but are only made sick by it.[4]

3. Gradual Progress Toward the Gate of Dao

The *Yijing* has a hexagram called *Jian*, "Progressive Advance" [no. 56]. Laozi speaks of the "Gate of all Wonders" [DDJ 1]. When working to cultivate perfection and master inner nature, do not expect sudden awakening. Rather, progress gradually and calmly practice. Thus you enter the gates of gradual progress: [CS: As I enter them through insight, Dao becomes visible.]:[5]

1. Fasting and abstention.   2. Seclusion.
3. Visualization and imagination.   4. Sitting in oblivion.
5. Spirit liberation.

What does fasting and abstention mean? It means cleansing the body-self and emptying the mind.[6]

What does seclusion mean? It means withdrawing deep into the oratory.

What does visualization and imagination mean? It means holding in the mind[7] and recovering inner nature.

What does sitting in oblivion mean? It means letting go of the form-body and completely forgetting the "I" [ZZ 6].

What does spirit liberation mean? It means the myriad concrete manifestations [dharmas] are pervaded by spirit.[8]

Practice according to these five gates of gradual progress and complete step one, then gradually move on to step two. Complete step two, then gradually move on to step three. Complete step three, then gradually move on to step

---

[4] The *Daoshu* includes this in the text and reverses the order of the two statements.

[5] The *Daoshu* summarizes this paragraph in one sentence and includes the following explanations in later sections (2.4b).

[6] Cf. the statement on "keeping the mind empty" in *Daode jing* 3 and Zhuangzi's "fasting of the mind" (ch. 4).

[7] This contains a reference to section 3 of the *Zuowang lun*.

[8] The *Zhuangzi* has: "Knowledge is pervaded by spirit" (29/12/14), and "Make yourself one with Great Pervasion" (19/6/92). Buddhists speak of "spirit pervasion" as the state of the deep and transcendent *samādhi* of the Buddha. He then emits a bright light and possess supernatural powers. See *Yuanjue jing* (T. 17.913a) and *Weimo jing* (T. 14.539a).

four. Complete step four, then gradually move on to step five. Thus you succeed at spirit immortality!

4. Fasting and Abstention[9]

Fasting and abstention not only mean to live on vegetables and mushrooms. Cleansing the body is not just bathing to remove the dirt. Rather, the method is to regulate food intake so that it is perfectly balanced, to massage the body so that it glows in health.

All people are endowed with the *qi* of the five phases.[10] They live on things that consist of them. From the time they enter the womb people breathe in and out; blood and essence circulate in their bodies. How could one stop eating and yet pursue long life?

Ordinary people do not understand that abstaining from grains and absorbing *qi* are only temporary measures of Daoists. These things do not mean that we completely abstain from all food forever. We speak of fasting and abstention from food, yes. But we refer to the purification of nourishment and the moderation of intake.[11] If one is hungry one eats—but never to satiation.[12] Thus we establish a balanced diet.

Don't eat anything not well cooked! Don't eat dishes with the five flavors in excess! Don't eat anything fermented or conserved! These are our basic abstentions.

Massage your skin with your hands so that it becomes moist and hot! This drives out cold *qi* and makes the body radiate with a glow.

Refrain from long sitting, long standing, long exhaustive labor! All these are basic abstentions.[13] They serve to balance and regulate the body. If the body is strong, *qi* is whole.

Thus fasting and abstention are the first gate to Dao.

---

[9] *Zhaijie*, lit. "purification and precepts." In the middle ages, this indicated days of retreat which involved fasting (see Kohn 2010, 99). Here it refers to dietary practices.

[10] *Zuowang lun* 11ab. See also *Huangdi neijing suwen* as cited in YQ 14.13b.

[11] The *Daoshu* shortens this and defines fasting as "purification" and abstention as "regulation." For Daoist diets, see Lévi 1983; Arthur 2006; Kohn 2010.

[12] Cf. *Cunshen lianqi ming* 1b.

[13] See Kohn 2008b, 71. This follows the *Daoshu* (2.5a). The DZ edition leaves out "no" (*wu* 勿) before every item. The same abstentions appear in Sima's *Fuqi jingyi lun* (YQ 57.19b; see Engelhardt 1987) with reference to the *Huangdi neijing suwen* (23.10b). Already the *Zhuangzi* contains warnings against physical exertion (see Robinet 1983, 79).

5. Seclusion

What is meant by seclusion?[14] It has nothing to do with living in ornate halls, in cavernous buildings, on double matting and thick carpeting. It means sitting with one's face to the south, sleeping with one's head to the east, complying in everything with the harmonious rhythm of yin and yang.[15]

Light and darkness should be in balance. The room should not be too high. If it is too high, yang is predominant and there will be too much light. The room should not be too low. If it is too low, yin is predominant and there will be too much darkness.

The reason for this precaution is that, when there is too much light, the material souls will be harmed. When there is too much darkness, spirit souls will suffer. People's spirit souls are yang, their material souls are yin. Harm them with light and darkness, and they will get sick.

When things are arranged in the proper balanced way, we have a chamber of seclusion. Still, don't forget how various the *qi* of Heaven and Earth can be. There may, for example, be violent [CS: primordial] yang that attacks the flesh. Or there may be a lascivious yin that overpowers the body. Be wary and guard against these! During the progressive advance of cultivation and nourishment there is no proper seclusion unless these instructions are carried out.

The Master of Heavenly Seclusion says: "The room I live in has windows on all four sides. When wind arises I close them; as soon as the wind has died down I open them again.[16] In front of my meditation seat a curtain is suspended; behind it a screen has been placed. When it is too light I draw the curtain to adjust the brightness inside. When it gets too dark I roll the curtain up again to let light in from outside.

"On the inside I calm my mind, on the outside I calm my eyes. Mind and eyes must be both completely at peace. If either light or darkness prevails, there are too many thoughts, too many desires. How could I ever calm myself inside and out?" Thus in studying Dao, seclusion marks the second step.

---

[14] The term for "seclusion" (*anchu* 安處) goes back as far as the *Shijing*. It also occurs in the "Xinshu" 心術 (Arts of the Mind) chapter of the *Guanzi* and in Buddhist literature. The *Yuanjue jing*, for example, mentions it in the context of a progressive system as the step to be taken after "meticulous observation of the precepts" (T. 17.914b).

[15] The *Daoshu* here has: "The place where one lives must be completely in accord with the harmonious rhythm of yin and yang" (2.5a).

[16] Closing and opening doors to match yin and yang is already mentioned in *Xià* I.11.

6. Visualization and Imagination

Visualization means to visualize my spirit. Imagination means imaging my body-self. [17] [DS: How to do this?] Closing the eyes and one can see one's own eyes. Collecting the mind one can see one's own mind. Mind and eyes never separate from my body-self and never harming my spirit: this is the gradual practice of visualization and imagination.

Ordinary people, to the end of their days, direct their eyes only toward others. Thus their minds wander outside and for their whole life is concerned only with outer affairs. Thus the eyes also continue looking at things outside.[18] Brightly sparkling they float around everywhere and never reflect back on themselves. How can people not become sick from this and end up dying prematurely?

Therefore "return to the root means stillness, and stillness means to recover destiny" [DDJ 16]. To recover destiny and be true to inner nature is called "the gate of all wonders" [DDJ 1]. Thus, with the step of visualization and imagination one is halfway to succeeding in one's study of Dao.

7. Sitting in Oblivion

Sitting in oblivion is attained after learning visualization and imagination. It also means the forgetting all about visualization and imagination.

Acting in Dao and not seeing oneself act—isn't that the meaning of sitting? Seeing something and not acting on it—isn't that the meaning of oblivion?

Why do we speak of not acting? Because the mind remains free from agitation. Why do we speak of not seeing? Because the body-form is completely obliterated.[19]

[DS: Someone asks: "If the mind is not agitated, does it have Dao then?" {CS: How do you attain the non-agitated state of mind?"} The Master of Heavenly Seclusion remains silent and does not answer. Another asks: "If the body is obliterated, does it have Dao then?" {CS: How do you attain the obliteration of the body?}]

---

[17] "Imagination" means the deliberate creation of images on the basis of actual experience. It stands in opposition to "fantasy" which refers to images largely devoid of reality. A similar usage of these terms is found in the psychology of Carl Jung.

[18] For more on the interaction of mind and yes, see below in the translation of Wu Yun's treatise "On Mind and Eyes."

[19] Cf. *Zuowang lun* 4b.

The Master of Heavenly Seclusion closes his eyes and does not look.

At some point, he wakes to Dao and withdraws, saying: "Dao is really in me. What person is this 'me'? What person actually is this Master of Heavenly Seclusion?"

Thus, self and other both forgotten, nothing is left to radiate forth.

8. Spirit Liberation

Step one, fasting and abstention, is called liberation through faith.[20] NOTE: Without faith, the mind cannot be liberated.

Step two, seclusion, is called liberation through withdrawal. NOTE: Without withdrawal, the mind cannot be liberated.

Step three, visualization and imagination, is called liberation through insight. NOTE: Without insight, the mind cannot be liberated.

Step four, sitting in oblivion, is called liberation through stability. NOTE: Without stability, the mind cannot be liberated.[21]

When the four gates of faith, withdrawal, insight, and stability have been pervaded by spirit, then we speak of spirit liberation. By "spirit" we mean that which "arrives without moving and is swift without hurrying" [ZZ 26/11/17]; what transforms along with yin and yang and is "as old as Heaven and Earth" [DDJ 7].

When the three forces of Heaven, Earth, and Humanity [*Yijing*, "Shuogua" 1] are combined, changes occur. NOTE: The *Xici* says: "When the changes come to an end, there is transformation. Where there is transformation, there is pervasion. Where there is pervasion, there is continuity" [II.2].

When the myriad "things are equalized" [ZZ 2], then Dao and inherent potency are active. NOTE: This refers to Laozi's *Daojing* and *Dejing*.

When the underlying inner nature of all is attained, there is perfect suchness.[22] NOTE: The *Lotus Sūtra*, the *Lankāvatāra Sūtra*, and the *Nirvāna Sūtra* of Sakyamuni all deal with "the underlying inner nature."

---

[20] "Liberation through faith" (*xinjie* 信解) translates the Sanskrit *adhimukti* (Soothill and Hudous 1937, 288).
[21] The order of the various kinds of liberation is different in the *Daoshu*: 1. faith; 2. absorption; 3. stillness; 4. insight (2.6a).
[22] This translates *bhūtatathata*, the eternal unchanging reality behind all phenomena (Soothill and Hudous 1937, 332).

[CS: Enter into suchness and return to nonaction. NOTE: The *Yuanjue jing* says: "Whether there is the threefold embodiment of the Buddha in action or in nonaction or the metamorphosis body of the Buddha which cannot fall back into mundane destiny, all is the one original nature" {T.17.921b}.]

The Master of Heavenly Seclusion says: "I am born with the changes; I will die with the changes. I move with the myriad things; I rest with the myriad things" [ZZ 34/13/14; 40/15/10]. Waywardness comes form the underlying inner nature; perfection comes from the underlying inner nature. [23] For this reason, life and death, movement and rest, waywardness and perfection: through spirit I am liberated from them all.

"Among human beings, I am called an immortal. In heaven, I am a celestial immortal. On earth, I am an earth immortal. [CS: In water I am a water immortal.] Thus the path to spirit immortality consists of these five progressive gates, leading to a single goal. NOTE: Meaning that through all five one ultimately returns to immortality.

Postface: Oral Instructions[24]

I recited the text *Tianyinzi* and after three years I had gained some vague understanding. Subsequently I used the five gates it outlines and very gradually approached the practice. After another three years, I awakened to the peace of body-form and mind and realized the insipidity of fame and profit. After yet another three years, the Master appeared to me and gave me the following oral instructions.

The central part of my teaching, he said, is the section on visualization and imagination. It deals with the return to the root, with recovering life and fulfilling one's inner nature in all its subtleties. The fundamental root of the human being grows from the elixir field. When one returns to this one can live long. Thus I say: Return to the root and recover destiny [DDJ 16]. The numinous consciousness of humanity is grounded in rational nature. When inner nature is pervaded by spirit, it is subtle and there will be no obstruction in dealing with the myriad things. Thus I say: Perfect nature in all its subtleties.

---

[23] Dao as the one original nature of the cosmos which underlies all existence is an important concept in Tang Daoism. The expression used is *daoxing* 道性, a direct take on the Buddhist *foxing* 佛性, "buddha-nature." See Kamata 1966.

[24] As found in Tao Zongyi's 陶宗儀 *Shuofu* 說郛 (Theory Land, ch. 75), Hu Wenhuan's 胡文煥 *Gezhi congshu* 格致叢書 (Integrated Research Collection) of the late Ming (1.5), and *Baizi quanshu* 百子全書 (Complete Writings of the Hundred Masters) of 1875 ("Daojia").

Breathing is activated by *qi*, so I provide instructions to expel the old and draw in the new [breath]. Saliva arises from the kidneys, so I teach to rinse the mouth and swallow the saliva. Thoughts and ideas stir in the mind and consciousness, so I instruct to practice visualization and imagination. The defensive *qi*, the blood, and the channels in the human body all turn toward the outside when one is awake and focus inside during sleep. In both waking and sleeping, inside and outside should nurture each other in harmony.

With harmony established, practice daily between midnight and noon [during the time of living *qi*]. Lie down flat on your back and stretch your arms and legs. Next, rise to undertake healing exercises, breathing strongly but steadily. The tap the front teeth together quietly, then click the molars to produce a loud sound. With both hands massage your face to the eyes, until the body feels warm and glowing.

Next, sit upright with legs folded under. With your tongue stimulate the Flowery Pond, then rise when saliva arises in the mouth. Silently count the times of rinsing and once in 300 swallow the saliva. Swallow only after you have inhaled fully and do not exhale before you have completed the swallowing. Practicing like this, the inhaled *qi* reaches the lower elixir field together with the saliva. Also, practice only between midnight and noon when all food is well digested and the mind is empty. Rinse and swallow without interruption—it does not matter how many times altogether. Just stop when you feel it is enough. Five says of this practice count as one cycle.

Next, light incense in your oratory. Visualize and imagine your body from head to foot, then again up from the feet to the [upper] elixir field, moving along the spinal column and into the Niwan [Palace in the head]. After this, turn again to rinsing the mouth and swallowing the saliva.

Also, cover your ears with the palms of your hands until you hear a drumming sound inside the head. After three sets of seven, stretch both legs, stand up, and bend forward. Stretch the neck, gripping it tightly with both hands. Then place your hands on your hips and raise your shoulders in alternation. Hold the breath. Stop when the *qi* is full and your face is red. Repeat this seven times. Pay close attention to make sure the *qi* enters all the way into the Niwan. This concludes the general outline of the practice.

There are, however, more essential and subtler practices which more careully align and synchronize the practice with the *qi* of Heaven and Earth. For this you must be able to recognize when the *qi* comes and clearly feel when it stops. This way you can be in harmony with Heaven and Earth, eventually attaining the same age. This is spirit immortality.

The practice ideally begins at midnight on the day of the winter solstice. This is when yang *qi* first arises. Regardless of whether it is early or late, make sure you can feel the arising of *qi* within yourself. One when you clearly feel that it has arrived can you begin circulating it within, always remaining fully aligned with the *qi* of Heaven and Earth. The next day again you wait for the *qi* to arrive, then work along with it. This is the sublest and most essential method of spirit immortality. Only few can practice it.

For 360 days circulate your *qi* in harmony with the perfect *qi* [of the cosmos]. Having done this three times over [for three years], you will feel clarity and harmony within. It will feel quite different from ordinary life. How much more so when you continue with the practice for even longer periods! Growing in subtle alignment, the way of spirit immortality is no longer hard to attain.

Recorded by Sima Chengzhen.

Text Seven

The Five Kitchens[1]

Preface[2]

[1a] I have heard that the *Yijing* says: "Penetrating [ultimate] meaning and entering into spirit promotes the utmost activation [of spirit]. Utilizing this activation and bringing peace to the body-self [self] allow for the veneration of inherent inherent potency."[3]

---

[1] This translates the *Wuchu jing* as found in DZ 763. Alternative readings in YQ 61.5b-10b are noted in brackets. The verses are in bold face with lines numbered from 1 to 20. The commentary is in plain text.

[2] Dated to the 12th month of Kaiyuan 開元 23 (735). See Mollier 2000, 64.

[3] This passage is found in the "Dazhuan" 大傳 (Great Commentary) to the *Yijing*, (2.5.3). The full passage runs: "The contraction of the measuring worm is done in order to try to stretch itself out, and the hibernation of dragons and snakes is done in order to preserve their lives. Perfect concepts come about by entrance into the numinous, which, once had, allows one to extend their application [activation] to the utmost. The use of these applications comes about by making one's person secure, which allows for the subsequent veneration of his inherent power. To go beyond this is something that no one has ever known how to do, for to plumb the numinous to the utmost and to understand transformation represent the very acme of inherent power" (Wilhelm 1950, 338).

Wang Bi comments: "'Perfect concepts' means 'the profound subtlety of the principles of things.' The numinous, being utterly still, does not act, but when it responds to something, that response is perfect and thoroughgoing. Thus one is able to take advantage of all the subtle secrets that underlie the world and gain unified and complete control over their applications. The Dao governing how to make use of applications means that one first makes one's position secure and only after that takes action. Perfect concepts derive from 'entrance into the numinous, which, once had, allows one to extend their application to the utmost' The use of these applications derives from 'making one's person secure, which al-

These words are truly valuable, truly wonderful! From them we know that first ultimate meaning must be penetrated, then one can join with spirit to reach its utmost activation. This activation in turn must be utilized, then one can bring peace to the body-self and venerate potency. To reach utmost activation while ultimate meaning is not penetrated, to bring peace to the body-self without utilizing its activation, to know Dao without having peace in oneself: this has never happened!

This being so, the pervasive activation [of *qi*] is the master of all life and transformations. Essence and *qi* forming living things we call concretized harmony. Vast and spaceless, they all stand together, forming the great potency of Heaven and Earth. Is this not what we call "life"?

The prime way to completing physical form in this life is to think less, reduce desires, embrace simplicity, and pursue harmony. Let the mind wander in dispassion, harmonize *qi* in cosmic vastness, and you will be clear and bright in your body, your will and *qi* like pure spirit. If ever there are any cravings or desires trying to get in, you can spot any potential opening and get ahead of them.

[1b] For this reason, the sages have handed down the teachings and arranged them, have expounded karmic functioning and controlled it. Therefore, you should stabilize your *qi* to utmost softness, thereby to find the path to cosmic harmony; turn to obscurity and calm your breath, thereby to stop all desires; cleanse your mind and live in seclusion, thereby to penetrate spirit and understand the hidden transformations. After all this, the body-self can be at peace and the state can be secure; inherent potency can be activated and the people be unknowing. Then you will naturally be able to fully benefit form all the good fortune spread by the blessings of Heaven.

Bow your head and recite the five stanzas of this scripture, and you will easily get the perfect essentials of cultivating the body-self and protecting life. To complete harmony and encompass universal oneness: penetrate [ultimate] meaning, so you can enter into spirit, sit in oblivion, and let go of brilliance; bring peace to the body-self, so you can venerate potency, investigate sensory experience, and nourish yourself forever.

---

lows for the subsequent veneration of his inherent power' As principles must derive from their progenitor; so each and every matter springs from the root. If one returns to the root of things, he will find quiescence there and discover all the world's principles available to him. However, if he enslaves his capacity for thought and deliberation just so he can seek ways to put things to use and if he disregards the need to make his person secure just so he can sacrifice himself to achievement and fine reputation, then the more the spurious arises, the more principles will be lost, and the finer his reputation grows, the more obvious his entanglements will become" (Lynn 1994, 81-82).

Arranging the text to include admonitions and explanations, I have humbly drafted an insignificant and worthless work. Receiving grace like a torrent of rain and noticing steady support [from Dao?], I cannot avoid the heavenly light shining on me and forget just how lowly and vulgar I am. Therefore, I bow to submit this work, trembling in shame and fear, feeling vague and indistinct as if totally lost. Always your servant, I, Yin, knock my head to the ground.

The Text

[1a] As long as you dwell in the *qi* of universal oneness and in the harmony of cosmic peace, the five organs are abundant and full and the five spirits are still and upright. When the five organs are abundant, all sensory experiences are satisfied; when the five spirits are still, all cravings and desires are eliminated.

This scripture expounds on how the five organs taking in *qi* is like someone looking for food in a kitchen. Thus its title: "Scripture of the Five Kitchens."

* * *

1 The *qi* of universal oneness merges with the harmony of cosmic peace.

"The *qi* of universal oneness" is the wondrous origin. In a state of pervasive function, it is called primordial *qi*. When this functions pervasively, it creates yang harmony in Heaven, yin harmony on Earth, and the harmony of cosmic peace in the exchange of these two. Thus when human beings receive life, they are always endowed with the harmony of *qi* of universal oneness. Therefore, the text speaks of the "harmony of cosmic peace." Only afterwards do physical form and concrete materials come together [1b] and the five constancies [senses] become active. Thus Laozi says: "The ten thousand things carry yin and embrace yang, pervading *qi* they come to a state of harmony" [42].

As a result, to maintain [a connection to] the origin: on the outside, eliminate the two forms of perception, thereby making life's allotment whole; on the inside, dwell in *qi* of universal oneness, thereby merging with the harmony of cosmic peace. Once merged with universal oneness, inner nature and destiny are complete. Therefore Laozi says: "Can you stabilize your *qi* and find complete softness, like an infant?" [10].

2 Attaining universal oneness, Dao rests in cosmic peace.

"Attaining universal oneness" means: on the inside, dwell in the *qi* of universal oneness to nourish essence and spirit; on the outside, make physical form and life whole to abide in cosmic peace. Then *qi* of universal oneness can be in pervasive activation and the body-self is filled with the harmony of cosmic peace. This is cosmic harmony. Thus it says "attaining universal oneness." Doing so, the various ways of cultivating the body and nurturing spirit all join in the harmony of cosmic peace. As Laozi says: "The myriad things rely on it to be born" [32]

3 Cosmic harmony really is neither universal oneness nor harmony.

[2a] This says, when people are first endowed with the *qi* of universal oneness, they are [innately] merged with the harmony of cosmic peace. By [later] dwelling in harmony and attaining universal oneness, they can merge with cosmic order and find overarching peace. As utmost harmony flourishes freely, not only is there no more [sense of] oneness, but there is also no [conscious awareness of] harmony any longer. It cannot be critically examined, but is like soil thrown on earth [complete natural]. As Laozi says: "I do not know its name" [25].

4 Mysterious cosmic order joins the mysterious moment of eternity.

"Mysterious" is wondrous; "cosmic order" is inner nature. This says: the *qi* of universal oneness forever dwells in the mysterious moment of eternity and, as it merges with cosmic order, brings forth inner nature. As inner nature is cultivated, one recovers inherent potency and wondrously begins to pervade cosmic harmony. Once wondrous inner nature is completely merged with cosmic harmony, one becomes mysteriously co-eternal with the mystery [source of all]. Laozi says: "Both may be called mysterious" [1].

* * *

5 Do not intentionally develop thinking and intention,

"Intention" here indicates delusory perception. This says, when trying to dwell in the *qi* of universal oneness and merge with the harmony of cosmic peace, [2b] be careful not to dwell in imaginary perception since it will condition you karmically toward projected reality and [discriminating] consciousness. Rather, concentrate spirit to a state of deep luminosity [like standing water] and wide radiance, making it vague and vacuous, and let it merge with the state before thoughts arise. Wisdom unfolds only after all knowledge is forgotten. Once one has seen this barrier, there is no more [perception of] good and bad fortune.

On the other hand, if you "intentionally develop thinking and intention," that intention will invite delusory perception of being in the world of dust and grime and cause cosmic harmony to vanish. How, then, will you attain [eternal] life and [pervasive] understanding? As Laozi says: "Cut off contacts, shut the doors, and to the end of life there will be peace without toil" [52, 56; ZWL 2a].

6 But do not pursue non-thinking either.

If you just stay away from being conditioned by delusory perception, radiant wisdom will unfold on its own. When that happens, you won't actually [consciously] know it. On the contrary, if you knowingly pursue non-thinking, you are already mired in delusory perception and are thus in a state no different from thinking, intending, and the like. Thus Laozi says: "Nameless and simple, and free from desires" [42].

7 Have intention but without any thinking or [conception of] existence:

[3a]On the inside, dwell in *qi* of universal oneness, just let it all be empty. When all is empty, cosmic harmony comes of itself and cosmic order naturally pervades all. Even if not conditioned by delusory perception, if you try to actively pull in cosmic harmony, you will be sucked into [conscious] intention toward, and the classification of, one-sided views [apparent reality]. Although this does not mean you then dwell in projections and consciousness, you yet need to be free from any thinking or [conception of] existence. As Laozi says: "Use its light to recover its brightness" [52].

8 Then any concrete manifestations are [immediately] controlled.

It is like this: On the inside dwell in the harmony of cosmic peace, and the concrete manifestations [dharmas] of the harmony of cosmic peace merge in complete pervasion. Then all these concrete manifestations will vanish. Vanished manifestations means that there is no more [perceiving] agent in the mind, so what would there be to control? Then not controlling becomes the very action of controlling. Thus it says: "Then any concrete manifestations are [immediately] controlled."

* * *

9 Never entangle mind with mind,

The mind is the raw material of unfolding wisdom and also the vessel of delusory perception. If it perceives correctly, it brings forth wisdom; [3b] if it perceives erroneously, it brings forth delusion. This says: If people can find energetic harmony within and their mind perceives correctly, their entire inner being will radiate with clarity and purity.[4] Then right wisdom[5] is deeply luminous. It mirrors [universal] light, and the [world's] dust and grime have no place to stick.[6] Like a deep abyss and unadulterated, it regards the myriad phenomena

---

[4] This might imply a reference to the *Qingjing jing*.
[5] Buddhist *samyak*. See Soothill and Hudous 1937, 192.
[6] This recalls the famous poem of Huineng, the Sixth Patriarch, on the mirror of the mind and the contention of the Northern School of Chan that one should polish it so that no dust and dirt can stick to it. SeeYampolsky 1967; McRae. 1983 The symbolic role of the mirror in medieval China is discussed in Lai 1979; Ching 1983; Demiéville 1987.

equally. Seeing all phenomena [equally] without a [perceiving] agent: this is the constant mind.

If, on the other hand, you try to attain this mind by working through the mind, you will only condition the mind to perceive defilements. On the outside, it dwells on all sorts of concrete manifestations; on the inside, it has no radiant wisdom. In this state the constant mind is already lost. Then any chance of merging with is ruined. Thus the *Zhuangzi* says: "Attaining this mind, with this mind attain the constant mind. How, then, can it perceive any outside things?" [ch. 4].

10 But recover a state of no perceiving agent and the elimination of conditioning.

Now, if you use the mind to condition the mind, you will perceive all sorts of concrete perceptions. If you perceive correctly, the mind will bring forth wisdom and you will naturally attain the constant mind. When both wisdom and mind are constant, then you reach the correct state of no-perception [no-mind]. How, then, could you still be conditioned? Once free from conditioned mind, there is no more conditioning to be eliminated either. Deeply translucent and utterly serene, where would there by a perceiving agent? Thus Laozi says: "Diminish and again diminish"[48]. **[4a]**

11 The mind dwelling in non-dwelling mind:

If wisdom radiates with deep luminosity and in constancy, we speak of mind dwelling in the elimination [of all]. When there is no agent present, we speak of "non-dwelling." Once the mind is radiant, it will not be tempted to pursue or receive any mental conditioning. Then there is nothing to eliminate, nor is there a perceiving agent.

12 In perfection, maintain perfect abyss-like quality.

"Perfection" is another word for the constant mind radiating in wisdom, full of clarity and purity and without any dilution. Deeply translucent and sharing in the source of wisdom, utterly serene without a trace of defilement, completely unknowing with regard to outward manifestations, and without a bit of karmic conditioning—now the harmony of cosmic peace encompasses perfection and one is never separate from the origin. Thus the text uses the word "maintain."

* * *

13 Cultivating cosmic order, the will becomes a detached will,

[4b] "Cosmic order" is inner [Dao] nature. "Will" is a state of mind without flow [content]. Once you eliminate all projected reality, you can perceive this mind. Then inner nature can be perceived as well. In other words, in cultivating inner nature, if there is a [state of] mind that still has content, just retreat to a position of all-round radiance. Once the world of dust and grime is fully eliminated on the outside, when projected reality and consciousness no longer have an active agent, you can "cast off form, do away with knowledge, and become one with Great Pervasion" [Zhuangzi 6]. With inner nature cultivated, you can recover the cosmic beginning and radiate all-round without obstruction. Utterly pure both on the inside and the outside, you can be "mysterious and again mysterious" [DDJ 1]. Thus you detach yourself from all [mental] content and [perceptive] delusion.

14 While accumulating cultivation will not get you to detachment.

First, by cultivating inner nature and developing a detached will, inside and outside are both serene and no perceiving agent arises any longer in the mind. Nor is there [any perception of] a vacuous mind. Sitting in oblivion and acting in oblivion at all times, things just arise and pass away one after the other.

On the other hand, if you accumulate cultivation practices, you will never be able to reach full oblivion and obliteration. Giving rise to even one thought of cultivation becomes the hair that pulls a thousand pounds: your internal radiance is shaken, the outside world of dust and grime arises, and you will be unable to properly merge with the detached will. [5a]

15. The will may be present but not as a cultivated will.

If the mind is completely free form any content, where would gradual awakening come from? [Tianyinzi 2]. A mind in a state of complete stability must be caused by some sort of content, thus the text speaks of "will." Without cultivating the will, just illuminate the detached will, and there will not be [the error of] accumulating cultivation. Just forget about cultivation, and inner [Dao] nature will be stable. This leads to serenity and all-round radiance.

16 There is just personal karmic functioning and no more self-based knowing.

Caused by mental content, wisdom and karma are clear are pure, thus the text speaks of "personal karmic functioning." On the inside, forget all about the self; on the outside, forget all about things [Cf. Qingjing jing]. In a state of radiant wisdom, without even a smidgeon of fluster and activity, there is just karmic functioning, and all knowledge is naturally forgotten. Thus the text says: "No more self-based knowing."

* * *

17 All food *qi* combines into *qi*

Now, *qi* of universal oneness coagulates and combines in the harmony of cosmic peace. With cosmic harmony and universal oneness both in place, radiant wisdom is constant and deeply translucent. Then you can let the mouth take in various flavors to satisfy the five organs; your body-self can assimilate different kinds of "foamy and frothy" [foods], **[5b]** thereby to support physical form and life.

We receive solidity from Earth, coagulate moisture from water, are endowed with warmth by fire, and rely on wind for our breath. These four conditioning factors combine and dissolve constantly, none having any part in the wondrous underlying solidity [of the universe]. Therefore they muddle and obscure *qi* of universal oneness, confuse and disturb the harmony of cosmic peace, and cause the arising of delusory perception. They stir up nothing but corruption and pollution.

18 But it won't stay combined and stable for long.

This says, people should have the harmony of cosmic peace to encompass universal oneness, remain completely free from all delusory perception, and maintain perfection in constant deep luminosity. Then they can join their physical structure with cosmic peace and harmony. They may also use all sorts of food for their combined *qi*, however, doing so, "they won't stay combined and stable for long."

19 All forms of [combined] *qi* return to original *qi*.

The four conditioning factors lead to [delusory] perception and [discriminating] consciousness; the six taints [of perception] bring forth corruption.[7] All made of earth, water, fire, and wind will eventually disperse and return to the origin. **[6a]** Once the root consciousness is defiled, how can one perceive karmic functioning?

20 If you pursue gathering it, you also must pursue its dispersal.

"Gathering" means perceive and take in; "dispersal" means unfold and activate. Now, delusion and [seeing things as] existing are two forms of mental content, which lead to two kinds of karmic causation. Pursuing anything that is perceived and thus taken [into the mind] will inevitably lead to unfolding and activation. If cosmic peace and harmony merge with universal oneness, then *qi* of

---

[7] The six taints of perception, *liuran* 六染, are Buddhist states of wrong ways to relate to apparent reality—1. being attached to it; 2. failing to eliminate it; 3. developing discriminating consciousness on its basis; 4. having sensory acceptance of it; 5. mentally seeing; and 6. living in a primal karmic relation to it. See Soothill and Hudous 1937, 135.

universal oneness is completely in harmony. Thereby reaching the point of utmost emptiness is called "recovering destiny" [DDJ 16]. Finding constancy by
recovering life is called "correct perception." In a state of correct perception
and purified karmic functioning, you can bring forth radiant wisdom. When
radiant wisdom is deeply translucent and perfectly constant, you rest in oneness,
free from all [perception of] existence. Then you can enter the spaceless.

On the other hand, if in universal oneness you eat [foods for] cosmic *qi*, hoping
to return to the origin, and rely on the four conditioning factors to complete
your karmic functioning, you will forever tumble around the six rebirths.

Text Eight

Mind and Eyes[1]

Introduction: The Problem

[1a] What makes people live is the spirit; what they are entrusted to is the body. The central square spot is called the numinous prefecture. When this is at peace, the spirit is vibrant and the body is harmonious; when it is agitated, the spirit is labored and the body declines. Only when the deep root is very calm, can one truly cultivate inner nature [to be free from] emotions.

However, what agitates the spirit is the mind; what disturbs the mind are the eyes. Through them one loses perfection and is separated from the foundation [of life]. There is nothing worse than this. Therefore I will now borrow the roles of the mind and the eyes and have them engage in disputation with each other—in order to remove obstructions and help the spirit toward purification. [1b] Let us therefore say, the mind strives for nonaction and the eyes disturb it.

The Mind: Obstructions

The mind reprimands the eyes, saying:

I wish to forget all emotions in withdrawal and retirement, lead inner nature to the invisible and inaudible. I want to hide in the sphere of great harmony, wan-

---

[1] This translates Wu Yun's *Xinmu lun* from DZ 1038. The text DZ 1051, 2.16b-19b is almost identical. Variants are notes in brackets marked "DZ." Subheadings are my own. I would like to thank Xu Yiming and Alan Chan for their perceptive comments on the translation, which was originally published, with more extensive explanations, in *Monumenta Serica* (see Kohn 1998b).

der along the path of the four attainments. I wish to leave the realm of life and death behind and enter the ultimate of spirit radiance. I want to ride on pure chaos and travel far-off, at one with the vast expanse and free from all bounds.

However, whenever I stop to rest, why do you still look at things? Whenever I am pure, why do you still make plans? Why do you glance at the myriad images and confuse my proper way? Why do you delight in beautiful sights and muddle my true essence? Why, when I am far off in nonseeing, radiant in free-floating vision, do you disturb me with terraces in spring and make melancholy with domains in autumn?

You focus on the soil of Yan and make the emotions get excited; you look afar at the gates of Wu and make the hair change [color with sadness]. You glance up at the country of Chu and make me ache with longing; you look down upon the suburbs of Qi and make me cry with yearning. Oh, how I am agitated by so many thoughts—and all because of the confusion caused by your tiny pupils.

The body dotes on beautiful ornaments; the mouth desires rich tastes; the ears are fond of harmonious sounds; **[2a]** and the nose delights in fragrant smells. But you agitate me most of all! All your various activities bring me nothing but distress! It is all your fault! If I wasn't at odds with you — who else would be my enemy?

The Eyes: Responsibility

The eyes retort with anger:

Have you not heard? When one man controls the realm, so that the multitude have standards to rely on, order must be established from above. Disorder is never the fault of those below. Thus under Yao even commoners could be given a fief, while under Jie anyone ran a chance to be put to death. In however many different places and of however many different kinds, people always follow the imperial rule.

Similarly the master who controls the body is you, the mind. You are the numinous prefecture. Someone goes against you and you get rid of him. Someone complies with your orders and you promote him. All praise and happiness issue from you alone; all regret and sorrow assemble only through you.

Therefore a ruler of men controls order before it is thrown into chaos; a preserver of the Dao overcomes all thoughts before they are confused. Otherwise, once all in the four seas has divided and collapsed, how can you chastise the rebels? How, when the five emotions have scattered and gone out of control, can you observe them with proper detachment?

Why don't you just stop your machinations and perfect your subtlety? Instead, you discriminate between beings and self, illuminate right and wrong. You rejoice in glory and grieve for shame, **[2b]** delight in surplus and regret insufficiency.

Like the wind raises the clouds and carries them far off, like the stars rush away with the lightning, you are drumming and dancing about in a muddle. This incites all kinds of desires, which confuse perfection and obscure the spirit. They in turn distort the spontaneous mind [within] and rebel against the lords [impartiality]of Heaven [without]. How can you not be overpowered by the wonders of creation and lose yourself in the swamp of existing things?

We, the eyes, are only your humble servants, following what you command. Having entangled us in deep defilement, now you turn around and put the blame on us! Alas, alas! What fault is it of ours?

The Mind: Vision

The mind thereupon weeps [DZ: chirps]. After a long time, it responds:

Should we, then, consider who among us, you or I, is clearer in his directions? How the hidden and the visible are so separate, yet so mysteriously one?

The manifold things are causing us affliction, so let us now decide what to do. Eventually we may transcend the boundaries of grime and trouble and step into the realm of pure serenity.

> Eating boundless *qi*,
> Breathing the morning light,
> Nibbling on blossoms of pure jade,
> Rinsing with jasper springs—
> We join the numinous transformations,
> In feathery wings go beyond the clouds and mist,
> And soar ever farther.

> Above, we rise to the Three Clarities,
> Below, we abolish the Eight Wilds—
> Trust Pine and Jump as our friends, **[3a]**
> Join Heaven and Earth in linked eternity!
> What ruin or praise can reach us?
> What gain or loss [abandon] not yet forgotten?

Such is my vision. Consider it and give me your comments.

The Eyes: Right Action

The eyes counter once more:

This is getting closer, but it is not quite there yet. You see, if you acted like this, you would desire stillness yet following things in haste; you would push out defilements yet stir up more dregs from the depth. Utterly in darkness about the means of returning to the root, you would just go far-off and set yourself up alone.

As for truly embodying the invisible and inaudible, you enwrap it and never find its core, expand with it and never find its end. Vast and open, it is without limit; dark and obscure, it is without equal. Merely giving up one thing while accepting another, you attain the small and let go of the great. Forgetfully resting in darkness to obliterate your shadow, you still do not escape from benefit and harm. Give forth nothing but emptiness and openness, and Dao and inherent potency will provide support. Eliminate all human plans before they even take shape, and the cosmic order of Heaven will come of itself.

Thus, Mysterious Prime blunted his sharpness and observed all that's wondrous; Wide Learning abolished all mentation and used only bodily form. The Yellow Emperor obtained it with the help of No-Shape; the Master of Vast Perfection joined it through Deepest Darkness. [3b] Yan Hui sat in oblivion and merged with Great Pervasion; Master Zhuang matched Heaven and could discover the Essence.

Listing the host of sages and examining their potency, [we find that] none of them ever planned [to reach that state] with wisdom. Rather, [they reached it] like water that stops waving and becomes clear all the way, like dust that does not settle and leaves the mirror bright. They never avoided the world in high loftiness but found deep peace in their square-inch [hearts]. Thus they could be relaxed [DZ: apprehensive] and remain forever, go along in pervasion and transcend all.

Without actively shining forth, they were radiant; without trying to be secret, they were well hidden. Mystically merging from beginning to end, who could tell they were separate from the myriad beings? They became one with all and never gained [anything over others]; because of this, they never lost [anything either].

If you sincerely follow in the steps of these sages on their level path, you will forever be protected by primordial good fortune. But if you abandon the center and serve the extraneous, you will make little progress and never get anywhere.

Why is this so?

Rivers rise, and dragons come to coil in them; woods grow, and wild beasts come to roam in them. Similarly the spirit rests in an empty hollow, the Dao assembles in mysterious emptiness. If you do not open yourself to their being, how can you ever match their nonbeing?

Unless the body is forgotten in stillness and serenity, unless the spots and dregs on the mirror are cleansed, unless the door to the mystery is spontaneously bright, and unless the dark depth [of the Dao] firmly contained—how can you ever go beyond all to utter nonattachment?

[4a] Without all this—how can you stride on the Eight Luminants, ascend to the Ninefold Empyrean? How can you gaze at the superb splendor of the Golden Towers, step on the solitary emptiness of the Purple Palace? How can you merge with the boundlessness of a grand kalpa and make ten thousand springtimes into a single morning?

The Mind: Realization

The mind thereupon adopts a relaxed attitude to the multitude of thoughts and becomes placid when faced with insecurity and hesitations. Purified of thoughts, it gradually becomes clear; controlling insecurity, it stops pursuing things.

In the end, the mind expresses his gratitude to the eyes and says:

> You favored me with the good Dao,
> And graced me with your perfect words.
> You woke me up from a great dream,
> And opened me to twofold mystery.
>
> You elevated me to the stages of perfection,
> and brought me to the gate of all that's wondrous.
> You made me roam in vast, deserted wilderness,[2]
> And let me wander freely around the boundless source.
>
> Neither a member of the crowd nor yet utterly alone,
> I am no longer tranquil or excited.
> I join utmost happiness in permanent accordance,
> Embrace the essence of perfection and find eternal life.
>
> Giving up things, there is nothing to give up,
> Deepening things, I go deeper yet again.
> I reach to the ancestor of all creation,

---

[2] Following DZ 1051 and reading *yu* ("in") instead of *yi* (particle).

Come to the heart of Heaven's and Earth's symbols.

You made me empty of desires,
See beyond the bounds of the five colors;
Blocking all protection,
I look into the forest of primordial dark and yellow. [4b]

I gaze at existence, but it is like looking at empty serenity;
I hear music, but it is like listening to the valley's sounds.
I make spontaneous nature my companion,
Join freedom from desires as my closest friend.

I no longer run around for emperors and lords,
Never again defend the rights of Later Heaven.
I block desires before they ever rise,
Cut off entanglements before they cause confusion.

I forget the vastness even of Heaven and of Earth,
Never mind the minuteness of the hair in autumn.
Resting in serenity and silence,
I listen to Pure Harmony.

Engulfed in obscurity and darkness,
I see the Light of Dawn.
Going along with all beings,
I too follow the cycle.

Containing inner radiance,
I close up all the gates.

Whirling storms, heaving oceans,
Rolling thunder,[3] tumbling mountains,
Sky-high floods, burning marshes—

Still, I am free, away from all!
Movement stilled, language silenced—

Why ever think?

---

[3] The word "thunder" (*ting* ö") is left out in the edition in DZ 1051.

Bibliography

Adamek, Wendy. 2007. *The Mystique of Transmission: On an Early Chan History and Its Contexts*. New York: Columbia University Press.

Altose, Murray A. and Yoshikatsu Kawakami, eds. 1999. *Control of Breathing in Health and Disease*. New York: Marcel Dekker.

Andersen, Poul. 1980. *The Method of Holding the Three Ones*. London: Curzon Press.

Andō Shunyū 安藤俊雄. 1970. "Shibyōhō to shite no tendai shikan" 治病方としての天台止觀. *Ōtani daigaku kenkyū nenpō* 大谷大学研究年報 23:1-58.

Aoki Gorō 青木五朗. 1979a. "Kaku Shō Sōshichu shisen" 郭象莊子註試權. *Kyōto kyōiku daigaku kiyō* 京都教育大学紀要 55:196-202.

_____. 1979b. "Shōshi Kaku Shō chu no shinshi mondai ni tsuite" 莊子郭象註のに真世問題ついて. *Kyōto kyōiku daigaku kokubungaku kaishi* 京都教育大学紀要 14:27-35.

Arthur, Shawn. 2006. "Life Without Grains: *Bigu* and the Daoist Body." In *Daoist Body Cultivation*, edited by Livia Kohn, 91-122. Magdalena, NM: Three Pines Press.

_____. 2009. "Eating Your Way to Immortality: Early Daoist Self-Cultivation Diets." *Journal of Daoist Studies* 2:32-63.

Assandri, Friederike. 2008. "Laozi's Eclipse and Comeback: The Narrative Frame of the *Benji jing*." *Journal of Daoist Studies* 1:1-27.

_____. 2009. *Beyond the Daode jing: Twofold Mystery in Tang Daoism*. Magdalena, NM: Three Pines Press.

Austin, James. 1998. *Zen and the Brain: Toward an Understanding of Meditation and Consciousness*. Cambridge, Mass.: MIT Press.

_____. 2006. *Zen-Brain Reflections: Reviewing Recent Developments in Meditation and States of Consciousness*. Cambridge, Mass.: MIT Press.

Baldrian-Hussein, Farzeen. 1984. *Procédés secrets du joyau magique.* Paris: Les Deux Océans.

_____. 2004. "The *Book of the Yellow Court*: A Lost Song Commentary of the 12th Century." *Cahiers d'Extrême-Asie* 14:187-226.

Bedell, Leila G. 1885. *The Abdominal Brain.* Chicago: Grass and Delbridge.

Begley, Sharon, ed. 2007. *Train Your Mind to Change Your Brain.* New York: Ballentine.

Benn, Charles D. 1977. "Taoism as Ideology in the Reign of Emperor Hsüantsung." Ph.D. Diss., University of Michigan, Ann Arbor.

_____. 1991. *The Cavern Mystery Transmission: A Taoist Ordination Rite of A.D. 711.* Honolulu: University of Hawai'i Press.

Benson, Herbert. 1976. *The Relaxation Response.* New York: Avon.

_____. 1996. *Timeless Healing: The Power and Biology of Belief.* New York: Simon & Schuster.

_____, and William Proctor. 1985. *Beyond the Relaxation Response.* New York: Times Books.

Bielefeldt, Carl. 1986. "Ch'ang-lu Tsung-tse's *Tso-Ch'an I* and the 'Secret' of Zen Meditation." In *Traditions of Meditation in Chinese Buddhism,* edited by Peter N. Gregory, 129-62. Honolulu: University of Hawaii Press,

Bodde, Derk. 1942. "Some Chinese Tales of the Supernatural." *Harvard Journal of Asiatic Studies* 6:338-57.

Bohm, David. 1951. *Quantum Theory.* New York: Prentice-Hall.

Bokenkamp, Stephen R. 1986. "The Peach Flower Font and the Grotto Passage." *Journal of the American Oriental Society* 106:65-79.

_____. 1994. "Time After Time: Taoist Apocalyptic History and the Founding of the T'ang Dynasty." *Asia Major* 7.1:59-88.

_____. 1997. *Early Daoist Scriptures.* With a contribution by Peter Nickerson. Berkeley: University of California Press.

_____. 2007. *Ancestors and Anxiety: Daoism and the Birth of Rebirth in China.* Berkeley: University of California Press.

Boltz, Judith M. 1987. *A Survey of Taoist Literature: Tenth to Seventeenth Centuries.* Berkeley: University of California, China Research Monograph 32.

Bono, Joseph, Jr. 1984. "Psychological Assessment of Transcendental Meditation." In *Meditation: Classic and Contemporary Perspectives,* edited by Deane H. Shapiro, Jr. and Roger Walsh, 209-19. New York: Aldine.

Borysenko, Joan, with Larry Rothstein. 1987. *Minding the Body, Mending the Mind*. Reading, Mass.: Addison-Wesley.

Braverman, A. 1989. *Mud and Water: A Collection of Talks by the Zen Master Bassui*. San Francisco: North Point Press.

Brazier, David. 1995. *Zen Therapy: Transcending the Sorrows of the Human Mind*. New York: John Wiley & Sons.

Brown, Daniel P. 1984. "A Model for the Levels of Concentrative Meditation." In *Meditation: Classic and Contemporary Perspectives*, edited by Deane H. Shapiro, Jr. and Roger Walsh, 271-80. New York: Aldine.

_____, and Jack Engler. 1984. "A Rorschach Study of the Stages of Mindfulness Meditation." In *Meditation: Classic and Contemporary Perspectives*, edited by Deane H. Shapiro, Jr. and Roger Walsh, 232-62. New York: Aldine.

Bucke, R.M. 1961 [1901]. *Cosmic Consciousness: A Study of the Evolution of the Human Mind*. Hyde Park, NY: University Books.

Bucknell, Rod, and Chris Kang, eds. 1997. *The Meditative Way*. Richmond, UK.: Curzon Press.

Bugault, Guy. 1968. *La notion de "prajñā" ou de sapience selon les perspectives du Mahāyāna*. Paris: Boccard.

Bumbacher, Stephan Peter. 2000. *The Fragments of the Daoxue zhuan*. Frankfurt: Peter Lang.

Cahill, Suzanne. 1990. "Practice Makes Perfect: Paths to Transcendence for Women in Medieval China." *Taoist Resources* 2.2:23-42.

_____. 2006. *Divine Traces of the Daoist Sisterhood*. Magdalena, NM: Three Pines Press.

Campany, Robert. 1996. *Strange Writing: Anomaly Accounts in Early Medieval China*. Albany: State University of New York Press.

Capra, Fritjof. 1975. *The Tao of Physics: An Exploration of the Parallels Between Modern Physics and Eastern Mysticism*. Boulder: Shambhala.

Cardoso, R., E. DeSouza, L. Camano, et al. 2004. "Meditation in Health: An Operational Definition." *Brain Research Protocols* 14:58-60.

Cedzich, Ursula-Angelika. 2001. "Corpse Deliverance, Substitute Bodies, Name Change, and Feigned Death: Aspects of Metamorphosis and Immortality in Early Medieval China." *Journal of Chinese Religions* 29:1-68.

Ch'en, Kenneth. 1973. *The Chinese Transformation of Buddhism*. Princeton, Princeton University Press.

Chan, Cecilia, Lai Wan, and Amy Yin Man Chow, eds. 2006. *Death, Dying and Be-reavement: A Hong Kong Chinese Experience.* Hong Kong: Hong Kong University Press.

Chan, Wing-tsit. 1963. *A Source Book in Chinese Philosophy.* Princeton: Princeton University Press.

Chatterjee, Ashok Kumar. 1962. *The Yogacara Idealism.* Delhi: Bhargva Bhushan Press.

Chen Banghuai 陳邦淮. 1982. "Zhanguo 'Xing*qi* yuming' kaoshi" 戰國行氣玉銘考試. *Guwenzi yanjiu* 古文子研究 20:485-576.

Chen Guofu 陳國符. 1975. *Daozang yuanliu kao* 道藏源流考. Taipei: Guting.

Chen, William Y. 1987. *A Guide to Tao Tsang chi yao.* Stony Brook: Institute for the Advanced Study of World Relgions.

Chen Yingning 陈撄宁. 2000. *Daojiao yu yangsheng* 道教与养生. Beijing: Huawen.

Chen Yuan 陳垣, Chen Zhichao 陳智超 , and Zeng Qingying 曾慶瑛, eds. 1988. *Daojia jinshi lue* 道家金石略. Beijing: Wenwu.

Ching, Julia. 1983. "The Mirror Symbol Revisited: Confucian and Taoist Mysticism." In *Mysticism and Religious Traditions,* edited by Steven T. Katz, 226-46. New York: Oxford University Press.

Cleary, Thomas. 1977. *The Blue Cliff Record.* 3 vols. Boulder: Shambhala.

_____. 1984. *The Flower Ornament Scripture.* Boston: Shambhala.

_____. 1993. *Unlocking the Zen Koan.* Berkeley: North Atlantic Books.

Cline, Erin M. 2010. "Mirrors, Minds, and Metaphors." In *Experimental Essays on Zhuangzi,* edited by Victor H. Mair, 154-76. Dunedin, FL: Three Pines Press.

Conze, Edward. 1978. *Selected Sayings from the Perfection of Wisdom.* Boulder, Co: Prajna Press.

_____. 1990. *The Large Sutra on Perfect Wisdom.* Delhi: Motilal Barnasidass.

Cook, Francis H. 1977. *Hua-yen Buddhism: The Jewel Net of Indra.* University Park and London: Pennsylvania State University Press.

Crandall, Michael M. 2010 [1983]. "On Walking Without Touching the Ground: 'Play' in the Inner Chapters of the *Zhuangzi.*" In *Experimental Essays on Zhuangzi,* edited by Victor H. Mair, 99-121. Dunedin, FL: Three Pines Press.

Dalai Lama. 2002. *How to Practice: The Way to a Meaningful Life.* New York: Pocket Books.

Davidson, Julian M. 1984. "The Physiology of Meditation and Mystical States of Consciousness." In *Meditation: Classic and Contemporary Perspectives*, edited by Deane H. Shapiro, Jr. and Roger Walsh, 376-95. New York: Aldine.

De Meyer, Jan. 2006. *Wu Yun's Way: Life and Works of an Eighth-Century Daoist Master.* Leiden: E. Brill.

Deikman, Arthur J. 1982. *The Observing Self: Mysticism and Psychotherapy.* Boston: Beacon Press.

Demiéville, Paul. 1987. "The Mirror of the Mind." In *Sudden and Gradual: Approaches to Enlightenment in Chinese Thought*, edited by Peter N. Gregory, 13-40. Honolulu: University of Hawai'i Press.

Despeux, Catherine. 2006. "The Six Healing Breaths." In *Daoist Body Cultivation*, edited by Livia Kohn, 37-67. Magdalena, NM: Three Pines Press.

_____, and Livia Kohn. 2003. *Women in Daoism.* Cambridge, Mass.: Three Pines Press.

Diamond, John. 1979. *Behavioral Kinesiology.* New York: Harper & Row.

Donner, Neal. 1987. "Sudden and Gradual Intimately Conjoined: Chih'i's T'ien-t'ai View." In *Sudden and Gradual: Approaches to Enlightenment in Chinese Thought*, edited by Peter N. Gregory, 201-26. Honolulu: University of Hawaii Press.

_____, and Daniel B. Stevenson. 1993. *The Great Calming and Contemplation: A Study and Annotated Translation of the First Chapter of Chih-i's Mo-ho chih-kuan.* Honolulu: University of Hawaii Press.

Dumoulin, Heinrich. 1965. *A History of Zen Buddhism.* New York: MacGraw-Hill.

_____. 1979. *Zen Enlightenment: Origin and Meaning.* Translated by John Maraldo. New York: Weatherhill.

_____. 1992. *Zen Buddhism in the 20ᵗʰ Century.* Translated by Joseph S. O'Leary. New York: Weatherhill.

Easwaran, Eknath. 1990. *Meditation.* Berkeley: Nilgiri Press

Eliade, Mircea. 1958. *Birth and Rebirth.* New York: Harper & Row.

Engelhardt, Ute. 1987. *Die klassische Tradition der Qi-Übungen. Eine Darstellung anhand des Tang-zeitlichen Textes Fuqi jingyi lun von Sima Chengzhen.* Wiesbaden: Franz Steiner.

_____. 1989. "*Qi* for Life: Longevity in the Tang." In *Taoist Meditation and Longevity Techniques*, edited by Livia Kohn, 263-94. Ann Arbor: University of Michigan, Center for Chinese Studies Publications.

_____. 1996. "Zur Bedeutung der Atmung im Qigong." *Chinesische Medizin* 1/1996:17-23.

Epstein, Gerald. 1989. *Healing Visualizations: Creating Health through Imagery*. New York: Bantam.

Eskildsen, Stephen. 1998. *Asceticism in Early Taoist Religion*. Albany: State University of New York Press.

———. 2004. *The Teachings and Practices of the Early Quanzhen Taoist Masters*. Albany: State University of New York Press.

———. 2007. "Mystical Ascent and Out-of-Body Experience in Medieval Daoism." *Journal of Chinese Religions* 35:36-62.

———. 2009a. "*Neidan* Methods for Opening the Gate of Heaven." In *Internal Alchemy: Self, Society, and the Quest for Immortality*, edited by Livia Kohn and Robin R. Wang, 87-104. Magdalena, NM: Three Pines Press.

———. 2009b. "Death, Immortality, and Spirit Liberation in Northern Song Daoism: The Hagiographical Accounts of Zhao Daoyi." In *The People and the Dao: New Studies in Chinese Religions in Honour or Daniel L. Overmyer*. edited by Philip Clart and Paul Crowe, 389-418. St. Augustin/Nettetal: Steyler Verlag, Monumenta Serica Monograph LX.

Esposito, Monica. 2009. "The *Daozang Jiyao* Project: Mutations of a Canon." *Daoism: Religion, History and Society* 1:95-156.

Faure, Bernard. 1986. "The Concept of One-Practice-Samadhi in Early Ch'an." In *Traditions of Meditation in Chinese Buddhism*, edited by Peter N. Gregory, 99-128. Honolulu: University of Hawaii Press.

———. 1997. *The Will to Orthodoxy: A Critical Genealogy of Northern Chan Buddhism*. Stanford: Stanford University Press.

Feinstein, David, Donna Eden, and Gary Craig. 2005. *The Promise of Energy Psychology*. New York: Penguin.

Forke, Alfred. 1972 [1907]. *Lun-Heng: Wang Ch'ung's Essays*. 2 vols. New York: Paragon.

Fried, Robert. 1993. *The Psychology and Physiology of Breathing: In Behavioral Medicine, Clinical Psychology, and Psychiatry*. With Joseph Grimaldi. New York: Plenum Press.

———. 1999. *Breathe Well, Be Well*. New York: John Wiley and Sons.

Fryba, Mirko. 1989. *The Art of Happiness: Teachings of Buddhist Psychology*. Boston: Shambhala.

Fujiwara Takao 藤原高男. 1980. "Rōshikai ni okeru chūgenha no kōei" 老子解における重玄派の後裔. In *Ikeda Suetoshi hakase koshi kinen Tōyōgaku ronshū* 池田末利博士古希記念東洋学論集, 657-72. Tokyo: Tōhō gakkai.

_____. 1962. "Kō Kan Rōshi chu kō" 顧歡老子注考. *Kangibunka* 漢魏文化 3:19-29.

Fujiyoshi Jikai 藤吉慈海. 1974. "Zazen to zabō ni tsuite" 坐禪と坐忘について. In *Zenshū sōshū no tenkai* 禪淨雙修の產開. Tokyo, 1974.

Fukui Fumimasa 福井文雅. 1987. *Hannya shingyō no rekishiteki kenkyū* 盤若心經の歷史的研究. Tokyo: Shunjusha.

Fukunaga Mitsuji 福永光司. 1954. "Kaku Shō no Sōshi kaishaku" 郭象の莊子解釋. *Tetsugaku kenkyū* 哲学研究 37:108-24 and 167-77.

_____. 1964. "Kaku Shō no Sōshi chu to Kō Shu no Sōshi chu" 郭象の莊子註と向秀の莊子註. *Tōhō gakuhō* 東方学報 36:187-215.

_____. 1969. "'No-Mind' in *Chuang-tzu* and Ch'an Buddhism." *Zinbun* 12:9-45.

_____. 1973. "Dōkyō ni okeru kagami to ken" 道教における鏡と劍. *Tōhō gakuhō* 東方學報 45:59-120.

Fung Yu-lan. 1952. *A History of Chinese Philosophy.* Translated by Derk Bodde. 2 vols. Princeton, Princeton University Press.

_____. 1964. *Chuang Tzu: A New Selected Translation with an Exposition of the Philosophy of Kuo Hsiang.* New York: Paradigm.

Gach, Michael Reed, and Beth Ann Henning. 2004. *Acupressure for Emotional Healing.* New York: Bantam.

Gallo, Fred, ed. 2004. *Energy Psychology in Psychotherapy.* New York: Norton..

Gass, Robert. 1999. *Chanting: Discovering Spirit in Sound.* New York: Broadway Books.

Gert, Bernard. 1970. *The Moral Rules.* New York: Harper & Row.

Gimello, Robert M. and Peter N. Gregory. 1983. *Studies in Ch'an and Hua-yen.* Honolulu: University of Hawai'i Press.

Girardot, Norman. 2009 [1983]. *Myth and Meaning in Early Daoism: The Theme of Chaos (Hundun).* Dunedin, FL: Three Pines Press.

Glassman, Bernie. 2000. *Infinite Cirle: Teachings in Zen.* Boston: Shambhala.

Goldstein, Joseph, and Jack Kornfield. 1987. *Seeking the Heart of Wisdom: The Path of Insight Meditation.* Boston: Shambhala.

Goleman, Daniel. 1988. *The Meditative Mind: The Variety of Meditative Experiences.* New York: Putnam.

_____, ed. 1997. *Healing Emotions: Conversations with the Dalai Lama on Mindfulness, Emotions, and Health.* Boston: Shambhala.

_____, ed. 2003. *Destructive Emotions: A Scientific Dialogue with the Dalai Lama.* New York: Bantam Books.

Goodrich, Charles. 1925. *The Invention of Printing in China and Its Spread Westward.* New York: Ronald Press.

Goossaert, Vincent. 2002. "Starved of Resources: Clerical Hunger and Enclosures in Nineteenth-Century China." *Harvard Journal of Asiatic Studies* 62.1:77-133.

Goullart, Peter. 1961. *The Monastery of Jade Mountain.* London: John Murray.

Graham, A. C. 1960. *The Book of Lieh-tzu.* London: A. Murray.

_____, 1961. "The Date and Compilation of the Liehtzyy." *Asia Major* 2. ser., 8:139-98.

_____. 1969. "Chuang-tzu's Essay on 'Seeing Things As Equal'." *History of Religions* 9:137-59.

_____. 1980. "How Much of *Chuang-tzu* Did Chuang-tzu Write?" *Studies in Classical Chinese Thought.* Journal of the American Academy of Religions Supplement 35:459-501.

_____. 1981. *Chuang-tzu: The Seven Inner Chapters and Other Writings from the Book of Chuang-tzu.* London: Allan & Unwin.

_____. 2010 [1983]. "Daoist Spontaneity and the Dichotomy of 'Is' and 'Ought'." In *Experimental Essays on Zhuangzi*, edited by Victor H. Mair, 3-22. Dunedin, FL: Three Pines Press.

Groner, Paul. 1984. *Saicho: The Establishment of the Japanese Tendai School.* Berkeley: Berkeley Buddhist Studies Series 7.

Hachiya Kunio 蜂屋邦夫. 1967. "Sōshi shōyoyū hen o meguru Kaku Shō to Shi Ton no kaishaku" 莊子逍遙遊篇をめぐつて郭象と支遁の解釋. *Hikaku bunka kenkyū* 比較文化研究 8:59-98.

Hansen, Chad. 2010 [1983]. "A Dao of 'Dao' in *Zhuangzi*." In *Experimental Essays on Zhuangzi*, edited by Victor H. Mair, 23-55. Dunedin, FL: Three Pines Press.

Happold, F.C. 1970. *Mysticism: A Study and an Anthology.* Baltimore: Penguin.

Harper, Donald. 1998. *Early Chinese Medical Manuscripts: The Mawangdui Medical Manuscripts.* London: Wellcome Asian Medical Monographs.

Harrison, Eric. 2000. *How Meditation Heals: A Scientific Explanation.* Berkeley: Ulysses Press.

Hawkes, David. 1959. *Ch'u Tz'u: The Songs of the South.* Oxford: Clarendon Press.

Hawkins, David R. 2002a. *Power Vs. Force: The Hidden Dimensions of Human Behavior.* Carlsbad, Calif: HayHouse.

_____. 2002b. *The Eye of the I.* Sedona: Veritas.

_____. 2003. *I: Reality and Subjectivity.* Sedona: Veritas.

_____. 2006. *Transcending the Levels of Consciousness: The Stairway to Enlightenment.* Sedona: Veritas.

_____. 2008. *Reality, Spirituality, and Modern Man.* Toronto: Axial Publications.

Heine, Steven. 2002. *Opening a Mountain: Koans of the Zen Masters.* New York: Oxford University Press.

Hendrischke, Barbara. 2006. *The Scripture on Great Peace: The Taiping jing and the Beginnings of Daoism.* Berkeley: University of California Press.

Hervouet, Yves, ed. 1978. *A Sung Bibliography—Bibliographie des Sung.* Hong Kong: The Chinese University Press.

Hewitt, James. 1977. *The Complete Yoga Book.* New York: Schocken Books.

Holzman, Donald. 1976. *Poetry and Politics: The Life and Works of Juan Chi (210263).* Cambridge: Cambridge University Press.

Homann, Rolf. 1971. *Die wichtigsten Körpergottheiten im Huang-t'ing-ching.* Göppingen: Alfred Kümmerle.

Hori, G. Victor Sogen. 2000. "Koan and Kensho in the Rinzai Zen Curriculum." In *The Koan: Texts and Contexts in Zen Buddhism* edited by Steven Heine and Dale S. Wright, 280-315. New York: Oxford University Press.

Horiike Nobuo 堀池信夫. 1972. "Sōshi no shisō to Kaku Shō no shisō" 荘子の思想と郭向の思想. *Kambun gakkai kaiho* 漢文學會會報 31:63-75.

Horner, I. B. 1977. *The Collection of the Middle Length Sayings.* 3 vols. Oxford: The Pali Text Society, Translation Series, vol. 31. Reprinted by Routledge and Kegan Paul.

Humphries, Christmas. 1968. *Concentration and Meditation.* Baltimore: Penguin.

Hurvitz, Leon. 1962. *Chih-i (538-597): An Introduction to the Life and Ideas of a Chinese Buddhist Monk.* Brussels: Institut Belge des Hautes Etudes Chinoises.

Huxley, Aldous. 1946. *The Perennial Philosophy.* New York and London: Harper & Brothers.

Jackowicz, Stephen. 2006. "Ingestion, Digestion, and Regestation: The Complexities of the Absorption of *Qi.*" In *Daoist Body Cultivation,* edited by Livia Kohn, 68-90. Magdalena, NM: Three Pines Press.

James, William. 1936 [1902]. *The Varieties of Religious Experience.* New York: The Modern Library.

Jan, Yün-hua. 1981. "The Mind as the Buddha-nature: The Concept of the Absolute in Ch'an Buddhism." *Philosophy East and West* 31:467-79.

Jarrett, Lonny S. 2006. "Acupuncture and Spiritual Realization." In *Daoist Body Cultivation*, edited by Livia Kohn, 19-36. Magdalena, NM: Three Pines Press

Kabat-Zinn, Jon. 1990. *Full Catastrophe Living*. New York: Bantam.

_____. 2005. *Coming to Our Senses: Healing Ourselves and the World through Mindfulness*. New York: Hyperion.

Kaltenmark, Max. 1979a. "Notes sur le *Pen-tsi king*. Personnages figurant dans le sutra." In *Contributions aux etudes de Touen-houang*, edited by Michel Soymié, 2:91-98. Paris-Geneva: Ecole Française d'Extrême-Orient.

_____. 1979b. "The Ideology of the *T'ai-p'ing-ching*." In *Facets of Taoism*, edited by Holmes Welch and Anna Seidel, 19-52. New Haven: Yale University Press.

Kamalashila. 1992. *Meditation: The Buddhist Way of Tranquility and Insight*. Birmingham: Windhorse.

Kamata Shigeo 鎌田茂雄. 1963. "Dōkyō kyōri no keisei ni oyoboshita bukkyō shisō no eikyō" 道教教理の形成におよぼした佛教思想の影響. *Tōyō bunko kenkyūjo kiyō* 東洋文化研究紀要 31:165-240.

_____. 1966. "Dōsei shisō no keisei katei" 道性思想の形成過程. *Tōyō bunko kenkyūjo kiyō* 東洋文化研究紀要 4:61-154.

Kamitsuka Yoshiko 神塚淑子. 1979. "Go Un no shōgai to shisō" 呉筠の生涯と思想. *Tōhōshūkyō* 東方宗教 54:33-51.

_____. 1982. "Shiba Shōtei Zabōron ni tsuite" 司馬承禎 坐忘論について. *Tōyō bunka* 東方文化 62:213-42.

Kasulis, Thomas P. 1981. *Zen Action/Zen Person*. Honolulu: University of Hawai'i Press.

Keenan, John P. 1993. "Yogacara in China." In *Buddhist Spirituality: Indian, Southeast Asian, Tibetan, and Early Chinese*, edited by Takeuchi Yoshinori, 365-72. New York: Crossroad.

King, Winston L. 1980. *Theravada Meditation: The Buddhist Transformation of Yoga*. University Park: Pennsylvania State University Press.

Kirkland, J. Russell. 1986. "Taoists of the High T'ang: An Inquiry into the Perceived Significance of Eminent Taoists in Medieval Chinese Society." Ph.D. Diss., Indiana University, Bloomington.

_____. 1991. "Huang Ling-Wei: A Taoist Priestess in T'ang China." *Journal of Chinese Religions* 19:47-73.

Kjellberg, Paul, and Philip J. Ivanhoe, eds. 1996. *Essays on Skepticism, Relativism, and Ethics in the Zhuangzi*. Albany: State University of New York Press.

Knaul, Livia. 1982. "Lost *Chuang-tzu* Passages." *Journal of Chinese Religions* 10:53-79.

_____. 1985a. "The Winged Life: Kuo Hsiang's Mystical Philosophy." *Journal of Chinese Studies* 2.1:17-41.

_____. 1985b. "Kuo Hsiang and the *Chuang-tzu*." *Journal of Chinese Philosophy* 12.4:429-47.

_____. 1985c. "The Habit of Perfection." *Cahiers d'Extrême-Asie* 1:71-85.

_____. 1986. "Chuang-tzu and the Chinese Ancestry of Ch'an Buddhism." *Journal of Chinese Philosophy* 13.3; 411-28.

Knoblock, John, and Jeffrey Riegel. 2000. *The Annals of Lü Buwei*. Stanford: Stanford University Press.

Kohn, Livia. 1987a. *Seven Steps to the Tao: Sima Chengzhen's Zuowanglun*. St.Augustin/Nettetal: Monumenta Serica Monograph XX.

_____. 1987b. "The Teaching of T'ien-yin-tzu." *Journal of Chinese Religions* 15:1-28.

_____. 1989a. "Guarding the One: Concentrative Meditation in Taoism." In *Taoist Meditation and Longevity Techniques*, edited by Livia Kohn, 123-56. Ann Arbor: University of Michigan, Center for Chinese Studies Publications.

_____. 1989b. "Taoist Insight Meditation: The Tang Practice of *Neiguan*." In *Taoist Meditation and Longevity Techniques*, edited by Livia Kohn, 191-222. Ann Arbor: University of Michigan, Center for Chinese Studies Publications.

_____. 1989c. "The Mother of the Tao." *Taoist Resources* 1.2:37-113.

_____. 1990a. "Eternal Life in Taoist Mysticism." *Journal of the Americal Oriental Society* 110:622-40.

_____. 1990b. "Transcending Personality: From Ordinary to Immortal Life." *Taoist Resources* 2.2:1-22.

_____. 1991. "Taoist Visions of the Body." *Journal of Chinese Philosophy* 18:227-52.

_____. 1992. *Early Chinese Mysticism: Philosophy and Soteriology in the Taoist Tradition*. Princeton: Princeton University Press.

_____. 1993a. *The Taoist Experience: An Anthology*. Albany: State University of New York Press.

_____. 1993b. "Quiet Sitting with Master Yinshi: Medicine and Religion in Modern China." *Zen Buddhism Today* 10:79-95.

_____. 1995. *Laughing at the Tao: Debates among Buddhists and Taoists in Medieval China*. Princeton: Princeton University Press.

_____. 1997. "Yin Xi: The Master at the Beginning of the Scripture." *Journal of Chinese Religions* 25:83-139.

_____. 1998a. *God of the Dao: Lord Lao in History and Myth*. University of Michigan, Center for Chinese Studies.

_____. 1998b. "Mind and Eyes: Sensory and Spiritual Experience in Taoist Mysticism." *Monumenta Serica* 46:129-56.

_____. 1998c. "Steal Holy Food and Come Back as a Viper: Conceptions of Karma and Rebirth in Medieval Daoism." *Early Medieval China* 4: 1-48.

_____. 2001. *Daoism and Chinese Culture*. Cambridge: Three Pines Press.

_____. 2003. *Monastic Life in Medieval Daoism: A Cross-Cultural Perspective*. Honolulu: University of Hawai'i Press.

_____. 2004a. *Cosmos and Community: The Ethical Dimension of Daoism*. Cambridge, Mass.: Three Pines Press.

_____. 2004b. *The Daoist Monastic Manual: A Translation of the Fengdao kejie*. New York: Oxford University Press.

_____. 2007 [1991]. *Daoist Mystical Philosophy: The Scripture of Western Ascension*. Magdalena, NM: Three Pines Press.

_____. 2008a. *Meditation Works: In the Daoist, Buddhist, and Hindu Traditions*. Magdalena, NM: Three Pines Press.

_____. 2008b. *Chinese Healing Exercises: The Tradition of Daoyin*. Honolulu: University of Hawai'i Press.

_____. 2009. *Readings in Chinese Mysticism*. Dunedin, Fla: Three Pines Press.

_____. 2010a. *Daoist Dietetics: Food for Immortality*. Dunedin, FL: Three Pines Press.

_____. 2010b. "Body and Identity." In *Riding the Wind with Liezi*, edited by Jeffrey Dippmann and Ronnie Littlejohn. New York: Oxford Univesrity Press.

_____, and Russell Kirkland. 2000. "Daoism in the Tang (618-907)." In *Daoism Handbook*, edited by Livia Kohn, 339-83. Leiden: E. Brill.

_____, and Robin R. Wang. 2009. *Internal Alchemy: Self, Society, and the Quest for Immortality*. Magdalena, NM: Three Pines Press.

Komjathy, Louis. 2002. *Title Index to Daoist Collections*. Cambridge, Mass.: Three Pines Press.

_____. 2007. *Cultivating Perfection: Mysticism and Self-Transformation in Quanzhen Daoism*. Leiden: E. Brill.

_____. 2008a. *Handbooks for Daoist Practice*. Hong Kong: Yuen Yuen Institute.

_____. 2008b. "Mapping the Daoist Body (1): The *Neijing tu* in History." *Journal of Daoist Studies* 1:67-92.

_____. 2009. "Mapping the Daoist Body (2): The Text of the *Neijing tu*." *Journal of Daoist Studies* 2:64-108.

Korn, Errol R., and Karen Johnson. 1983. *Visualization: The Uses of Imagery in the Health Professions*. Irvine, Calif.: American Institute of Hypnotherapy.

Krech, Gregg. 2002. *Naikan: Gratitude, Grace, and the Japanese Art of Self-Reflection*. Berkeley: Stone Bridge Press.

Kroll, Paul W. 1978. "Ssu-ma Ch'eng-chen in T'ang Verse." *Society for the Study of Chinese Religions Bulletin* 6:16-30.

_____. 1996. "Body Gods and Inner Vision: *The Scripture of the Yellow Court*. In *Religions of China in Practice*, edited by Donald S. Lopez Jr., 149-55. Princeton: Princeton University Press.

Kusuyama Haruki 楠山春樹. 1979. *Rōshi densetsu no kenkyū* 老子傳說の研究. Tokyo: Sōbunsha.

Lagerwey, John. 1981. *Wu-shang pi-yao: Somme taoïste du VIe siecle*. Paris: Publications de l'Ecole Française d'Extrême-Orient.

_____. 2004. "Deux écrits taoïstes anciens." *Cahiers d'Extrême-Asie* 14:131-72.

Lai, Whalen. 1979. "Ch'an Metaphors: Waves, Water, Mirror, Lamp." *Philosophy East and West* 29:243-55.

Lévi, Jean. 1983. "L'abstinence des céréals chez les taoïstes." *Etudes Chinoises* 1:3-47.

Li Ling 李零. 1993. *Zhongguo fangshu kao* 中國方術考. Beijing: Renmin Zhongguo.

Lincoln, Bruce. 1975. "The Indo-European Myth of Creation." *History of Religions* 15:121-45.

Link, Arthur E., and Timothy Lee. 1966. "Sun Cho's *Yü-tao-lun*: A Clarification of the Way." *Monumenta Serica* 25:169-96.

Littlejohn, Ronnie. 2010. "Kongzi in the *Zhuangzi*." In *Experimental Essays on Zhuangzi*, edited by Victor H. Mair, 177-94. Dunedin, FL: Three Pines Press.

Liu, Xun. 2009. "Numinous Father and Holy Mother: Late-Ming Duo-Cultivation Practice." In *Internal Alchemy: Self, Society, and the Quest for Immortality*, edited by Livia Kohn and Robin R. Wang, 122-41. Magdalena, NM: Three Pines Press.

Lo, Vivienne. 2005. "Pleasure, Prohibition, and Pain: Food and Medicine in Traditional China." In *Of Tripod and Palate: Food, Politics and Religion in Traditional China*, edited by Roel Sterckx, 163-85. New York: Palgrave MacMillan.

Loehr, James E., and Jeffrey A. Migdow. 1986. *Breathe In, Breathe Out: Inhale Energy and Exhale Stress by Guiding and Controlling Your Breathing*. Alexandria, VA: Time Life Books.

Loon, Piet van der. 1984. *Taoist Books in the Libraries of the Sung Period*. London: Oxford Oriental Institute.

Loori, John Daido, ed. 2006. *Sitting With Koans: Essential Writings on the Practice of Zen Koan Introspection*. Boston: Wisdom Publications.

Lu, Kuan-yü. 1964. *The Secrets of Chinese Meditation*. London: Rider.

Luttgens, Kathryn, and Katherine F. Wells. 1989. *Kinesiology: Scientific Basis of Human Motion*. Dubuque, IA: Wm. C. Brown Publishers.

Lynn, Richard John. 1994. *The Classic of Changes: A New Translation of the I Ching as Interpreted by Wang Pi*. New York: Columbia University Press.

Mahony, William K. 1987. "Karman: Hindu and Jain Concepts." In *Encyclopedia of Religion*, edited by Mircea Eliade, 8:261-66. New York: Macmillan.

Mair Victor H. 2010 [1983], ed. *Experimental Essays on Zhuangzi*. Dunedin, FL: Three Pines Press.

Malek, Roman. 1985. *Das Chai-chieh-lu*. Frankfurt: Peter Lang.

Maspero, Henri. 1981. *Taoism and Chinese Religion*. Translated by Frank Kierman. Amherst: University of Massachusetts Press.

McMillin, David L., Douglas G. Richards, Eric A. Mein, and Carl D. Nelson. 1999. "The Abdominal Brain and the Enteric Nervous System." *Journal of Alternative and Complementary Medicine* 5.6. www.meridianinstitute. com.

McRae, John R. 1983. The Northern School and the Formation of Early Ch'an Buddhism. Honolulu: Hawai'i University Press.

_____. 2003. *Seeing Through Zen: Encounter, Genealogy, and Transformation in Chinese Chan Buddhism*. Berkeley: University of California Press.

Miller, James. 2008. *The Way of Highest Clarity: Nature, Vision and Revelation in Medieval Daoism*. Magdalena, NM: Three Pines Press.

Miura, Isshu, and Ruth Fuller Sasaki. 1965. *The Zen Koan*. New York: Harcourt Brace Javonovich

Mollier, Christine. 2000. "Les cuisines de Laozi et du Buddha." *Cahiers d'Extrême-Asie* 11: 45-90.

_____. 2008. *Buddhism and Taoism Face to Face: Scripture, Ritual, and Iconographic Exchange in Medieval China*. Honolulu: University of Hawai'i Press.

Motoyama, Hiroshi. 1990. *Toward a Superconsciousness: Meditational Theory and Practice*. Berkeley: Asian Humanities Press.

Mugitani Kunio 麥谷國雄. 1982. "Kōtei naikeikyō shiron"黄庭內景經試論. *Tōyōbunka*東洋文化 62:29-61.

_____. 1987. "Yōsei enmei roku kunchu" 養性延命錄訓註. *Report of the Study Group on Traditional Chinese Longevity Techniques*, no. 3. Tokyo: Mombushō.

_____. 2004. "Filial Piety and 'Authentic Parents' in Religious Daoism." In *Filial Piety in Chinese Thought and History*, edited by Alan K. L. Chan and Sor-hoon Tan, 110-21. London: RoutledgeCurzon.

Nadeau, Robert, and Menas Kafatos. 1999. *The Non-Local Universe: New Physics and Matters of the Mind*. New York: Oxford University Press.

Nakajima Ryūzō 中島隆藏. 1970. "Kaku Shō no shisō ni tsuite" 郭象の思想について. *Shūkan tōyōgaku* 集刊東洋学 24:43-60.

_____. 1984a. *Dōkyō gishu sakuin*道教義樞索引. Manuscript, private distribution.

_____. 1984b. "Taijō gyōhō innenkyō ni okeru ōhōron" 太上業報因緣經における應報論. In *Makio Ryōkai hakase shoju kinen ronshū Chūgoku no shūkyō to kagaku* 牧尾良海博士頌壽記念論集: 中國の宗教思想と科學, 335-54. Tokyo: Kokusho kankōkai.

Nakano Tōru 中野通. 1990. "Kaku Shō ni okeru zabō" 郭象における坐忘. *Tōhō-shūkyō* 東方宗教 75:1-19.

Nattier, Jan. 1992. "The *Heart Sutra*: A Chinese Apocryphal Text?" *Journal of the International Association of Buddhist Studies* 15.2:153-223.

Needham, Joseph, et al. 1976. *Science and Civilisation in China*, vol. V.3: *Spagyrical Discovery and Invention—Historical Survey, from Cinnabar Elixir to Synthetic Insulin*. Cambridge: Cambridge University Press.

Ng, Yu-Kwan. 1993. *T'ien-t'ai Buddhism and Early Mādhyamika*. Honolulu: University of Hawai'i Press.

Nickerson, Peter. 1996. "Abridged Codes of Master Lu for the Daoist Community." In *Religions of China in Practice*, edited by Donald S. Lopez Jr., 347-59. Princeton: Princeton University Press.

Nomura Shigeo 野村茂夫. 1970. "Sōshi no muyō no yō o megutte" 莊子の無用の用をめぐって. *Tōhōshūkyō* 東方宗教 35:36-48.

O'Brien, Elmer. 1964. *The Varieties of Mystic Experience*. New York: Holt, Rinehart & Winston.

Ōfuchi Ninji 大淵忍爾. 1979. *Tonkō dōkei: Zuroku hen* 敦煌道經圖錄篇. Tokyo: Kokubu shoten.

Oschman, James. 2000. *Energy Medicine: The Scientific Basis*. New York: Churchill Livingstone.

Oshima, Harold H. 2010 [1983]. "A Metaphorical Analysis of the Concept of Mind in the *Zhuangzi*." In *Experimental Essays on Zhuangzi*, edited by Victor H. Mair, 62-82. Dunedin, FL: Three Pines Press.

Ospina, Maria B., et al. 2007. *Meditation Practice for Health: State of the Research*. AHRQ Publication No. 07-E010. Rockville, Md: Agency for Healthcare Research and Quality. www.ahrq.gov.

Otis, Leon. 1984. "Adverse Effects of Transcendental Meditation." In *Meditation: Classic and Contemporary Perspectives*, edited by Deane H. Shapiro, Jr. and Roger Walsh, 201-09. New York: Aldine.

Park, Song Bae. 1983. *Buddhist Faith and Sudden Enlightenment*. Albany: State University of New York Press.

Pas, Julian F. 1986. "Six Daily Periods of Worship: Symbolic Meaning in Buddhist Liturgy and Eschatology." *Monumenta Serica* 37:49-82.

Phillips, Scott P. 2008. "Portrait of an American Daoist: Charles Belyea/Liu Ming." *Journal of Daoist Studies* 1:161-76.

Poceski, Mario. 2007. *Ordinary Mind as the Way: The Hongzhou School and the Growth of Chan Buddhism*. New York: Oxford University Press.

———. 2009a. "Review of Wendy Adamek, *The Mystery of Transmission*." *Journal of Chinese Religions* 36.

———. 2009b. "Review of Albert Welter, *The Linji Lu and the Creation of Chan Orthodoxy*." *Philosophy East and West* 59.

Pregadio, Fabrizio. 2006. *Great Clarity: Daoism and Alchemy in Early Medieval China*. Stanford: Stanford University Press.

———, ed. 2008. *The Encyclopedia of Taoism*. London: Routledge.

Price, A.F. and M. L. Wong. 1969. *The Diamond Sutra and the Sutra of Hui-neng*. Boulder, Col: Shambhala.

Proudfoot, Wayne. 1985. *Religious Experience*. Berkeley: University of California Press.

Qing Xitai 卿希泰. 1988. *Zhongguo daojiao shi* 中國道教史. Chengdu: Sichuan renmin.

Rao Zongyi 饒宗頤. 1992 [1956]. *Laozi xianger zhu jiaojian* 老子想爾注校箋. Shanghai: Wenyi.

Ratey, John J. 2002. *A User's Guide to the Brain: Perception, Attention, and the Four Theaters of the Brain*. New York: Vintage Books.

Reiter, Florian C. 1990. *Der Perlenbeutel aus den drei Höhlen: Arbeitsmaterialien zum Taoismus der frühen T'ang-Zeit.* Wiesbaden: Harrassowitz.

Ren Jiyu 任繼愈. 1990. *Zhongguo daojiao shi* 中國道教史. Shanghai: Renmin.

_____, and Zhong Zhaopeng 鐘肇鵬, eds. 1991. *Daozang tiyao* 道藏提要. Beijing: Zhongguo shehui kexue chubanshe.

Reynolds, David K. 1983. *Naikan Psychotherapy: Meditation for Self-Improvement.* Chicago: University of Chicago Press.

Rinaldini, Michael. 2008. "How I Became a Daoist Priest." *Journal of Daoist Studies* 1:181-87

Robinet, Isabelle. 1976. "Les randonées extatiques des taoïstes dans les astres." *Monumenta Serica* 32:159-273.

_____. 1977. *Les commentaires du Tao to king jusqu'au VIIe siècle.* Paris: Mémoirs de l'Institute des Hautes Etudes Chinoises 5.

_____. 1979. "Metamorphosis and Deliverance of the Corpse in Taoism." *History of Religions* 19:37-70.

_____. 1983a. "Kouo Siang ou le monde comme absolu." *T'oung Pao* 69:87-112.

_____. 1983b. "Chuang-tzu et le taoïsme religieux." *Journal of Chinese Religions* 11:59-109.

_____. 1984. *La révélation du Shangqing dans l'histoire du taoïsme.* 2 vols. Paris: Publications de l'Ecole Française d'Extrême-Orient.

_____. 1989. "Visualization and Ecstatic Flight in Shangqing Taoism." In *Taoist Meditation and Longevity Techniques*, edited by Livia Kohn, 157-90. Ann Arbor: University of Michigan, Center for Chinese Studies Publications.

_____. 1993. *Taoist Meditation.* Translated by Norman Girardot and Julian Pas. Albany: State University of New York Press.

_____. 1997. *Taoism: Growth of a Religion.* Translated by Phyllis Brooks. Stanford: Stanford University Press.

Robinson, Richard H. 1967. *Early Mādhyamika in India and China.* Madison: University of Wisconsin Press.

Rosenberg, Larry. 1999. *Breath by Breath: The Liberating Practice of Insight Meditation.* Boston: Shambhala.

Roth, Harold D. 1997. "Evidence for Stages of Meditation in Early Taoism." *Bulletin of the School of Oriental and African Studies* 60: 295-314.

_____. 1998. "Mysticism in the *Laozi*." In *Essays on Religious and Philosophical Aspects of the Laozi*, edited by P. J. Ivanhoe and M. Csikszentmihalyi.

_____. 1999. *Original Tao: Inward Training and the Foundations of Taoist Mysticism*. New York: Columbia University Press.

_____. 2010 [2000]. "Bimodal Mystical Experience in the "Qiwulun" Chapter of *Zhuangzi*." In *Experimental Essays on Zhuangzi*, edited by Victor H. Mair, 195-211. Dunedin, FL: Three Pines Press.

Rousselle, Erwin. 1933. "Seelische Führung im Taoismus." *Eranos Jahrbuch* 1:135-99.

Sakade, Yoshinobu. 1989. "Longevity Techniques in Japan: Ancient Sources and Contemporary Studies." In *Taoist Meditation and Longevity Techniques*, edited by Livia Kohn, 1-40. Ann Arbor: University of Michigan, Center for Chinese Studies Publications.

_____. 2007a. "Sun Simiao et le bouddhisme." In *Taoism, Medicine, and Qi in China and Japan*, edited by Yoshinobu Sakade, 9-28. Suita: Kansai University Press.

_____. 2007b. "Methods and Ideas on Increasing Vitality in Ancient China: The Transition form *Neiguan* to *Neidan* in the Sui and Tang Dynasties." In *Taoism, Medicine, and Qi in China and Japan*, edited by Yoshinobu Sakade, 50-68. Suita: Kansai University Press.

Sakauchi Shigeo 坂内榮夫. "Taidōron kō: Tōdai dōkyō to Kōshū zen" 大道論考: 唐代道教と洪州禪. *Chūgoku shisōshi kenkyū* 中國思想史研究 19:173-89.

Samuels, Mike, and Nancy Samuels. 1975. *Seeing with the Mind's Eye: The History, Technique, and Uses of Visualization*. New York: Random House.

Santee, Robert. 2008. "Stress Management and the *Zhuangzi*." *Journal of Daoist Studies* 1:93-123.

Sasaki, Ruth Fuller. 1975. *The Record of Lin-chi*. Kyoto: Institute for Zen Studies.

Saso, Michael. 2000. *Zen is for Everyone: The Xiao Zhiguan Text by Zhiyi*. Carmel, Calif.: New Life Center.

_____. 2010 [1983]. "The *Zhuangzi neipian*: A Daoist Meditation." In *Experimental Essays on Zhuangzi*, edited by Victor H. Mair, 137-53. Dunedin, FL: Three Pines Press.

Schafer, Edward H. 1965. "The Idea of Created Nature in T'ang Literture." *Philosophy East and West* 15:153-60.

_____. 1977a. *Pacing the Void*. Berkeley: University of California Press.

_____. 1977b. "The Restoration of the Shrine of Wei Hua-ts'un at Lin-ch'uan in the Eighth Century." *Journal of Oriental Studies* 15:124-38.

_____. 1979. "A T'ang Taoist Mirror." *Early China* 4:387-98.

_____. 1980. *Mao-shan in T'ang Times*. Boulder: Society for the Study of Chinese Religions.

_____. 1981. "Wu Yün's 'Cantos on Pacing the Void'." *Harvard Journal of Asiatic Studies* 41:377-415.

_____. 1982. "Wu Yün's 'Stanzas on Saunters in Sylphdom'." *Monumenta Serica* 35:1-37.

Scharfstein, Ben-Ami. 1973. *Mystical Experience*. Indianapolis: Bobbs-Merrill.

Schipper, Kristofer M. 1975. *Concordance du Houang-t'ing king*. Paris: Publications de l'Ecole Française d'Extrême-Orient.

_____. 1979. "Le Calendrier de Jade: Note sur le *Laozi zhongjing*." *Nachrichten der deutschen Gesellschaft für Natur- und Völkerkunde Ostasiens* 125:75-80.

_____. 1985. "Taoist Ordination Ranks in the Tunhuang Manuscripts." In *Religion und Philosophie in Ostasien: Festschrift für Hans Steininger*, edited by. G. Naundorf, K.H. Pohl, and H. H. Schmidt, 127-48. Würzburg: Königshausen and Neumann.

_____, and Franciscus Verellen, eds. 2004. *The Taoist Canon: A Historical Companion to the Daozang*. 3 vols. Chicago: University of Chicago Press.

Schloegl, Irmgard. 1976. *The Zen Teaching of Rinzai*. Boulder: Shambhala.

Seki Masao 關雅夫. 1965. "Kaku Shō no Sōshi chu ni mirareru shizen to sono hoka" 郭象の莊子註に見られる自然とその他. *Niigata daigaku jimbun kagaku kenkyū* 新潟大学人文科学研究 28:31-71.

_____. 1974. "Kaku Shō, Sei Gen'ei no Sōshi kaishaku" 郭象.成玄英の莊子解釋. *Niigata daigaku kokubun gakkai shi* 新潟大学国文学会誌 18:50-59.

Sekida, Katsuki. 1975. *Zen Training*. New York: Weatherhill.

Sekiguchi Shindai 關口真大. 1957. *Tendai shōshikan no kenkyū* 天台小止觀の研究. Tokyo: Shinjūsha.

_____. 1974. *Tendai shōshikan: zazen no zahō* 天台小止觀:坐禪の作法. Tokyo: Iwanami shoten.

_____, ed. 1975. *Shikan no kenkyū* 止觀の研究. Tokyo: Iwanami.

Shapiro, Deane H., Jr.. 1984. "Classic Perspectives on Meditation." In *Meditation: Classic and Contemporary Perspectives*, edited by Deane N. Shapiro, Jr. and Roger Walsh, 5-13. New York: Aldine.

_____, and Roger Walsh, eds. 1984. *Meditation: Classic and Contemporary Perspectives*. New York: Aldine.

_____, and Steven M. Zifferblatt. 1984. "Zen Meditation and Behavioral Self-Control: Similarities, Differences, and Clinical Applications." In *Meditation:*

Classic and Contemporary Perspectives, edited by Deane H. Shapiro, Jr. and Roger Walsh, 585-98. New York: Aldine.

Sharf, Robert. 1991. "The Treasure Store Treatise (*Pao-tsang lun*) and the Sinification of Buddhism in Eighth-Century China." Ph. D. Diss, University of Michigan, Ann Arbor.

Shi, Jing. 2005. "An Interview with Liu Xingdi." *The Dragon's Mouth* 2005.3:2-8.

_____. 2006. "Sitting and Forgetting: An Introduction to *Zuowang*." *The Dragon's Mouth* 2006.1:10-13.

_____. 2007. "An Interview with Eva Wong." *The Dragon's Mouth* 2007.1:4-8

Sivin, Nathan. 1967. "A Seventh-Century Chinese Medical Case History." *Bulletin of the History of Medicine* 41.3:, 267-73.

_____. 1968. *Chinese Alchemy: Preliminary Studies*. Cambridge, Mass.: Harvard University Press.

Solé-Leris, Amadeo. 1986. *Tranquility and Insight: An Introduction to the Oldest Form of Buddhist Meditation*. Boston: Shambhala.

Sommer, Deborah. 2002. "Destroying Confucius: Iconoclasm in the Confucian Temple." In *On Sacred Ground: Culture, Society, Politics, and the Formation of the Cult of Confucius*, edited by Thomas A. Wilson, 95-133. Cambridge, Mass.: Harvard Asia Center.

_____. 2003. "Ritual and Sacrifice in Early Confucianism: Contacts with the Spirit World." In *Confucian Spirituality*, edited by Tu Weiming and Mary Evelyn Tucker, 197-219. New York: Crossroads.

_____. 2008. "Boundaries of the *Ti* Body." Asia Major 21:293-324.

_____. 2010. "Concepts of the Body in the *Zhuangzi*." In *Experimental Essays on Zhuangzi*, edited by Victor H. Mair, 212-27. Dunedin, FL: Three Pines Press.

Soothill, William E., and Lewis Hudous. 1937. *A Dictionary of Chinese Buddhist Terms*. London: Kegan Paul.

Spencer, Colin. 1993. *Vegetarianism: A History*. New York: Four Walls Eight Windows.

Stace, Walter. 1987 [1960]. *Mysticism and Philosophy*. Los Angeles: Jeremy P. Tarcher.

Stein, Rolf A. 1963. "Remarques sur les mouvements du taoïsme politico-religieux au IIe siecle ap. J.-C." *T'oung Pao* 50:1-78.

Stevenson, Daniel B. 1986. "The Four Kinds of Samādhi in Early T'ien-t'ai Buddhism." In *Traditions of Meditation in Chinese Buddhism*, edited by Peter N. Gregory, 45-98. Honolulu: University of Hawai'i Press.

Strickmann, Michel. 1979. "On the Alchemy of T'ao Hung-ching." In *Facets of Taoism*, edited by Holmes Welch and Anna Seidel, 123-92. New Haven: Yale University Press.

Sunayama Minoru 沙山捻. 1980. "Sei Gen'ei no shisō ni tsuite" 成玄英の思想について. *Nihon Chūgoku gakkaihō* 日本中国学会報 32:125-39.

_____. 1987. "Ku Dō tōsenkō" 瞿童登仙考. *Tōhōshūkyō* 東方宗教 69:1-23.

Suzuki, Shuryu. 1970. *Zen Mind, Beginner's Mind*. New York: Weatherhill.

Swanson, Paul L. 1989. *Foundations of T'ien-t'ai Philosophy: The Flowering of the Two Truths Theory in Chinese Buddhism*. Berkeley: Asian Humanities Press.

Switkin, Walter. 1987. *Immortality: A Taoist Text of Macrobiotics*. San Francisco: H. S. Dakin Company.

Tang Junyi 唐君毅. 1966. *Zhongguo zhexue yuanlun: Daolun pian* 中國哲學原論: 道論篇. Taipei: Xuesheng shuju.

Thera, Nyanaponika. 1962. *The Heart of Buddhist Meditation*. New York: Samuel Weiser.

Togawa Yoshi 戸川義男. 1966. "Kaku Shō no seiji shisō to sono Sōshi chu" 郭の政治思想とその莊子註. *Nihon Chūgoku gakkaihō* 日本中国学会報 18:142-60.

Tsukamoto, Zenryū, and Leon Hurvitz. 1985. *A History of Early Chinese Buddhism*. 2 vols. Tokyo: Kodansha.

Underhill, Evelyn. 1911. *Mysticism*. London: Methuen & Co.

Verellen, Franciscus. 1992. "Evidential Miracles in Support of Taoism: The Inversion of a Buddhist Apologetic Tradition in Tang China." *T'oung Pao* 78:217-63.

Von Euler, Curt, and Hugo Lagercrantz, eds. 1987. *Neurobiology and the Control of Breathing*. New York: Raven Press.

Wallace, B. Alan. 2005. *Genuine Happiness: Meditation as a Path to Fulfillment*. Hoboken, NJ: John Wiley & Sons.

Walsh, Roger. 1984. "An Evolutionary Model of Meditation Research." In *Meditation: Classic and Contemporary Perspectives*, edited by Deane H. Shapiro, Jr. and Roger Walsh, 24-32. New York: Aldine.

_____, and Deane H. Shapiro, Jr. 2006. "The Meeting of Meditative Discipline and Western Psychology: A Mutually Enriching Dialogue." *American Psychology* 61:227-39.

Wang Zongyu 王宗昱. 2001. *Daojiao yishu yanjiu* 道教義樞研究. Shanghai: Shanghai wenhua.

Ware, James R. 1966. *Alchemy, Medicine and Religion in the China of AD 320*. Cambridge, Mass.: MIT Press.

Watson, Burton. 1968. *The Complete Works of Chuang-tzu*. New York: Columbia University Press.

_____. 1999. *The Zen Teachings of Master Lin-Chi: A Translation of the Lin-chi lu*. New York: Columba University Press.

Watts, Alan. 1957. *The Way of Zen*. Harmondsworth: Penguin.

Welter, Albert. 2008. *The Linji Lu and the Creation of Chan Orthodoxy: The Development of Chan's Records of Sayings Literature*. New York: Oxford University Press.

Wilhelm, Hellmut. 1948. "Eine Zhou-Inschrift über Atemtechnik." *Monumenta Serica* 13:385-88.

_____. 2010 [1983]. "*Zhuangzi* Translations: A Bibliographical Appendix." In *Experimental Essays on Chuang-tzu*, edited by Victor H. Mair, 228-32. Dunedin, FL: Three Pines Press.

Wilhelm, Richard. 1950. *The I Ching or Book of Changes*. Princeton: Princeton University Press, Bollingen Series XIX.

Wong, Eva. 1992. *Cultivating Stillness: A Taoist Manual for Transforming Body and Mind*. Boston: Shambhala.

Wu Shouju 吳受濾. 1981. *Sima Chengzhen ji jijiao* 司馬承禎集集輯校. Beijing.

Wu, Chi-yu. 1960. *Pen-tsi king, Livre du terme originel: Ouvrage taoïste inedit du VII siecle*. Paris: Centre National des Recherches Scientifiques.

Yamada Takashi 山田俊. 1992. *Kohon Shōgenkyō* 古本昇玄經. Sendai: Tōhōku daigaku.

Yamano Toshio 山野俊郎. 1984. "Moka shikan byōkankyō no kenkyū" 摩訶止觀病患境の研究. *Ōtani daigaku daigakuin kenkyū kiyō* 大谷大学研究年報 1:105-24.

Yampolsky, Philip B. 1967. *The Plaform Sutra of the Sixth Patriarch*. New York: Columbia University Press.

Yan Lingfeng 嚴靈奉. 1983. *Jingzi congzhu* 經子叢註. Taipei: Xuesheng shuju.

Yearley, Lee. 2010 [1983]. "The Perfected Person in the Radical *Zhuangzi*." In *Experimental Essays on Zhuangzi*, edited by Victor H. Mair, 122-36. Dunedin, FL: Three Pines Press.

Yixuan. 1976. *The Zen Teaching of Rinzai: The Record of Rinzai*. Berkeley: Shambhala.

Yoshikawa Tadao 吉川忠夫. 1987. "Seishitsu kō" 靜室考. *Tōhō gakuhō* 東方學報 59:125-62.

Yoshioka Yoshitoyo 吉岡義豐. 1959. *Dōkyō to bukkyō* 道教と佛教, vol. 1. Tokyo: Kokusho kankōkai.

Yu Feiwu 予非吾. 1983. "Du *Tianyinzi yangsheng shu*" 讀天隱子養生書. *Qigong zazhi* 氣功雜誌 3:129-33.

Yü, Ying-shih. 1987. "O Soul, Come Back: A Study of the Changing Conceptions of the Soul and Afterlife in Pre-Buddhist China." *Harvard Journal of Asiatic Studies* 47:363-95.

Zhu Yueli 朱越利. 1982. "*Qi qi* erzi weitong bian" 炁氣二字韋同辨. *Shijie zongjiao yanjiu* 世界宗教研究 1982/1:50-58.

Ziporyn, Brook. 2003. *The Penumbra Unbound: The Neo-Taoist Philosophy of Guo Xiang*. Albany: State University of New York Press.

_____. 2004a. "Tiantai School." In *The Encyclopedia of Buddhism*, edited by Robert Buswell, 845-51. New York: Macmillan.

_____. 2004b. "*Mohe zhiguan*." In *The Encyclopedia of Buddhism*, edited by Robert Buswell, 548-49. New York: Macmillan.

_____. 2009. *Zhuangzi: The Essential Writings with Selections from Traditional Commentaries*. Indianapolis: Hackett Publishing.

Zürcher, Erik. 1959. *The Buddhist Conquest of China: The Spread and Adaptation of Buddhism in Early Medieval China*. 2 vols. Leiden: E. Brill.

_____. 1980. "Buddhist Influence on Early Taoism." *T'oung Pao* 66:84-147.

Index